INSIDE

BASEBALL

THE BEST OF
TOM VERDUCCI

SPORTS ILLUSTRATED BOOKS

Copyright 2006
Time Inc. Home Entertainment

Published by
Sports Illustrated Books

Time Inc.
1271 Avenue of the Americas
New York, NY 10020

ISBN: 1-933405-00-7

Sports Illustrated Books is a trademark of Time Inc.

To my mother, Vita,
and to the memory of my father, Anthony

Contents

Introduction

BY ROGER CLEMENS

YOU MIGHT SAY THAT TOM VERDUCCI AND I BROKE into the big leagues together. It's hard to remember a time when Tom wasn't known around the game as one of the best baseball writers in the country; but in 1984, when I was a rookie with the Red Sox, he was enjoying his first full season on the baseball beat, as a backup to the regular Mets and Yankees writers for *Newsday*. Our paths have crossed often since then, and we've had a lot of great conversations, particularly since he joined SPORTS ILLUSTRATED in 1993. I really got to know him over the years, but I only began to understand why I've always enjoyed his work so much in the spring of 2003.

I was pitching for the Yankees, getting close to my 300th win, and one day Tom asked me about the exercise regimen I follow between starts. He wondered how a guy in his 40s was still able to generate a 95 mph fastball. Lots of reporters have asked about my workouts, and I figured this would just be another one of those stories. *Roger runs, blah blah blah.* "No, I don't want you to *tell* me about what you do," Tom said. "I want to *see* it."

I'd never heard that from a writer before. Of course, I hadn't seen many writers who were in the kind of shape Tom appeared to be in, either. (Just to give him a hard time, I tell him he looks like Jason Sehorn, the former New York Giants cornerback.) "Forget watching it," I replied. "How about you *do* it with me?"

Tom laughed, but the next morning he was standing outside my apartment in Manhattan, dressed in full workout gear and ready to go. It was a damp, gray day, the kind of morning that makes you want to sleep in or flip the channels until it's time to head to the ballpark. But Tom, my trainer, another workout buddy and I headed over to an empty soccer field and got after it, far from the spotlights of any big-league stadium. We went right into what I call the SEAL Deal, a 33-minute drill where I alternate abdominal work—a total of about 950 crunches—with quarter-mile runs. I don't care what kind of shape you're in, that program will get your attention. I won't mention any names, but through the years I've invited many of my teammates to that workout. Most of them got through maybe half of it . . . and then they never wanted any part of that again.

My trainer and I were ready to have some fun with Tom, but he stayed right with us, running and doing crunches like he was the one making a start in a few days. All right, maybe he skipped a few of the crunches. But he didn't bow out. That impressed me, though I shouldn't have been surprised. Tom wasn't chasing *me* around that soccer field. He was chasing a story, trying to find out how I do what I do, and he's always willing to go a little further and dig a little deeper than most writers. When he wants to chat in the clubhouse or behind the batting cage, players know his questions will have a little more on them than what we usually hear. Not in a nasty way; one of the things that stands out about Tom is how calm and even-keeled he is and how fair he is in what he writes. Everything he does is above the belt. Players appreciate that, especially in a business where sometimes what's said in an interview can be spun out of context. You know whatever Tom asks will be well thought out and what he writes will reflect what was said, even when he hears it while grinding through the last lap of a 6:40 mile.

Maybe the fact that Tom is a pretty good athlete accounts for why he so accurately captures the personalities of the players he writes about, whether it's Sandy Koufax or Rickey Henderson. And as this collection shows, Tom writes stories that stick with you long after you've read them. I remember thinking about one during, of all times, a spring training drill when I was with the Yankees. Dwight Gooden, who was also a rookie in '84, was in camp with us as a part-time coach. As we were taking PFP (Pitchers' Fielding Practice) I couldn't help but think that instead of hitting me grounders, Doc should have been getting ready to go into the Hall of Fame. I thought back a few years, to when Tom had told the stories of Gooden and Darryl Strawberry in *The High Price of Hard Living*, one of the pieces in this book. It's a reminder that talent isn't enough to guarantee success in this game.

The same goes for writing, and few reporters I've met combine natural talent with a work ethic the way Tom does. He's the rare writer who has as much to offer those of us inside the game as we do him, which is one of the reasons I've enjoyed going back and reading the stories in this book again. I'm not just talking about trade news or tidbits about guys on other teams that come up in conversation. I'm talking about stories like *Totally Juiced*, Tom's ground-breaking piece on baseball's steroid problem, and the Marvin Miller piece, *The Players' Most Valuable Player*, a short profile of the man who made it possible for today's players to live the lives they do. Those stories were eye-openers for players as well as fans.

Tom and I have talked a lot about that subject: about how power pitchers approach their craft, about mechanics, about the difference between eras like Koufax's and mine. In a way, pitching and writing are similar. No matter what happens in a game, the guy on the mound is the one who gets the *W* or the *L* next to his name. And a writer, especially one who writes with substance, puts himself on the line, too. And like a good pitcher, a writer can't be afraid to fail.

In Tom's case, there's nothing to be afraid of: The stories in this book are proof that he rarely, if ever, fails. Anyone who has worked with him knows that Tom takes his stories to heart. When you read them, I think you will too.

Houston, Texas
November 2005

Preface

My Life in Baseball

BY TOM VERDUCCI

THE WAY I REMEMBER IT, THE FIRST TIME I LAID EYES on a major league ballplayer he was larger than life, or at least bigger than a charter bus. It was 1967, a little more than a month before my seventh birthday. I have no memory that it was the summer Carl Sandburg and Edward Hopper died, that the United States bombed Hanoi, that Thurgood Marshall was named a Supreme Court justice and that Newark, N.J., only a few miles from our home in Glen Ridge, was one of the many American cities torn apart by race riots.

What I do vividly remember is that it was the summer I discovered the music of the Monkees, the friendly comfort of *Mister Rogers' Neighborhood* and the magic of baseball cards.

Life, as far as I knew it anyway, was very good. And it was never better than when I watched the Washington Senators play the New York Yankees at the vast man-made canyon known as Yankee Stadium.

One of my father's cousins was married to the great Gil Hodges, then the manager of the Senators. "Uncle Gil," as we called him, left tickets that day for me, my two older brothers, and our aunt and uncle. I remember looking at those monuments in centerfield—a batted ball happened to roll behind them during the game—and thinking people were

11

buried beneath them. I remember that Frank Howard and Dick Nen hit back-to-back homers for the Senators, who won the game, 6–3, but I did not remember until I researched the game that a guy named Mickey Mantle of the Yankees also a hit a home run that day.

After the game we waited next to the Senators' team bus, parked behind the rightfield bullpen, to say hello (and goodbye) to Uncle Gil. What happened then made a bigger impression on me than anything that happened in the game. Howard stopped to shake my hand before he got on the bus. I looked up. Way up. At 6-foot-7, Howard was the biggest man I'd ever seen, and from the perspective of a six-year-old kid, he was taller than that great big green bus behind him. Three words came to mind, all of which I was incapable of actually speaking.

Oh.

My.

Goodness.

I learned long ago that looking up to major league ballplayers in a figurative sense is about as dangerous as looking head-on at a moving charter bus: You're bound to get hurt. But that lesson was nowhere to be found in the accumulated experience of a six-year-old back in 1967. It was impossible then for baseball to disappoint me, and the towering figure of Frank Howard, blotting out the team bus and the afternoon sun, confirmed to me that these men were giants.

Truth is, I was hooked even before I saw what a major league ballplayer looked like up close, back when I first began to walk. When my dad, a teacher and coach, would tune in a baseball game on our black-and-white console TV and watch from the floor, I would grab four pillows and arrange them in a diamond around him. I'd watch closely while standing next to the pillow that was home plate. When the batter swung, I would pantomime a swing of my own and then tear off in my cloth diaper for the bases, touching all the pillows and sliding into home.

Why baseball? Who knows? The perfect geometry of the diamond? The easy pace of the game? Or, more likely, is it about me, about my DNA? Baseball seems as much a part of who I am as brown eyes. The book you are holding springs from my lifelong love for the game, an affection that grows deeper as I continue to learn more about baseball and the people who play it.

I played the game, in its various forms, at every opportunity and, as kids did back then, usually without adults around: Wiffle ball with my brothers in front of the house, stickball at the elementary school and one-ole-cat or a full-blown pickup game at the park where I spent virtually every day of my summers, bothering to come home only when the gas streetlamps began to glow.

My father was a beloved high school football and baseball coach at Seton Hall Prep in South Orange, N.J., and from him I learned about sport not from the top down, by trying to emulate the pros, as most kids do, but from the inside out: the importance of team play, fundamentals, preparation, commitment, humility. Having him for my dad was like having one of those teachers' textbooks that include the answers to all the questions. His lessons served me well through high school ball, as a bench-warming walk-on outfielder at Penn State, as a professional writer and as a father myself.

It quickly became apparent that writing, like baseball, was another love hard-wired into my system. I always liked words and all you can do with them.

Here are a couple of DNA tests. First, go to your local sporting goods store and walk down the aisle where they keep the baseball equipment. If you can't make it to the end of the aisle without slipping a glove onto your hand and pounding the pocket with your fist, we share a gene.

Second, read something. Anything written professionally: a book, a magazine, a newspaper. If you do more than just absorb the information—if you also hear and feel the rhythm with which the words were assembled—then we've got another genetic match.

All I've ever wanted to do was to combine my love for sports, especially baseball, and writing. How fortunate I've been to realize that passion, first at *Today* newspaper in Cocoa, Fla., on the Miami Dolphins beat, where coach Don Shula treated everyone, including this 21-year-old rookie reporter, with respect and class, and then to *Newsday* in New York and now SI. As I begin my 25th year on the job, writing baseball is still fresh and exciting and challenging because every day, every game, every story and every combination of words is different.

Baseball writing has introduced me to fabulous places, interesting people and unforgettable moments, most of which—blessedly, as if to heighten the experience—I never saw coming. Sure, I've covered grand moments such as the resumption of the Pine Tar Game at Yankee Stadium in 1983, the great home run race of 1998 and every World Series since 1985 except one (1989, due to a broken foot). But some of the smaller moments stay with me just the same.

I once watched Yankees pitcher Tommy John commit three errors on one play, which began as a groundball to the mound.

I saw Dale Berra dry his tears with a sanitary sock in the clubhouse at old Comiskey Park after his father, Yogi, was fired as Yankee manager. And speaking of sanitary socks—this is one image I wish I could shake—I saw another Yankee manager, Stump Merrill, remove his sock after a game in broiling Florida heat and use it to clean the clods of tobacco from between his teeth.

I saw Cal Ripken's consecutive-game streak nearly end after he twisted his knee in an on-field brawl. I knew something was up when Mr. Reliable, who is so punctual he wore a wristwatch during batting practice, failed to meet me for a lunch we had planned the next day. (He eventually did send word to the restaurant that he wouldn't make it—for lunch, of course, not that night's game.)

I shagged flies with other Yankees and Mets beat writers during some early batting practice sessions and quickly learned that when big leaguers hit the ball you have to change the mental calculus you've used your whole life and add about 15 feet to where you think it will come down.

I lost some clams to Greg Maddux playing golf, somehow kept my lunch down while working out with Roger Clemens, lifted weights with Mark McGwire as he prepared for the 1998 season, ran with Pedro Martinez in Santo Domingo, trailed Billy Martin on the field and in the bars (which became a vital part of the Yankees beat), sat with Pete Rose in his New York hotel and listened to him confess to betting on baseball, and, in a Manhattan nightclub after the 2000 World Series, had my shins kicked repeatedly by a woman with a cast on her leg who was trying to make more space for herself at Derek Jeter's very crowded private party.

I've worked in 46 major league ballparks, not including the Tokyo Dome, where I covered the only postseason series played in 1994 and was so impressed by a young hitter for the Yomiuri Giants named Hideki Matsui that I brought home for my son a Matsui bank, with a coin slot in the back of its neck.

This book does not span all those years and all those ballparks. It begins with 1993, my first year at SI, a time when steroids were becoming the drug of choice in baseball, just as cocaine had been in the 1980s. Both drugs are accounted for here, as is the arc of what will be known (fairly with regard to some players, unfairly to many others) as the Steroid Era, when the bodies changed and so did the way the game was played.

As in any era, though, the wonders of the game shine through the corruption. There is still time—a need, even—to think along with Maddux, to laugh with Rickey Henderson, to cry with the people whose lives were changed by the 2004 Red Sox, and to stay cool while trying to hit a 94-mph fastball in a major league game. I've done all that, and it's been my job to take you with me. Former commissioner Fay Vincent likes to remember his days spent watching baseball games with his predecessor, the late commissioner Bart Giamatti, who called Vincent, his deputy commissioner, Dep. Giamatti would turn to Vincent and say, "You know, Dep, you've got to remember that this is work." I know the feeling.

Last October, on an unusually warm, bright fall afternoon, I sat in the open-air press box of the new Comiskey Park (as I still call it) in Chicago. It was Game 1 of the American League Division Series between the White Sox and Red Sox. I never have been a fan of any team as an adult. Instead, I'm a fan of the game and I root for extra innings, good stories and a perfectly choreographed relay, outfielder to infielder to catcher. Sitting in the sunshine, the field and players lit with that distinctive golden glow of the postseason sun, I was excited by the possibilities of another October.

It is a long way from that Senators bus to the Comiskey press box—I have a better view now, and a perspective that allows me to see inside baseball—but I still carry with me some of the wonder of that six-year-old boy. Come, have a look yourself.

Montgomery, N.J.
November 2005

INSIDE

BASEBALL

The Amazin' Collapse Of the Mets

*A team's fall from perennial contender to laughingstock is a
testament to the destructive power of mismanagement*

I T WAS 1988, ONE OF THOSE YEARS OF IMPERFECT GLORY FOR
the New York Mets, before the upper deck of Shea Stadium
was closed for lack of interest and before any of the team's
players were slapped with felony charges. Deep into the chilly
night of Oct. 9, Dwight Gooden stood on the mound with the baseball
in his hands and a two-run ninth-inning lead over the Dodgers. Three
outs and the Mets would lead the National League Championship Series three games to one.

"It's in the bag," thought Mets senior vice president Al Harazin. Good-
en had permitted the Dodgers only three hits—all singles, none of them
after the fourth inning. "Doc's going to win his first postseason game."

Gooden quickly had an 0-and-2 count on John Shelby, the easiest
hitter in the league to strike out. Yes, the Mets were nearly a lock to play
the Athletics in a titanic World Series, the first matchup of 100-win
teams in 18 years. Except something began to go wrong. Gooden
walked Shelby in an eight-pitch at bat. He seemed to labor on the last

two deliveries, fastballs high and away. He had thrown 125 pitches.

Reserve infielder Dave Magadan squirmed in the Mets dugout and thought, "Scioscia's up, Myers is in the bullpen. . . . Please put him in the game." But the lefthanded Randy Myers was not ready to face the lefthanded Mike Scioscia. Myers wasn't even warming up. No one was.

"He's still in control," manager Davey Johnson thought about Gooden. "If I bring in Myers, they'll pinch-hit Rick Dempsey anyway. He's more of a home run threat than Scioscia."

Scioscia had hit three home runs all year, only one since June. Mets catcher Gary Carter, knowing Scioscia liked to take a pitch or two with a runner on first, flashed his index finger to Gooden. After walking Shelby, the pitcher knew exactly what was needed: just a good get-ahead fastball squarely over the plate. It was 11:02 p.m. when Gooden threw the pitch. It arrived slightly above belt high. It would have been strike one, absolutely.

But then Scioscia swung.

THERE IS a line of demarcation that runs roughly along the crest of the Rocky Mountains through North America. Water on one side of the line flows toward the Pacific. On the other it flows in the opposite direction. The moment Scioscia hit that two-run home run, the Mets had reached their Continental Divide. "If we had won that game, we would have won that series," says Joe McIlvaine, then the Mets vice president of baseball operations and now an executive vice president with the team. "There's no doubt in my mind. It was a flash point."

The Mets lost that night in 12 innings and again the next afternoon. They lost the series in seven games, and they have not played another postseason game since. The course of the franchise's fortunes began flowing the wrong way, first in a trickle and then in a rush.

Two second-place finishes followed, though those turbulent years were more corrosive than anyone knew. It was the end to the dynasty that never was. The Mets were one of eight teams to finish first or second for seven consecutive seasons, but the only one of that group to not emerge from such a run with more than one pennant. Then came three losing seasons, each worse than the last. No team in baseball has been worse over those past three years, especially the most recent, a 103-loss horror in which the Mets, with conduct even more odious than their play, were reduced to being the pathetic objects of late-night television humor. So offensive was the 1993 team that on Aug. 26 an angered and pained Fred Wilpon met with his players for the first time in his 14 years of what had been his laissez-faire co-ownership with Nelson Doubleday. He scolded them for embarrassing the franchise and the city in which he had grown up. "You should feel privileged to be able to play baseball in New York," he told them. "If you don't feel that way and you want out, let us know. We'll get you the hell out of here."

Then came the landmark moment of the descent. Wilpon marched to a podium at a news conference and fired one of his players on the spot, essentially for acting like a jerk for the better part of three years. Wilpon simply blurted out that outfielder Vince Coleman, who had come to represent all that was wrong with the team, would never wear a Mets uniform again. The club still owed Coleman a 1994 salary of $3 million, but Wilpon would worry about that later.

"Businesswise," he says, "it wasn't a very smart thing to say. I didn't plan on saying it. Certainly I knew it in my mind. But, yes, I reached a point where I had to say enough is enough."

In the past three years three teams have gone from worst to first in successive seasons. Another, Oakland, took the reverse route last year. "A lot has changed since 1988," Wilpon says. "It's a much more volatile business now." The crash of the Mets, though, took on historic proportions. They became only the fourth team in history to lose 100 games within five seasons of winning 100. But unlike Oakland last season, the Mets collapsed without the excuse of fiscal restraint. They are a monument not so much to the vagaries of modern baseball as to the destructive forces of mismanagement.

The most ruinous of their mistakes took three basic forms: miscalculation or outright ignorance of the intangibles winning players need, particularly in New York; quick-fix trades that recklessly disregarded long-term effects; and the disastrous breakup of what was supposed to be a seamless passing of the front-office command from chief operating officer and general manager Frank Cashen to his lieutenants, McIlvaine and Harazin. Wilpon is positively penitential in acknowledging all three elements. "Not enough emphasis was placed on the mix of people and the chemistry that are essential to winning," Wilpon says. "It was almost like Rotisserie baseball."

LESS THAN two months after winning the 1986 World Series, the Mets traded outfielder Kevin Mitchell, who finished third in the Rookie of the Year balloting, to the Padres in a deal for outfielder Kevin McReynolds. It established the pattern for a series of errors in which the Mets progressively spoiled the chemistry of the team. Too often they overlooked players' mental toughness, approach to the game and suitability to the pressures in New York.

Mitchell was a kid from the San Diego ghetto who liked to tell stories of various escapades involving bullets and knives that had scarred his flesh. "Some people here thought Mitchell was a time bomb ready to explode," one Mets official says. Well, there was something of a detonation in 1989. Mitchell hit 47 home runs that year, won the Most Valuable Player award and led the San Francisco Giants to the pennant.

McIlvaine had coveted McReynolds since he scouted him as a collegian at Arkansas. But McReynolds's skills and production diminished annually after 1988. He never lost a step, though, in his haste to leave the clubhouse after games. McReynolds was more interested in beating traffic than in sharing with his teammates the joy of big victories or the crush of difficult defeats. So miscast was McReynolds in New York that he once said of its fans, "It's almost like people are miserable, and they want to bring you down to their level."

"Yes, I am disappointed with how McReynolds turned out," McIlvaine says. "He should have been a superstar. I can't tell you in all my years of scouting if I ever saw a player with tools like that. He didn't use that talent as much as he should have. Darryl Strawberry was the same way. They've both been good players. But they should have been excellent. They had Hall of Fame tools."

The Mets were wrong so many times about the makeup of their players that by 1992 they had a paranoid, distracted club. They put the likes of first baseman Eddie Murray and Coleman in the same clubhouse, where people like outfielder Bobby Bonilla and pitcher Bret Saberhagen quickly caught their contagious contempt for the media. "If there is one place in the entire world where that attitude can't work, it's New York City," Wilpon says. "It's the media capital of the world."

The Mets signed free agent Bonilla after the 1991 season. They invested $29 million in him to be their cornerstone player when baseball insiders knew he was nothing more than a good, complementary player given to self-absorption. Once, while with the Pirates, Bonilla was batting in the bottom of the ninth inning of a tie game when the winning run scored on a wild pitch. Despite the victory Bonilla was angry that he had lost a chance to pad his RBI total. "Why does it always happen to me?" he said.

New York has exposed the worst in him. He has threatened a reporter, worn earplugs at home games, called the press box with his team down 7–0 to complain about the scoreboard display of an error call against him, and whined so much that the New York *Daily News* ran a cartoon of Baby Bo in diapers on its back page. On top of all that he has batted .257—26 points lower than his lifetime average before going to New York. Last season his agent, Dennis Gilbert, wondered aloud to Harazin if maybe both the Mets and Bonilla might be better off if they traded him. Bonilla was not the leader or impact player the Mets had paid for.

"I think there are very few people in the game you can ask to do that," Harazin says. "Against the backdrop of success the Mets had for so many years, asking him to come in and do that was probably asking too much."

So sensitive was his rightfielder that former manager Jeff Torborg feared Bonilla would only be a worse wreck if he dared criticize him. "I tried to protect him as much as I could," Torborg says, "to the point where I got myself in trouble." Both Bonilla and Torborg were caught in lies trying to cover up the 1992 press box phone call.

It was Harazin who negotiated the free-agent contracts of Bonilla, Coleman and Murray, prompting former Mets pitcher Frank Viola to say in retrospect, "Money doesn't make a winning team. Al knows money, but he docsn't know baseball."

In three seasons Coleman missed more than half the team's games, cursed out a coach, was suspended for shoving his manager, caused Gooden to miss a start when he accidentally whacked him with a golf club, was a target of a rape investigation (no charges were brought), prepared for games by throwing dice in the clubhouse and, on July 24 this year, threw an M-100 firecracker out of a car window as he was leaving Dodger Stadium with some other players. The explosion injured three people, including a two-year-old girl who suffered corneal damage. Coleman originally was charged with a felony; in November his attorney negotiated a plea bargain in which Coleman pleaded guilty to a misdemeanor charge of possession of an explosive device.

"Vince Coleman was a total mistake by this organization," says Wilpon.

Murray produced admirable statistics for the Mets, but his hatred for the media poisoned the clubhouse. Although he was on his way to batting .285 with 27 home runs and 100 RBIs last season, and though the Mets would gladly and easily have parted with him, his venomous attitude had become so notorious that not a single team called to express interest in acquiring his bat down the stretch.

"Guys like Vince and Eddie copped this attitude that reporters were there only to screw up the team," says Magadan, who now plays for the Marlins. "I don't think there's any question that their attitudes affected the clubhouse. I realize reporters have a job to do, but believe me, you notice when you're talking to reporters and Eddie Murray walks by and says, 'Why are you talking to *them*?' Some guys would say, 'I don't want Eddie getting on me,' and they'd change their opinions about the press."

Saberhagen, with no history of such behavior, became a boor. On July 7 he tossed a lighted firecracker near reporters, and later he brashly admitted doing it, saying, "What are they going to do? Fine me?" Just three days after Coleman exploded his M-100 in Los Angeles, Saberhagen squirted bleach at reporters.

The Mets were wrong about their choice of managers too. After Davey Johnson was fired 42 games into the 1990 season, his seventh with the club, neither of his successors, Bud Harrelson or Torborg, made it through two seasons. Harrelson lost respect in the clubhouse when he quit his radio show because he thought the questions were too pointed and when he admitted sending coach Mel Stottlemyre to make a pitching change out of fear of being booed.

"That had an effect on the team," Magadan says. "The thing that hurt Buddy was when he showed vulnerability. Jeff wanted to control the media. We had so many meetings with Torborg and Buddy that were about the press, especially with Torborg. Those were just about the only team meetings we ever had with him."

At one meeting Torborg tried so hard to convince his players that they should not be distracted by the media that pitcher Pete Schourek finally piped up, "If we're not supposed to be worried about the media, why are we having all these meetings about the media?" Torborg was so preoccupied with covering up the slightest controversies that pitcher David Cone called him Oliver North.

"Jeff was put into a situation so different from Chicago," Harazin says, referring to Torborg's three years as manager of the White Sox, including a 94–68 season in 1990. "There he had a young, scrappy club with a college-style eagerness to succeed that suited him. I put him in a very different situation here. I didn't give as much thought to that as I should have."

When the Mets traded Cone to Toronto, on Aug. 27, 1992, he called it "the end of the arrogant Mets. The end of the mid-'80s, flourishing Mets." When Cone was asked that day if he knew how that end came about, he replied, "Well, yeah, the heart and soul was bred out of it. Numbers and production have taken a front seat while what a guy's intangibles are, what personality he brings to the Mets, is left on the backseat. You need people who are fixtures, with personality and guts. When things are down, those are the type of guys who fight back."

There is no more damning statistic indicative of how soft the Mets turned than this: They have a losing record in one-run games every year after 1988. They have been bullies in games decided by three or more runs in that time, with a .539 percentage in such games (215–184). In one- and two-run games, though, they have played .417 baseball (171–239). Trying to explain the disparity, Cone once attributed it to the Mets' "tight booty."

Of the 23 players to appear in the 1988 National League Championship Series for the Mets, 10 were gone by the end of the next year. Today only one of them is left: Gooden.

Cashen and Johnson now admit they acted rashly in trying to fuel the Mets' run at the top of the National League East and fulfill the pervasive and enormous expectations. "We traded so many good young players to try to keep the thing going," Cashen says. "We got caught up in it. I probably should have been more forceful in not letting that happen. I should have stopped a couple of trades." It is the temporary-insanity defense. Says Johnson, "Nobody was willing to take a step back and say, 'Wait a minute. What are we doing? Let's not panic.' We lost sight of what got us there."

Within a 44-day span of the 1989 season, the Mets traded centerfielders Lenny Dykstra and Mookie Wilson plus pitchers Rick Aguilera, Roger McDowell, Kevin Tapani and David West for three players who, as it turned out, would be gone from the club in little more than two years.

Late on the night of June 17, 1989, as the Mets rode their team bus back to their hotel after a game in Philadelphia, McIlvaine whispered to Johnson that he had a chance to obtain outfielder Juan Samuel from the Phillies for Dykstra and McDowell. "Think about it," McIlvaine told him. The manager shot back, "I don't have to think about it. I want you to make it if you can. It's that simple."

Why would Johnson be so eager to move the 26-year-old Dykstra? Because Johnson was no longer concerned about developing players. He had become a different manager ever since Cashen nearly fired him after the 1987 season—the two had clashed over personnel moves—even though the Mets won 92 games while their pitchers spent a combined 457 days on the disabled list.

"I thought I had a hell of a year managing," Johnson says of that second-place finish. "And then I had that problem with Frank. That told me they had taken the attitude, 'We have to win every year. We're great.' Now I'm thinking, Jeez, no matter what I've done before, that don't mean diddly-squat. So any time a trade came along that could make the ball club better immediately, I was for it because I could be gone at any moment.

"Sometimes you've got to take a step back to go forward," Johnson says. "The plan had been to eventually trade Mookie and give the job to Lenny. He'd struggle for a while, and the team wouldn't be as good without Mookie, but we'd be better off down the road. We stopped worrying about that. I'm as guilty as anybody."

McIlvaine made the trade the day after running it past Johnson and after Cashen—much to his subsequent regret—endorsed it. There was one unmentioned element that clinched the deal. Samuel was

Latin. "We were desperate to have a Latin on the team," says one Mets official, "especially with the great Latin American population in the city. We thought New York would love him."

Problem was, Samuel hated New York and was even less comfortable in centerfield. Since trading Dykstra and then Wilson (for Jeff Musselman) six weeks later, the Mets auditioned 17 players in centerfield, and none held the job for a full season.

By July 31, 1989, the Mets were seven games out. They panicked again. McIlvaine traded Aguilera, Tapani, West and two lesser pitching prospects to the Twins for Viola. Again Cashen would come to regret his endorsement.

With McIlvaine as director of scouting in the early '80s, the Mets built the foundation for their winning teams from a superlative farm system. A snapshot of their minor league system at the start of the '83 season included Aguilera, Dykstra, Gooden, Magadan, McDowell, Mitchell, Myers, Strawberry, Mark Carreon, Ron Darling, Tim Leary, Randy Milligan, Greg Olson, Calvin Schiraldi, Walt Terrell and other future big leaguers. Since the time Scioscia hit that home run off Gooden (and as McIlvaine had become more involved on the major league level), the Mets have not had a single player in their system who has 100 hits in a big league season and only one pitcher who has won as many as 10 games in a given year. That pitcher, Tapani, has done so four times—for Minnesota. "I didn't want to give up Aguilera," McIlvaine says. "He was just getting comfortable closing games. West had a good arm, but I knew he didn't have what it takes inside. Tapani is the one who surprised me. I thought he was a five-inning starting pitcher who couldn't go two days in a row if you put him in the bullpen."

The Mets' farm system was drying up, and here was McIlvaine

squandering what little was left. "This one," he said at the time, "could backfire right in my face if Viola doesn't perform up to expectations." The Mets made up just one game on the first-place Cubs after the trade, with Viola going 5–5. He spent two more years in New York—going 38–32 overall, including a combined 13–20 in August, September and October—before leaving as a free agent. "That's the kind of thinking," Wilpon says of the shortsighted trade, "that doesn't work out."

Viola was tormented by the carousel of grotesque fielders the Mets annually put on display. "I'm not surprised to see what's happened to the Mets," says Viola, who bolted after the 1991 season to sign with the Red Sox. "I saw it coming. What happened is they had too many people out of position. And I mean starting from the front office on down." Gregg Jefferies, a hitting phenom who was touted by McIlvaine as a future batting champ, came up in 1988 as a third baseman, moved to second base and then back to third—he displayed not a bit of elegance at either position—before the Mets moved him one last time: to Kansas City, following the '91 season. Howard Johnson began 1990 at third base, '91 at shortstop and '92 in centerfield. During those three seasons the Mets' Opening Day lineup featured different players at six positions every year. "The Mets have always been an offensive-minded club," says Dallas Green, who last season became the Mets' fifth manager in three years. "I could never understand why they ignored defense, with all the good pitching they had. It's a mistake we're not going to continue to make."

Midway through the 1989 season McIlvaine and Harazin were telling Cashen that he had to fire Davey Johnson. "The team is getting away from him," McIlvaine said. Johnson knew it was a stressful, transitional year. The co-captains, Carter and first baseman Keith

Hernandez, repeatedly broke down physically in what would be their last season with the club. Gooden, the emotional cornerstone of the franchise, tore a muscle in his throwing shoulder. Cashen chose to bring back Johnson to start the '90 season, and McIlvaine continued trading. He sent Myers to Cincinnati for John Franco because he feared Myers was weightlifting himself out of baseball. Myers has since won an NLCS Most Valuable Player award and set the league save record for a single season. Franco has been hurt or ineffective much of the past three seasons. Less than two months into the season Cashen agreed that Johnson had to go.

Initially the Mets responded to Johnson's successor, Harrelson, and on Sept. 3, 1990, they were in first place, one-half game ahead of the Pirates. They lost their next five games, though, including three crucial games in Pittsburgh. In the third game of that series, on the recommendation of McIlvaine, Harrelson started Julio Valera, a 21-year-old righthander with one career start in the big leagues, rather than the veteran Darling. Valera allowed five runs while getting only six outs in a 7–1 defeat. Except during the first three weeks of a season, the Mets have not been in first place since.

AFTER THE 1988 season Wilpon and Doubleday wanted Cashen to begin a transition into a consultant's role, allowing McIlvaine to assume full control of the baseball operations and Harazin the business side. "We wanted it to be a gradual process," Wilpon says. But two years later Cashen was still the ultimate authority in the organization, with no official change imminent, though McIlvaine and Harazin were doing much more of the spadework. While Cashen grew comfortable running the club in a patriarchal manner, the owners were content to stretch out the front-office transition another year. Finally, when the Padres asked McIlvaine in September 1990 to be their G.M., he figured, "If I'm going to do all the work, I might as well get all the blame or credit, and make the decision myself." So on Oct. 2, 1990, McIlvaine signed a five-year contract to be general manager of the Padres. His departure was provoked in part by the razzing his nine-year-old son, Timmy, took in school. "Your dad traded Lenny Dykstra," kids would say—and worse.

"All of a sudden, the plan of succession was no plan at all," Wilpon says. "We were stunned when Joe left." No one was more stunned than Cashen, who was 65 and having a house built in Florida to accommodate a more leisurely life. Suddenly he had to run the team again on a full-time basis. He had neither the energy nor the interest for it.

Cashen was a self-proclaimed "dinosaur" who was growing increasingly bitter about the explosion in players' salaries. "I admit," he says, "that I look at the money being spent as if it were mine." He had built winning teams in Baltimore and New York, but now the business and its players were changing, and Cashen was not. One month after McIlvaine left, Strawberry left too—in part because of Cashen.

In midsummer of '90, just when the Mets and Strawberry—a moody outfielder prone to lapse into stretches of indifferent play—were rolling, Cashen had scoffed in a television interview that Strawberry, a potential free agent, wasn't worth the money Oakland slugger Jose Canseco was getting. The tone and timing of the comments were inappropriate, especially with a player like Strawberry, who never seemed to be sure what he wanted. McIlvaine, who played minor league ball and studied at a seminary, had a better touch with players. But contrary to the owners' plan, this was Cashen's team.

"At that point Darryl was leaning toward staying with us," McIlvaine would say later. "But after that it all changed. Darryl just wants to be loved. When Frank said what he said, Darryl felt his friends had deserted him. That did it."

It was in September, with the Mets trailing Pittsburgh by three games with six to play, that Cashen finally decided he wanted Strawberry gone. Strawberry had said his back was too sore to play, and he watched the Mets lose two of their next three games and be eliminated. He never played again for them. "That," Cashen says, "was the last straw. Here was a guy who didn't want to play with the season on the line. Darryl had had great Septembers for us. But I think he lost some of his hunger for winning."

Strawberry decided to sign a five-year, $20.25 million contract with the Dodgers in November '90. Cashen was relieved to be rid of Strawberry, who seemed to launch as many controversies as home runs. (He holds the franchise record, 252.) "We'll be a better team without him," Cashen promised, obviously unprepared for the team's 208–277 free-fall since then.

For 10 years Cashen had disdained the free-agent game, insulated by that rich farm system. He quickly changed that posture after his best player and best baseball mind left him in the space of five weeks in 1990. At the urging of Harrelson and Harazin, he signed Coleman to a four-year, $11.95 million contract. It was an act of desperation that accelerated the decline of the Mets as much as any other single move.

By the end of the 1991 season Cashen finally agreed to step aside. Against their better judgment, Wilpon and Doubleday turned the entire operation over to Harazin, a bookish former management labor lawyer who admitted to never having owned a pair of blue jeans. More important, as Wilpon knew, Harazin's baseball knowledge was dangerously shallow.

"Al was running both sides of the business," Wilpon says. "I think that was a mistake. The days of one general manager doing everything are over. Nelson and I knew it then. But we liked Al and decided to give it a shot. It was a costly shot for us."

The Mets' problems deepened. Last June, Wilpon realized that putting Harazin at the helm of the entire organization had been a mistake, just as his gut had forewarned him. He was entertaining Doubleday, his neighbor, at his Long Island home one day when the two men resolved to take action. "We have to go back to our plan," Wilpon said of their old intention to separate the baseball and business operations of the club. Doubleday agreed. Harazin, though, wasn't so amenable. He quit rather than be confined to running the business operations.

McIlvaine was rehired to run the baseball operations on July 8, after having left the Padres four weeks earlier in a dispute over a directive from the San Diego owners to trade the club's high-salaried players. The Mets considered no one else for the job. It was a curious choice, given McIlvaine's checkered trading record in his first tour in New York. Wilpon, though, believed McIlvaine's expertise at evaluating young talent was what the Mets needed most as they started rebuilding. McIlvaine has already allowed oft-injured pitcher Sid Fernandez, Howard Johnson and Murray to leave as free agents, while considering trades involving Bonilla and Saberhagen that will bring the Mets some prospects.

This October, McIlvaine sat behind the backstop at Veterans Stadium and watched Dykstra star in the World Series, another obvious reminder of his and the franchise's failings. Yes, Scioscia had kept the Mets out of the World Series in 1988. But since then Aguilera, Cone, Dykstra, Mitchell, Myers, Tapani and West had helped their teams get there. Of course, none of those teams was the Mets.

"COME HERE, let me show you something," Wilpon says. He rises from a chair in the Fifth Avenue office of his real estate company and walks across the room to a white rectangular box that is so large it is resting across four chairs. There is a great sense of purpose in his walk now. He is finished watching others run his baseball team. The Mets won't embarrass him again the way they did in 1993.

"It was," he says, "one of the most painful years of my life. To see what happened with this team was very, very painful. That's why I tell you this is a whole new thing we're starting."

Wilpon wants former Mets such as Tom Seaver, Mookie Wilson, Lee Mazzilli and Rafael Santana to come work for the organization. He wants "the greatest community outreach program" in sports. He wants grand entranceways and redesigned fan services at what has been a tacky Shea Stadium. He wants updated, cheery uniforms for the ushers. He has ordered intensive customer-relations training for all of the organization's business managers, including himself. He has talked with the Disney people, Universal Studio executives and other resort managers to learn how to attract and treat customers.

"Go to any of my buildings right now," he says. "I guarantee you, you won't find a piece of paper on the floor."

Wilpon pulls away the lid from the large white box. Inside is an architectural model of a sprawling entertainment complex. The centerpiece is a grass-surface stadium with a retractable dome, to be built within five years near the current Shea Stadium site and financed by state and city bonds. The stadium is surrounded by several pavilions that resemble huge tents. Wilpon explains they are state-of-the-art exhibit halls that he intends to be the permanent home of the World's Fair. That portion of the complex will be privately funded.

Wilpon opens and closes the little retractable dome, which splits open at the center like dual sliding doors. It is a perfectly happy and orderly place. The little plastic trees are always full and green. There is never any traffic on the access roads. It is kept immaculately clean. This is the world Fred Wilpon wants for the Mets. He wants the litter of a five-year decline swept up. He wants not a single piece of paper on the floor.

Postscript: The Mets still have not won a division title since 1988, though they twice earned wild-card berths, and owner Fred Wilpon still does not have his new ballpark. To this day the 1993 Mets, with the sixth-highest payroll at the time, stand as a monument to poorly constructed ball clubs.

Early Riser

*On a midsummer night in Boston, teenage sensation Alex Rodriguez
made his big league debut with the Mariners*

UNDER THE FOG-SHROUDED LIGHT TOWERS OF historic Fenway Park last Friday, the Seattle Mariners sent out as their starting shortstop a kid 13 months removed from his high school graduation and who shaves once a month. "If it doesn't work out," said Mariners manager Lou Piniella before the game, "I'm the one who's going to be criticized." No one could know for certain whether someone 18 years old was ready for the big leagues.

"No," said Alex Rodriguez. "I know I'm ready."

So when he took his infield position with the old stadium bursting with its usual summertime crowd, Rodriguez turned to 43-year-old teammate Rich Gossage, who was walking past him toward the right-field bullpen, and cracked, "You nervous, kid?" Then he winked. Empowered as much by self-assurance as by his remarkable talent, Rodriguez showed on first impression that his promotion was no rush job. Last Friday he handled all three of his chances in the field splendidly, especially the one that required a backhand stop and a long throw from the outfield grass. The next day he made an even more spectacular play; he dove headlong toward third for a smash, righted himself quickly and nearly got an impossible out at first base with a laser of a throw.

After going 0 for 3 in his debut, Rodriguez got his first two hits on Saturday, and the first time he reached base, Piniella gave him the green light. Rodriguez easily swiped second on the second pitch. But on Sunday, he had a rough afternoon, going 0 for 4 with three strikeouts and making a wild throw for an error.

Even though Rodriguez, who will turn 19 on July 27, is the youngest player to make the major leagues since Jose Rijo joined the Yankees 37 days short of his 19th birthday in 1984, he carried himself like a veteran. There were only occasional lapses when he gave away his age. That happened, for example, when he told Gossage he had played Class A ball this year in Appleton, Wis. "I played there once, too," the ancient Mariner said.

"When was that? Back in '88?" Rodriguez asked.

"Uh, no, 1971," Gossage said.

"Wow," said Rodriguez. "I was *born* in 1975."

Seattle selected Rodriguez with the first pick of the amateur draft in June 1993 and signed him to a three-year, $1.3 million contract on Aug. 30—too late for him to play in the minors last season. This year the Mariners had planned to give him half a season at Appleton and half a season at Class AA Jacksonville before calling him up in September, as his contract stipulates. Rodriguez did play 65 games for Appleton, where he hit .319, but he lasted only 17 games with Jacksonville, hitting .288 there, before Piniella convinced Seattle general manager Woody Woodward that the young shortstop was needed immediately.

Piniella pressed hard for the move after an ugly 9–3 loss to the Orioles on July 4 in which second baseman Rich Amaral made a critical double error. Amaral was one of four Seattle second basemen who had combined for 16 errors this season. Piniella knew that Rodriguez was a wizard on defense and that Felix Fermin, who had played solidly at short but lacked range, could move to second base. When Rodriguez made his debut, the Mariners ranked 12th in the league in fielding and were 12 games under .500 (36–48).

"Let's face it," said Piniella, "if we were close to .500 and playing well, this wouldn't have happened. We thought he'd be our shortstop next year anyway, and he was going to be here in September, so we've only moved his timetable up by six or seven weeks." Rodriguez was immediately welcomed by Ken Griffey Jr., the first pick of the 1987 draft, who reached the majors five years ago at 19. Griffey insisted that Rodriguez take a locker next to his own, whereupon he proceeded to needle the kid relentlessly. Griffey handed him coupons for McDonald's, saying, "You're making one-point-three; when you get sent down after the All-Star break, take the guys out to lunch down there."

But the 6' 3" Rodriguez would appear to have staying power. "It's funny," he said. "Last year I would have paid anything to go watch a major league game. This year I'm playing in one."

Postscript: Even at 18, Rodriguez had the poise and polish of a 10-year veteran, and not just between the white lines. I remember how he asked questions—about me, my job, the major leagues, anything. It was apparent even then that this was not just the debut of another phenom, but the coming out of a player who could be among the alltime greats.

The Players' Most Valuable Player

A snapshot of Marvin Miller, the former trade unionist who became baseball's pioneering labor leader

H E WAS A '60S RADICAL IN A SHIMMERING SHARKSKIN suit. He was an outsider who dared challenge one of America's most cherished and, to his great consternation, most unwavering institutions: the game of baseball. Viewed through the corrective lens of history, though, Marvin Miller advanced an ideology that wasn't all that radical, even if in the buttoned-down world of baseball, his wardrobe was.

Miller held that a ballplayer should not be bound to one club for life. He thought a $1,000 increase in the minimum annual salary over 20 years was grossly insufficient. Is that such extremist thinking? Well, it was in 1966, when Miller began what would be his 17 undefeated years as executive director of the Major League Baseball Players Association.

Miller, more than anyone else in the past 40 years, changed baseball's very structure, and he did so with the logic of someone not hidebound by the mythology and blind customs of the game. "I believe this was the first time the players reached out and got an experienced trade unionist," he says. "It wasn't that it was me. It was my background and expertise that were essential." He had come from the United Steelworkers of America, where he had gained vast experience in collective bargaining. When Miller first looked at baseball's standard player's contract, he thought it was "one of the worst labor documents I'd ever seen." It would have to be changed.

Starting with one battered filing cabinet and $5,400 in the association's checking account, Miller piled victory upon victory. "It's not difficult to make major strides," he once said, "in an industry a hundred years behind in labor relations." In 1968 he obtained an increase in the minimum salary from $6,000 a year (it had been $5,000 in '47) to $10,000; over time he assembled for the players what Ray Grebey, the former owners' representative, called "the best pension plan in America"; he secured the salary arbitration system in '73; and he held his membership together through a 50-day strike in '81—"the association's finest hour," as he called it in his memoirs.

Miller's agenda was aided mightily when, following the 1969 season, outfielder Curt Flood of the Cardinals made his courageous stand to protest baseball's reserve clause, under which a club was allowed to control a player's services until it decided to release or trade him. Flood refused to accept a trade to Philadelphia after his contract had expired, claiming that the reserve clause constituted a violation of antitrust law. Flood fought his case all the way to the Supreme Court, which ultimately ruled against him. It was, however, a short-lived victory for baseball owners. On Dec. 23, 1975, when arbitrator Peter Seitz ruled that pitchers Andy Messersmith and Dave McNally were free agents after playing the previous season without contracts, the reserve clause was effectively struck down. "The reserve clause was the most abominable thing I'd ever seen," says Miller. "I didn't think it would stand up."

He was better at labor relations than the owners—and he knew it. Baseball's most powerful man was just 5' 8", had a withered right arm since birth and never raised his voice in negotiations, relying instead on deep sighs or tiny laughs at things unfunny, and on a sense of righteousness that infuriated the owners. "He is a prisoner of his own ego above all things," wrote former commissioner Bowie Kuhn. *The St. Louis Globe-Democrat* said that Miller "would do baseball a favor if he disappeared or got lost or found the nearest hole and jumped into it."

He is 77 now, still living in his 32nd-floor apartment on the East Side of Manhattan and available to the players' association whenever it should seek his wisdom. Having established for the players both purpose and freedom, he is the association's George Washington and Abraham Lincoln all in one. "It's rightfully been called the most solid labor organization in the country, and not just in sports," he says. "Considering where we began, I think I'm proudest of that."

Strangely, while the game's labor wars have reached new heights of contentiousness, Miller's own image has seemingly been enhanced over time—from, at worst, that of some activist heaving homemade bombs at baseball to, at best, that of a champion of reason, who gradually earned the grudging respect of even his adversaries.

Postscript: I interviewed Miller in his New York apartment and admired both for their understated elegance. I always had considered him an undefeated champion—until 2003, that is, when the Hall of Fame Veterans Committee, composed mostly of Hall of Fame players, rejected his nomination to the Hall. I still don't understand how that could happen.

The High Price of Hard Living

*Reckless years in the fast lane, fueled by alcohol and cocaine,
cost former New York Mets phenoms Darryl Strawberry
and Dwight Gooden the prime years of their careers*

THE HOOD OF THE SILVER-BLUE MERCEDES RESTING IN the circular driveway of the new $1.2 million house in Rancho Mirage, Calif., is still warm. On this Wednesday afternoon in mid-January, Darryl Strawberry has just returned from providing a urine sample at a local hospital as part of his drug-testing agreement with Major League Baseball.

"There's a lot of sobriety out here," Strawberry says of the Coachella Valley as he offers up bottled water and stretches out on a leather sofa. The valley also has perfect desert weather, streets named after movie stars and more than 80 golf courses, 600 tennis courts and 10,000 swimming pools, one of which is on the other side of the patio doors just over Strawberry's left shoulder. Strawberry chose this resort community as his home last May after seeking treatment for cocaine abuse. "And I don't even play golf," he says. He is living in self-imposed exile, talking about his former home cities, New York and Los Angeles, as his versions of Sodom and Gomorrah.

"It became a lifestyle for me," Strawberry says. "Drink, do coke, get women, do something freaky . . . all that stuff. I did it for so long. I played games when I was drunk, or just getting off a drunk or all-night partying or coming down off amphetamines.

"With alcohol and drugs it was the excitement. That's how I got addicted. It was an exciting way to escape from everything else. Coming to the major leagues at such a young age and coming to New York . . . maybe someplace else it would be a little different, but New York is a party place, an upbeat place.

"Man, I put up some good numbers. But I look back and wish I could've done it like I'm doing it now: clean. I just got tired of [the lifestyle] after eight, nine, 10 years. They would have never caught me because I'd done it [drugs] for so long. I grew up in a fast place, L.A."

Strawberry had provided a urine sample the previous day as well. The day before that, on Monday, Strawberry had spoken at a Martin Luther King Day rally at the El Cerrito Community Center, a few miles north of Oakland. He had talked about the importance of keeping children off drugs and alcohol, referring to them several times as "the young youth today."

"I've been through drugs and alcohol myself," he had said into the microphone. "I overcame that through the grace of God." The cocaine he had scored less than 48 hours earlier, on Saturday night, lingered in his system as he spoke at the rally. More fatefully, it was in the urine samples he provided on Tuesday and Wednesday. He didn't realize, as he sprawled across his couch, telling a reporter he was clean, that he'd been caught.

IT BEGINS with one beer, the way a massive freeway pileup begins with one car or the way an inferno starts with a spark. Dwight Gooden's pattern of self-destruction continues when he orders another beer and then another. On this night, in June 1994, the lights and the music and mostly the alcohol at the Manhattan nightclub are soothing him.

He has been a hard drinker since 1986, when he was 21 and in his third year in the majors—abstaining from alcohol only on the two nights before a starting assignment and, flushed with youth, money and stardom, indulging on all the others. At 22 he landed in a drug rehab center after testing positive for cocaine. Now, nearing his 30th birthday and into his third straight losing season, he is drinking out of self-pity. The alcohol hits him like Novocain; it numbs the pain but cannot remove it.

The beers are not enough, so, as he often has, he switches to something harder. Vodka has always been a favorite. It makes him forget about his combined 22–28 record for the Mets in 1992 and '93, about how terrible his team has become and about the injured toe on his right foot, which has kept him on the disabled list for the past five weeks. The drinks keep coming.

Man, I'm hammered, he thinks. He presses on deep into the night, so deep that he still is drinking when he notices the place is closed, the doors are locked and everybody else except the people who work in the club have gone home. That's when one of the employees pulls out the bag of cocaine. You want some?

I know I shouldn't, he thinks. But that notion passes quicker than one of his old fastballs, dissolving completely into the fuzziness of his alcohol-polluted mind. What the hell, he thinks. I'm on minor league rehab for my toe. They won't test me. Within 48 hours a representative of the testing agency used by Major League Baseball arrives in Binghamton, N.Y., home of the Mets' Double A affiliate, to collect a urine sample from Gooden.

THE CAREER paths of Darryl Strawberry and Dwight Gooden began as parallel lines—unbending inclines headed straight to Cooperstown. How could it be that instead we are left with this ugly tangle of trouble? They both were National League Rookies of the Year, the 21-year-old Strawberry in 1983 and Gooden, at 19, the following season. When Gooden started his first major league game, in '84, Strawberry ripped a home run to centerfield for the game-winning RBI. Before either one of them had turned 25, they were stars, millionaires and, in '86, world champions as members of one of only four National League teams in this century to win as many as 108 regular-season games. How did those parallel lines wind up as twisted as those on a New York City subway map, the two of them intersecting over and over again?

Intersections: In the off-season following the Mets' World Series victory, Gooden was arrested for brawling with Tampa police and Strawberry was ordered by a Los Angeles court to stay away from his wife, Lisa, whose nose he had broken with a punch to the face. So when Strawberry reported to spring training in 1987 and discovered he had been assigned a locker next to Gooden's, he cracked in his typical dark humor, "Look, it's Assault and Battery together."

Six weeks later Gooden spent Opening Day in Smithers Alcoholism and Treatment Center in New York City, being treated for cocaine use, while Strawberry, wearing Gooden's uniform pants, drove in the winning runs with a three-run home run. Three years after Gooden checked into Smithers seeking treatment for drug abuse, Strawberry checked into Smithers for alcohol abuse. Both of them now admit they sought treatment halfheartedly. Little wonder then that last year Strawberry and Gooden both checked into the Betty Ford Center in Rancho Mirage for cocaine abuse. One going and the other coming, they missed each other by only 79 days.

Last Aug. 14, Strawberry picked up Gooden upon his release from the Betty Ford Center and drove him the one mile down Bob Hope Drive to Strawberry's new home. He escorted Gooden through the grand marbled foyer and into the living room.

"Doc, you've got to get out of Florida," Strawberry said. "You've got to change your environment to keep from using. The most important thing they told me at Betty Ford was to change the whole atmosphere and get away from the people who use."

Gooden has maintained his home in St. Petersburg since moving there in 1987 from his birthplace, Tampa. Within a week after leaving the Betty Ford Center last summer—and three days after attending a counseling session in New York with Robert Millman, a psychiatrist who represents Major League Baseball, and Joel Solomon, a psychiatrist who represents the players' union—Gooden was drinking and using cocaine again with friends in Tampa. And five months after that, Strawberry tested positive for cocaine.

"It just goes to show you," Gooden says now, "it doesn't matter where you are. Drugs, alcohol . . . it's everywhere. What's more important is that you can never let your guard down."

Another intersection: Today neither Strawberry nor Gooden has a team to call his own. They are suspended from baseball. They are the eighty-sixed Mets.

And yet they are so different. Strawberry is a complex puzzle. None of the Mets was better around children at charity events. Even now he is pouring a healthy portion of what's left of his money—he's estimated to have earned about $25 million as a baseball player—into the Strawberry Patch Youth Project, a San Francisco Bay Area drug and alcohol prevention program that he founded with Ron Jones, one of his closest friends and a former drug dealer. Strawberry is, even as he approaches his 33rd birthday, as naively eager for love and acceptance as a puppy in a pet-shop window. He has a natural capacity to charm people. He can turn any room into a happy place merely by strolling in with that cool, smooth, long-legged glide, and he can energize any ballpark, hit or miss, with that beautiful, looping swing.

Sadly, he can just as easily transform himself into something rotten. His transgressions contradict—even obliterate, for many people—that core of goodness. Alcoholic, drug abuser, batterer and now convicted tax cheat. His career has been a long screech of tires during which all you could do was wait for the crash. The chronic tardiness, the enormous mood swings and the erratic behavior offered a cacophonous prelude to disaster for all to hear. "A walking stick of TNT," says Strawberry's former Mets teammate Ron Darling.

Contrasted against Strawberry's dark streak was the apparent benevolent light of Gooden: accommodating, consistent, industrious, quiet. Indeed, after 1985 the tight friendship between the two ballplayers loosened to a comfortable acquaintance. They were not as close as the public thought. As Strawberry says, "I never partied with Doc."

"The few times Dwight was late for anything," Darling says, "everyone would ask, 'Is the cab stuck in traffic? Was he in an accident?' When Darryl was late, you thought right away, Darryl screwed up again. Doc was Teflon and could do no wrong. Darryl was a ticking time bomb."

THE WAY Strawberry remembers it, his first experience with cocaine was in 1983, soon after he was promoted to the major leagues. He liked to drink beer and he smoked pot sometimes, but now two of his veteran teammates were asking him to try something new. "There's a couple of lines in the bathroom for you, kid," he remembers them saying. "This is the big leagues. This is what you do in the big leagues. Go ahead. It's good for you."

Strawberry tried the cocaine. Damn, he thought, that's *good*.

So began the volatility that became the trademark of his career. He did not create a new controversy every day; it only seemed that way. In a seven-day span in June 1987, Strawberry overslept twice, and was rousted from his hotel bed both times by a teammate's phone call from the ballpark; was fined $250 and benched for two games for his tardiness; charged the mound after almost being hit by a pitch; and blasted a 450-foot home run. So often did he drop bombs that when asked about his weird week, he replied in all earnestness, "Weird? Why? Just because I was late twice, got benched, was fined and had a fight? It's part of the game."

Still, what happened within a four-day span this month was shocking even by his standards: Between Feb. 6 and 9 Strawberry received a 60-day suspension from baseball because of the positive drug tests, was released by the Giants and pleaded guilty to the charge of failing to report and pay tax on more than $350,000 in income from appearances at card shows from 1986 to '90. As part of the plea arrangement Strawberry is expected to be sent to prison for three months and be under house arrest for another three months.

Last week, according to Jones, Strawberry entered his third rehabilitation center in the past five years.

"Every time I think he's coming out of it, something else happens," said Richie Bry, Strawberry's agent from 1980 to '88, even before learning about this month's positive drug tests. "You don't know what to believe from him anymore. I think Darryl is basically a good person but

very immature and subject to being influenced heavily by other people, some good and some not. He's easily misled and easily succumbs."

The recent bout with cocaine cost Strawberry what appeared to be
an opportunity with a team that seemed to be a perfect fit for him.
During his 29 games with the Giants, who signed him after his release from the Dodgers last May, Strawberry enjoyed the benefits of
playing for an understanding manager, Dusty Baker; having Barry
Bonds and Matt Williams in the lineup, which allowed him to play
a supporting role for the first time in his career; and having his older
brother, Michael, on the team payroll as his personal chaperon. Strawberry lost all of that on Jan. 14, when he hooked up with some friends
for a Saturday night out in San Diego.

"He had all of that riding and still went back to cocaine," says Jones,
who says he changed his ways after going to prison twice, once on a
drug charge and once on a weapons charge. "That's how powerful
that s--- is. Darryl told me [he used again because] he felt a lot of
pressure was on him."

Until the recent relapse Strawberry said he had been clean since
last April 2. That night began with a private lecture in the office of
Dodgers manager Tommy Lasorda, before an exhibition game in Anaheim against the Angels. "Get yourself going," Lasorda barked. "We
need you to carry us."

How many times have I heard that? Strawberry thought. Only my
whole career. Why is it always on me? I'm tired of it. I don't want to
hear it anymore.

He hit a home run in his last at bat that night and then disappeared
into his own black hole of despair, drinking and drugs. He got so high
he never went home. His new wife, Charisse, called his mother, Ruby,
late the next morning, which was a Sunday. Darryl had weekend cus-

tody of his two children from his first marriage, Darryl Jr. and Diamond, but after staying at his house they were to return that day to his ex-wife, Lisa. Did Ruby know where Darryl was? Ruby was rushing off to church, so she let her daughter Regina talk to Charisse and left without being clear as to what the call was about.

When Ruby arrived at the Blood Covenant Christian Faith Center in Pomona, Calif., where she also works as a secretary, the parishioners comforted her. They had heard news reports that Darryl was missing. "It's going to be O.K.," they said. Ruby had no idea what they were talking about.

Strawberry remembered that the Dodgers had an exhibition game in Anaheim that afternoon—the last before the regular season began on April 5—but he could not muster the energy to go. I'm tired, he thought, too tired. I am not going through another season like this. The partying, the drinking. . . . I'm just so tired.

Late in the day he phoned his lawyer, Robert Shapiro, and agreed to meet with him the next morning. Shapiro, who two months later would be on national TV representing a fugitive named O.J. Simpson, brought Darryl into his office while Ruby, Charisse and Michael waited outside. Shapiro told Strawberry it was time he admitted he was an alcoholic and a drug user. For years Strawberry had been afraid to make that admission because he was worried, for one thing, about how it would be received by his family, his team and the media.

Shapiro told him he would take care of everything, including how it played out in the press. When the door opened, Shapiro gestured toward the family and asked Strawberry, "Is it O.K. to share it with them?" Strawberry nodded and told them.

"Tears welled up in my eyes, and I had a big lump in my throat," Ruby says. "It made me realize some of the things that were happening with him. He didn't care what was going on with the family. He was not in touch with us.

"Now that I look back I can understand a lot of his behavior. I used to wonder why he never made eye contact with me when he talked. I kind of brushed it off. You know, he was always on the go, never had much time. He was always kind of looking over my head, looking for someplace else to go or something.

"I remember one of the first things he did after he left the Betty Ford Center. We were sitting in my home, on opposite sides of a room. I told him, 'You know, that's something you never used to do.' And he said, 'What's that? What are you talking about?' And I said, 'You can look me in the eyes when you're talking to me. You never used to do that.'

"From what I understand now, a lot of things were going on before he came back to L.A. That was something we weren't aware of."

Marking the point at which a life went wrong is an inexact science. When did the downward spiral begin for Darryl? With that night after his rookie season when he met Lisa Andrews at a Lakers game at the Forum? With that first powerful hit of coke? With his sophomore year at Crenshaw High in South Central L.A., when he was disciplined by his baseball coach for having a bad attitude and quit the team? Or with those childhood nights when his father, Henry, would come home loud and angry after drinking and gambling? Darryl, the middle of five children, remembers being hit by his father "for little things" before Henry left Ruby in 1974, when Darryl was 12.

"It starts with abuse: verbal and physical abuse," Darryl says. "It leaves scars you carry to adulthood." Ruby doesn't remember Henry's striking Darryl so much, saying, "I'm not that kind of mother. I would not have allowed it with my kids." But she does concede it's important if "that's the way he remembers it." Teammates and friends always have noticed how Darryl has sought love, often desperately.

"Yes," Ruby says, "because Darryl didn't have the father he wanted, or one who acted the way he thought a father was supposed to, it caused him to act out in different ways. Some children need that father figure, especially boys. Darryl needed it, but he didn't have it and looked for it in other places."

The Mets selected Strawberry with the first overall pick of the 1980 draft, their decision clinched when Strawberry, then fresh out of Crenshaw High, posted an impressive score on a test that measures aggressiveness, mental toughness and self-confidence. After giving Strawberry a $200,000 signing bonus, New York had scout Roger Jongewaard accompany him to its Kingsport, Tenn., rookie league team. "I went with him as a buffer because of all the attention he was getting," Jongewaard says. "Darryl did such a great job handling it, he really didn't need me."

Less than three years later, in 1983, Strawberry was in the big leagues. He had 26 home runs that season, beginning an unprecedented run of hitting more than 25 home runs in his first nine seasons, all but one of them with the Mets. Only two other players had hit that many homers in more than their first *four* seasons: Frank Robinson (seven) and Joe DiMaggio (six). During that span Strawberry never hit 40 home runs in a season, and he averaged 92 RBIs—a relatively low total for someone with his power. He also missed an average of 21 games a season in those years. And he played just 75 games over the 1992 and '93 seasons because of a herniated disk that required surgery.

"He should have averaged 100 RBIs and 40 home runs," Jongewaard says. "He has underachieved. And that's a hard thing to say because he put up some very good numbers, but that's how much talent he had."

Those sort of expectations alternately inflated Strawberry with pride and wore him down. In typical Straw-speak, one day he would promise "a monster season" and the next he would complain about having to carry too big a load. His quotes were often outrageous and hollow. He continually drifted, as if pulled by the current, and if he ever sought mooring during his years with the Mets, he did not find it at home or in the clubhouse.

"I was at their wedding," a friend says of Darryl and Lisa's marriage, "and they were at each other's throats from Day One. It was like they hated each other from the start. And his mother didn't like her at all. That put a drain on Darryl. And it was no secret how they went through money. It was almost like a contest to see which one could outspend the other."

Darryl married Lisa in January 1985, two months before signing a six-year contract worth $7.2 million. The Strawberrys would separate and reconcile routinely over the next seven years. Once, at dinner with another couple, Darryl and Lisa shouted obscenities at each other so loudly in a restaurant that "we were embarrassed," says one of the other diners. "I said to Lisa, 'Why don't you try being nice to him?' And she said, 'If you only knew what he puts me through.' "

One of Lisa's attempts at reconciliation occurred in Houston during the 1986 National League Championship Series. Darryl says he spent one night drinking with friends at the hotel bar, and when he returned to their room he found Lisa had chained the door. He banged on it furiously as they screamed at each other. When she finally opened the door, Darryl uncorked a punch to her nose that sent her to a hospital. "It was scary," he says. "I did some of the same things in my marriage that I felt my father did to me and our family. It's unfortunate it had to happen like that, but I was turning into him. That's what I found out later from the people at Betty Ford."

Lisa filed for legal separation and an order of protection on Jan. 29, 1987. She and Darryl reconciled eight months later. On June 2, 1989, Lisa began divorce proceedings. The Strawberrys reconciled again later that year. At 3:45 in the morning of Jan. 26, 1990, during a fierce argument in which Lisa whacked Darryl in the ribs with an iron rod, he pulled out a .25 caliber pistol and pointed it at her. He was arrested and jailed briefly on suspicion of assault with a deadly weapon, but no charges were filed.

Recalling that night in his 1992 autobiography, *Darryl,* he wrote, "Just be glad, I remember saying to myself as I tried to find something positive in this whole mess, that you aren't involved with drugs." That, of course, was a lie. Eight days after the fight, at the Mets' recommendation, Strawberry checked into Smithers for alcohol abuse. As it turned out, this was a convenient move to avoid prosecution. That was another one of Darryl's lies. "Going to Smithers was my cover-up," he admits now. "I never even bothered telling them about the drugs."

Strawberry continued to drift. On Nov. 8, 1990, he signed as a free agent with the Dodgers. "My first choice was to be back home," he said at the ensuing press conference, only to turn around moments later and say, "The Mets were the only organization I wanted to play for."

He tried religion, claiming in January 1991 that he was born again. He was free of drugs and alcohol, he said, while rationalizing, "I can have a glass of wine or beer if I choose. I choose not to." An L.A. teammate said that was a lie and that Strawberry still was sucking down beers. Born-again teammates on the Dodgers, Brett Butler and Gary

Carter, would invite him to breakfast, but Strawberry wouldn't show.

"It wasn't a farce," his mother says. "I think he was genuinely try-ing to get his life together. But at the same time he did not want to admit to anyone how much trouble he was in."

Darryl and Lisa split again in January 1991, and she resumed di-vorce proceedings on May 28, 1992. The divorce was finalized on Oct. 15, 1993. Lisa was awarded the couple's house in Encino, a 1991 BMW 750i, a 1989 Porsche 928, a 1991 Mercedes SL, $300,000 in cash, $40,000 in attorney's fees (in addition to the $55,000 Darryl had al-ready paid for her attorneys and accountants) and $50,000 a month in spousal support. Darryl was ordered to pay another $30,000 a month in child support.

"His marriage was a bad one from the beginning," Ruby said in 1991. "Darryl wasn't that kind of person until he got involved with Lisa."

Lisa Strawberry did not respond to SI's attempts to reach her through her attorney.

On Dec. 3, 1993, less than two months after his divorce was final-ized, Strawberry married Charisse Simon. The wedding occurred three months after Strawberry was arrested on a battery charge for allegedly striking her. Simon did not press charges. The couple has an 11-month-old son, Jordan, and is expecting another child in June, the fifth for Strawberry by three women. (In 1990 Strawberry was found by means of a blood test to be the father of a child by Lisa Clay-ton, of Clayton, Mo., who had filed a paternity suit against him.)

Strawberry's domestic problems affected him on the field. He ad-mitted during spring training in 1987 that there were periods of "sev-eral days, even weeks where I didn't concentrate at all." Then his de-portment grew worse. That year he reported late to work at least four times (once remarking, "It's tough getting up for day games"), walked out of training camp once and begged out of a critical game against the first-place Cardinals with a virus after spending the afternoon recording a rap song. After that, Mets teammate Wally Backman remarked, "Nobody I know gets sick 25 times a year." To which Strawberry responded, "I'll bust that little redneck in the face." And all of that happened in a year when he had career highs in batting average (.284) and home runs (39).

"When a guy gets to the ballpark at five-thirty, six o'clock at night and he's sending somebody out for a burger or chicken and it's his first meal of the day, that's a sign of trouble," says Steve Garland, a former Mets trainer. "And that happened a lot."

"You could always tell the days Darryl didn't want to play," says former Met Dave Magadan. "He'd show up looking as if he was knocking on death's door. You knew he wasn't going to play or you'd get nothing out of him."

On those days Garland or one of the New York coaches would mention to manager Davey Johnson that Strawberry appeared as if he wanted to sit the game out. "F--- him," Johnson would snap back.

"That's right," Johnson says now. "I'd get the farthest away from him that I could so that he had no chance of getting the day off. My attitude was, he was going to play—screw him. Maybe he'll understand he has to keep himself ready to play and get his damn rest. Usually he'd be so mad at me, he'd go out and hit two home runs. It happened more than once."

"I don't know about that," Magadan says. "Most of those times Darryl was a nonfactor."

Johnson knew Strawberry was cheating himself on the field and called him into his office on numerous occasions. The speech, Johnson says, was always the same: "You've got to take care of yourself.

You've got to get your rest. You can't keep this up." Strawberry would nod and say, "Thanks, skip. I hear you. I'm going to turn things around." And the minute Strawberry walked out the door he would forget what he had heard.

Says Bry, Strawberry's former agent: "Management is so afraid to say anything to players, especially the high-paid ones. They see them on a daily basis. They're scared to death of the players, afraid to confront them if they know something's wrong. That's what happened with Darryl."

On Sept. 18, 1989, in anticipation of a New York loss, Strawberry and Kevin McReynolds began undressing in the clubhouse in the ninth inning of a game at Wrigley Field. The Mets staged a rally, however, forcing the two players to scurry back into their uniforms as their turns in the batting order approached. Johnson fined them $500 each and called a meeting the next day.

"Mac knew he was wrong, but what he really didn't like was being linked with Strawberry," Johnson says. "What really upset me was that during the meeting Darryl was saying, 'What's the big deal?' " Johnson and Strawberry nearly came to blows. Several players, including Darling, prevented a fistfight only by stepping between them. "What most people don't know," Darling says, "is that that kind of confrontation happened on planes and buses and in the clubhouse between Darryl and Davey maybe 20 times."

Strawberry could be mean and antagonistic, especially from his usual spot in the back of the team bus. He would shout loud enough so that Johnson, sitting in the first row, could hear him. He once ridiculed Johnson so viciously for not giving enough playing time to outfielder Mookie Wilson that Johnson had to fight back an urge to run to the rear of the bus and pummel Strawberry. On another day Mackey

Sasser, a Met catcher troubled by an embarrassing hitch in his throwing motion, was not as restrained. He charged Strawberry and came away from the assault with blood gushing from his nose.

"Darryl always thought [ragging on people] was funny," Magadan says. "But a lot of times it was vicious. And he wasn't always drunk. A lot of times it was on the bus right after a game."

Nobody caught more heat from Strawberry than Carter, the veteran catcher who struggled with injuries from 1987 through '89, his last three seasons with the Mets. "It got to the point of being very malicious," says Carter. "But a lot of it had to do with his drinking. You just let it go. I knew what it was all about. It was about money. He hated it that I was making more money than he was, even though I'd tell him, 'Darryl, you're going to make 10 times as much money in this game as I ever did.' It was the same thing with Keith Hernandez. That's why they had the fight."

In spring training of 1989, while lining up for a team picture, Strawberry suddenly took a swing at Hernandez, the Mets first baseman, shouting, "I've been tired of you for years!"

"That was where it really started to unravel for Darryl," Darling says. "He lost a lot of respect, and I think he was embarrassed. Keith and Gary were at the ends of their careers, and the team was passing to Darryl and Dwight. And they were never able to lead the team in the same way."

As the pressure grew and as the Mets failed again and again to make it back to the World Series, Strawberry began to see himself more and more as a victim. "Other guys would have a bad year and people would make excuses for them," he says, "but if we didn't win it was my fault. My own teammates would say things about me. I could never figure that out.

"Listen, I hold myself accountable for all that's happened. I take full responsibility for what I did. But me and Doc were two young stars, black players, who came to New York, and the expectations were extremely high. I don't think any other two players in any sport came to New York at that age with expectations so high. The pressure, it was so great. That's why I want to help kids now. I didn't have anyone say, 'Let me help you.' If I had had someone like that around, maybe I'd have had a different way of dealing with it."

WHEN STRAWBERRY, at 21, and Gooden, at 19, joined the Mets, they became part of a team that played hard and lived harder. That group evolved into a ball club fueled by an intense desire to be the best but very often driven also by alcohol, amphetamines, gambling and drugs. Young, impressionable and unsophisticated, Strawberry and Gooden were driftwood in the current.

"When Doc came out of Smithers in 1987," Garland says, "he talked to me about how prevalent the drug use was on the team. He started calling off names. He rattled off more than 10—more than half the team. Probably around 14 or 15. And I thought the '84, '85 and '86 teams were wilder."

Gooden recalls the time on a team charter in 1986 when the door to one of the bathrooms popped open, revealing a teammate inside using cocaine. "A lot of us saw it," Gooden says. "We just looked at each other and said, 'Nobody saw nothing.' "

Between 1986 and '91, of the 22 Mets players who appeared in the 1986 World Series, eight were arrested following incidents that were alcohol- and/or battery-related (Strawberry, Gooden, Darling, Rick Aguilera, Lenny Dykstra, Kevin Mitchell, Bob Ojeda and Tim Teufel) and a ninth was disciplined by baseball for cocaine use (Hernandez).

The charges against Aguilera, Mitchell and Ojeda were eventually dropped.

Johnson, the New York manager from 1984 through part of the '90 season, has admitted he drank too much in those years. He kept a refrigerator stocked with beer in his Shea Stadium office. A former Mets player even remembers one of the coaches smoking pot on a beach in Florida during one spring training.

Moreover, Johnson says he knew "a couple of the New York veterans, not including Strawberry, were using amphetamines." Says Garland, "The guys who used amphetamines, maybe the numbers weren't great, but those who did use them used them almost every day. They depended on them so much they felt like they couldn't play without them."

After the 1986 season the Mets traded Mitchell, who had grown up around gangs in San Diego, because he scared the suits in the front office. They worried he was corrupting Strawberry and Gooden. "It was a mistake," Johnson says. "Mitch would have one or two drinks, but that's it. He was a good influence on them. He played hard. He had the street smarts they lacked. He could spot trouble and tell people to get lost. They needed that."

The most influential player on those Mets teams of the mid- to late-1980s was Hernandez, the smarmy first baseman who, during 1985 drug trials in Pittsburgh involving 23 baseball players, admitted using cocaine while he was with St. Louis in the early '80s. Hernandez advised Strawberry on how to break out of a batting slump: Go out and get totally smashed. Strawberry remembers the time Hernandez told him he'd found the perfect drink, of which he needed only five or six in a night: "Dry martini," Strawberry says, laughing.

The other veteran pillar of the team, Carter, was ignored or, worse, ridiculed. His crime? He was a conservative family man. "There was a lack of respect for Gary Carter," Garland says. "He was clearly in an overwhelming minority—or I should say an underwhelming minority."

The game was changing in those years, what with salaries and the memorabilia business beginning to boom; with the social status of players shifting, as revered icons became disposable celebrities; and with cocaine, as it was in the rest of American society, readily available.

Says Darling, "Darryl and, to a lesser extent, Dwight were the first athletes I'd ever seen who surrounded themselves with an inner circle of about eight to 10 associates. I felt like I never really knew either one of them. These people will tell the big star whatever he wants to hear. Their whole existence is contingent on one thing: making the man happy. It was not a real world."

The vortex of these changes—the money, the empty adulation, the cocaine—spun more quickly for a team from New York. The Mets became such a sexy, star-studded team that they were chased by fans carrying video cameras, the newest high-tech assault weapon of an increasingly aggressive audience. Just getting out of a hotel became an exercise in subterfuge.

The Mets were a portable party. Who among them would dare to be the grinch who turned down the music? What stick-in-the-mud would confront a teammate about drinking too much? The dynamics of the baseball clubhouse, especially the New York clubhouse, would not allow that. "All ballplayers like their beer," says a Mets insider. "The difference with this team was they liked all the stuff harder than beer."

And so any talk about overindulging was done with a wink and a chuckle. Strawberry would see Gooden with liquor and say, "Man, you drinking again?" And Gooden would catch Strawberry doing likewise and remark, "Man, you're an alcoholic." Just something else to laugh about, that's all it was.

When Gooden got out of Smithers in 1987, his counselor there, Allan Lans, was given added responsibility as the Mets' psychiatrist. But Lans was distrusted by many players, who figured he was a spy for management. Gooden would joke to Strawberry, "Doctor Lans says you're a time bomb waiting to go off," and later Doc would simply say, "Tick, tick, tick. . . ." as he walked by Strawberry.

Strawberry often left the clubhouse after games with cans of beer in a paper bag. On travel days, he and Gooden would pack large bottles of vodka in their carry bags to take aboard the team charter planes.

"If we wouldn't have partied so much, we would have won more," Strawberry says. "We had a team full of drunks. We'd go into a town and couldn't wait to go out drinking and partying, always asking each other, 'Hey, where you going tonight?' If we had 24 guys on the team in those days, at least half of them were hard drinkers or drug users. That was a hard-living team."

"What I remember," Gooden says, "is we'd be on the road and we'd come back into the clubhouse after batting practice and we'd be saying, 'Yeah, let's kick some ass and then go out and show everyone we own this town.' Whether it was Montreal or St. Louis or whatever, we wanted people to know it, like we were taking over the place."

Several players were so heavily involved with poker that Johnson or one of his coaches occasionally sat in for a few hands in the clubhouse. "My fear," Johnson says, "was that the stakes were getting out of control, and one player would be into another player for a dangerous amount of money. I didn't want to see guys get hurt financially. Then there'd be animosity."

Johnson was fired during the 1990 season, in great part because Mets management saw the players getting away from him. He disputes Strawberry's assessment that the team drank itself out of more titles. "I enjoyed those teams, and we were in contention every year," he says.

But Magadan, sometimes one of Strawberry's harsher critics, says, "I would agree with Darryl on that. We just lost perspective. I think a lot of guys lost sight of what our goals were. We'd go on a six-game road trip, say to Chicago and St. Louis. And instead of thinking, Let's win five out of six or six out of six, guys would be thinking, In Chicago I can go out to this restaurant and this bar, and in St. Louis I can go here and there. It was almost as if the games were getting in the way for some guys. They'd rather skip them and just go out."

LAST AUGUST, on one of his first nights back home in St. Petersburg after his stay at the Betty Ford Center and his counseling sessions in New York, Gooden grabbed a cold beer from his refrigerator and jumped into his black Mercedes. One for the road. He headed north on I-275 to Tampa for a night out with friends. Already under a 60-day suspension from major league baseball, he was risking an even harsher sentence. So what? He was feeling worthless and alone. Everyone seemed to be giving up on him.

The beer started his familiar chain reaction: a few more beers that led to hard liquor that led to cocaine. "If I don't drink, I have no desire to use coke," Gooden says. "You could put a bag of coke in front of me right now and I'd have no desire for it at all. Once I drink, especially when I get drunk, the desire is there. The hard stuff leads to coke. It was the same thing over and over.

"My problems have never been here in St. Pete. I was always getting into trouble in Tampa. It's strange. I have a son in Tampa, and I go there all the time to see him. If I go to Tampa during the day, I'm fine. But in Tampa after the sun goes down, it's like I'm a vampire. I change. Get a beer for the ride, meet my friends, go to a club, and I'm in trouble.

"Why did it happen? That's one of the things I'm trying to work out with my counselor. It's tough trying to pinpoint it. It's not any one thing. It's not that simple. Why go out and get s--- faced to the max? I still can't pinpoint it."

Gooden was the greatest pitching prodigy ever. He struck out more batters (276), in 1984, than any rookie ever had. At 20 he was the youngest Opening Day pitcher this century and the youngest Cy Young Award winner ever. He is the only pitcher this century to have 200 strikeouts in each of his first three seasons. Of the first 100 games he started in the big leagues, he lost only 19.

"He was by far the greatest pitcher I'd ever seen," Darling says. "I pitched behind him in the rotation, so I always charted his pitches. Those first two years, I swear, it seemed like he was 0 and 2 on 75 percent of the hitters. It was like Little League, where the other team has no chance except to bunt. If you told me Dwight was going to win 300 games and strike out 400 people one year, I'd have believed it. That's how good he was."

In the months after he was voted Rookie of the Year in 1984, Gooden, then living in Tampa, began using cocaine occasionally behind closed bedroom doors at house parties. Life was so easy. It had to be celebrated. "My nearest sister is 13 years older than me," says Gooden, who has five older siblings. "I don't want to say I was spoiled, but I had what I wanted growing up. Once I got to the big leagues, it happened so quickly for me. I got caught up in it."

Says Strawberry, "Doc came into the big leagues at 19. By 20 he was a big drunk hanging out in strip clubs."

"Not true," Gooden says. "It was my third year when I started to drink heavily."

By then, 1986, rumors about his drug use began to swirl. People called the Mets front office claiming to have knowledge of it. Gooden missed an exhibition game because of a friend's car accident, he claimed. He missed the team's ticker-tape parade following the World Series victory because, he says now, he was hung over from the night before and overslept. He called off his engagement to Carlene Pearson and fathered a son, Dwight Jr., by another woman, Debra Hamilton of Tampa. Then he had a brawl with the Tampa police after they stopped his car.

So on March 24, 1987, at Gooden's urging, his agent, Jim Neader, met with Mets vice president Al Harazin to work out a voluntary drug-testing plan. Gooden was supposed to attend the meeting but did not show. "Test for everything," Neader said. The next day, Neader told Harazin, "Go ahead, test away." So the following day, the Mets took a urine sample and sent it to St. Petersburg General Hospital.

"I feel like I have to do it," Gooden said at the time. "I want to convince the Mets more than I do anyone else."

On March 30 a test came up positive for cocaine. On April Fools' Day the Mets confronted Gooden with the test result. His first reaction was to deny it. Then he broke down and cried. "It was an absolute bombshell," Johnson says. "I thought it wasn't true. He was on time, worked hard and set a good example for the other pitchers. He had one of the best work ethics I've seen."

Gooden's life was a lie, and the Mets unwittingly helped perpetuate it. Under the overzealous mothering of the front office and its publicity staff, Gooden was told when to speak, whom to speak to and, sometimes, what to say. Such was management's paranoia that during Gooden's first workout at Shea Stadium after his first drug rehabilitation, reporters were sequestered in an auxiliary locker room with a guard posted at the door. The press was even refused access to the press box. The Mets weren't about to let Gooden become a loose cannon like Strawberry. Problem was, they failed to let Gooden be himself.

"I became this person I really wasn't," he says. "People said I was this quiet, nice, shy kid. Sometimes I just wanted to yell, 's---' or 'f---' or just blow somebody out. But I'd always stop myself and say, 'I'm not supposed to be like this.' Jay [Horwitz, the team's public relations director] would ask me to do an interview, and even if I didn't want to do it, I'd say, 'O.K., I'll do it.' "

"The problem with Dwight," Johnson says, "is he couldn't say no. He was too nice. Evidently he knew people in Tampa who could get you in trouble. It was like he was the lucky one, and it would be wrong for him not to be their friend, like he wanted to prove to them he wasn't acting like a big shot and turning his back on them."

Says Gooden, "That's 100 percent true. I have to be more vocal—in any situation." Gooden, despite Horwitz's concern, decided on his own to be interviewed for this story. "I'm not going to sit back and just take things in anymore," he says. "I have to be me. I'm going to be a little more selfish."

Gooden checked into Smithers in April 1987 immediately after testing positive for cocaine. He felt awkward being there and refused to open up to Lans. I can handle this by myself, he thought. You're not much of a man if you have to go to someone else with your problems.

The counselors tried to teach him how alcohol acted as his gateway to cocaine, but the lesson didn't stick. Three weeks after he checked out of Smithers he was drinking again. "If I won, I went out drinking to celebrate," he says. "And if I lost, I went out drinking to forget about it."

After Gooden's four weeks in Smithers, Major League Baseball began testing him for drugs as often as three times per week. As he continued to test clean over the years, baseball officials relaxed their vigilance. First they stopped taking samples on the days that he pitched. Eventually the frequency of the testing shrank to four random tests over each half of the baseball season. And, Gooden says, Lans began cutting back on Gooden's aftercare, excusing him from Alcoholics Anonymous meetings in New York because Gooden was such a celebrity that his appearances there were a distraction.

Meanwhile, Gooden's drinking problem deepened. With Strawberry gone to Los Angeles, the Mets plummeted to fifth place in 1991 with a 77–84 record. It was the first time Gooden had played on a losing big league team. New York's deterioration continued, with 90 losses in '92 and 103 losses and a last-place finish in '93. Gooden suffered the first two losing seasons of his big league career in those years. He tried finding solace in a bottle of beer or vodka. It was in those years too that his arm started feeling unresponsive.

"I didn't think it happened before, but in '92 and '93 all the drinking started to affect my performance," he says. "After a while, abusing your body catches up to you."

In December 1993, after one of his nocturnal sojourns into Tampa, another drug test turned up positive. Inexplicably, according to a high-ranking major league official, baseball's medical people chose to let it slide without informing the executive council or the players' union. "They didn't do him any favors by doing that," former trainer

Garland says. "It does make you wonder if there were any other times they did the same thing."

But the dirty test last June was not ignored. The Mets told Gooden he was facing probable suspension for violating his aftercare program. Gooden, in deep denial, told friends that it was no big deal, that he simply had missed a test because he'd overslept. He learned of his 60-day ban on June 24, a day he was scheduled to start against the Pittsburgh Pirates. The Mets, paranoid as ever, coaxed him into going ahead with his start. After all, baseball wasn't ready to announce the suspension, so what would people think if Gooden was scratched from his start? It turned out to be the worst performance of his career. "If I had to do it again," he says, "there's no way I'd go out there."

At first, Gooden says, Millman and Solomon, his counselors in New York, did not recommend that he undergo another inpatient rehabilitation. His aftercare program, including the testing regimen, needed to be stepped up. Gooden, after meeting with the doctors on July 1, went home to St. Petersburg. At an outing over that Fourth of July weekend, he decided, "Well, I'll just have a couple of beers."

He continued to slide. "I always knew one or two guys who had the coke," he says. "It wasn't like I had to go driving through some bad neighborhood and roll the window down." Once, on the morning of scheduled drug tests, he called up Lans and said, "I was using last night. Should I still go ahead with the test?" Lans advised him, yes, he should let himself be tested.

Finally, on July 22, he checked into the Betty Ford Center. When he broke the news to his wife, Monica, that he was heading to the clinic, she looked puzzled and asked, "Why?"

"She didn't know how bad it was," he says. "She'd always be asleep in bed when I'd be coming home late."

But three weeks after Gooden left the clinic, his depression returned and his cocaine use resumed. "Looking back on it," he says, "I should have called Jim [Neader] and told him what I was feeling. It's almost like you want to isolate yourself from the world. I didn't want to see anybody, even my family."

Then on Sept. 15 the Mets confirmed that Gooden had again violated his aftercare program. Baseball deferred any further action, essentially allowing him more time to pull himself together. But more samples came back dirty. On Nov. 4 he was suspended for the 1995 season.

"People ask, 'How can you use when you know you're getting tested?'" Gooden says. "It's not that easy not to. I remember when Otis Nixon tested positive again (in 1991, while with the Braves). I was like, Oh, man, how could a guy do something like that with so much on the line? Now I understand."

Gooden claims he has remained clean since then and has the test results to prove it. "I want the tests," he says. "It's one thing to say it and another to have the proof."

He has devoted himself to his three-times-a-week Alcoholics Anonymous meetings and his two-times-a-week sessions with a personal counselor in New Port Richey, Fla. One of the members of his AA group is a 70-year-old man who has been attending such meetings for the past 30 years. Gooden was shocked to hear him talk about episodes of still wanting to go back to alcohol. Another AA group member explained he has had nine relapses and is working hard to stave off a 10th.

"I see why," Gooden says. "You can never have this thing beat. I have to accept that. I still have my days where I get down. The difference is it doesn't stay with me as long as it did in August and September."

On Jan. 27 Gooden flew to New York to meet with Millman and Solomon. As the plane descended to LaGuardia Airport, the side on which Gooden sat banked toward Shea Stadium, as if genuflecting. Gooden caught sight of the giant horseshoe with the great expanse of green laid out so invitingly. Overwhelmed, not with sadness but with joy, he nearly cried. At that moment he wanted to be standing on the mound, a fresh baseball in his hand, the possibilities all new again.

"C'MON, LET'S get inside and talk," Gooden says, gesturing toward his Mercedes as the rain begins to fall. The wheels are equipped with brilliant rims that gleam even in the late-morning gloom. Gooden selected the rims and ordered another set for Monica's Mercedes convertible. To keep himself occupied, he has turned his love for customizing cars into a serious hobby. At the moment he is tinkering with a 1974 Porsche and a 1969 Chevy. Renovation. It is what he's doing with his life.

Slipping behind the steering wheel, Gooden is still perspiring slightly from one of his typically grueling workouts with his personal trainer. He appears to be in terrific shape, and when he throws the baseball, he says, it feels like it is flying out of his hand again. "Not having alcohol in your system," he says, "it seems like it makes you meaner, quicker."

Wearing blue Mets shorts and a blue nylon Mets training jacket, he looks and talks as if he were still the Mets ace. In fact, he has no employer, which would seem to be a daunting proposition for someone who supports an extended family. Beginning in 1987, with a $320,000 house for his parents and a $530,000 house for himself and Monica, Gooden has purchased five of the seven homes on his block, a waterfront cul-de-sac. One of the houses is the home of his nephew, Marlins outfielder Gary Sheffield. Gooden wants to buy the remaining two houses and then erect a security gate at the entrance to the street, though he says, "It's Gary's turn to buy."

Gooden, who last year finished a three-year contract originally worth $15.45 million and has earned about $25 million during his major league career, says he is financially secure. What he wants is simply to pitch in the major leagues again—even before his suspension is scheduled to end in November. He says he has been told by baseball officials that he could be reinstated by midsummer if he shows he has put his life in order, a claim Major League Baseball does not confirm. He has a standing offer from the Mets to start talking about a new contract as soon as he is reinstated to the game. He wants nothing other than that.

"It just feels like New York is my home," he says. "I belong to New York. It seems like I did all my growing up in New York.

"Obviously, I'd like to apologize to the fans for my actions, but I can honestly say I'm on the right track. I'm getting myself in the best possible shape physically so when that chance comes I'll be ready. It may be time to quit feeling like it can be 1985 again. But I'd be lying if I said I don't want to win 20 games again.

"I keep having these daydreams about coming back. If they let me come back in June or July, I can picture winning Comeback Player of the Year and going to a dinner to get the award and giving a speech. I go over that speech all the time."

The rain has let up and the faintest bit of sunshine appears. He has to be on his way now. He has an appointment with his counselor this afternoon and an AA meeting in the evening.

Before he goes, he is asked about being paired in infamy with Strawberry. The two of them started out as stars and were going to be the dominant players of their era, sure as sunrise. Now here they are, on the outside looking in, with messy lives to clean up and careers as uncertain as they were once assured. Doc and Straw. Teammates once again.

"It's sad," Gooden says. "The stories are kind of similar. Except Darryl was more vocal and I wasn't. Maybe if I was more vocal and if he wasn't, maybe it would have turned out better for both of us. Maybe."

Postscript: I began my professional career covering the major leagues at the same time and in the same city as Strawberry and Gooden, and I saw goodness in each of them, which makes their stories all the more tragic. I also knew this piece, one of the longest to run in SI in the past 20 years, was not the end of the ballad of Darryl and Doc. New chapters of their troubled tale never stop coming. In the fall of 2005 Strawberry admitted to filing a false police report and his wife filed for divorce. Gooden, with his son in jail on a probation violation, was sentenced to three years probation for fleeing a traffic stop.

Alone on
The Hill

In this era of muscular hitters and minuscule strike zones, pitchers get hammered all the time. A few, however, don't just survive, they thrive. Here are their secrets

LISTEN VERY CAREFULLY. IF YOU STAND CLOSE ENOUGH to the plate, you can hear the best weapon a pitcher can wield in his bid to survive in one of baseball's greatest offensive eras. A good fastball announces itself in flight with an angry whisper. "It goes *sssssssss*," says Braves righthander Greg Maddux, softly blowing air through his teeth in what sounds like the preamble to a steaming teakettle's whistle. "You can *hear* the good ones."

When a baseball spins fast enough, it creates a hiss as it cuts through the air. The faster the spin, the louder the hiss, which explains why the sinking 93-mph fastball thrown by Marlins righthander Kevin Brown sounds like air rushing out of a punctured tire. "I stood and watched Kevin Brown throw on the side at the All-Star Game last year," Maddux says. "His ball didn't go *sssssssss*. It went *SSSSSSSSS!* It was the loudest ball I've ever heard. You can see why his stuff is so nasty."

Says Marlins backup catcher Greg Zaun, "His sinker hurts your hands when you don't hit it on the good part of the bat. And just catching it isn't easy. You can't get too cute with it or else you'll hurt your thumb. You don't worry about framing it or anything like that. You just try to catch it."

Brown had a 1.89 ERA last season—2.32 better than the National League average (one of the biggest such differentials in the game's history)—and held batters to the lowest slugging percentage (.289) in the majors. While more taters flew out of ballparks than ever last season, Brown permitted just eight home runs over his 233 innings. He faced 906 batters and walked only 31 unintentionally. "With the kind of movement he has on the ball," says Florida pitching coach Larry Rothschild, "that's the most amazing statistic from last season."

Heard any good fastballs lately? Not likely. Pitchers such as Brown, 24-game winner John Smoltz of the Braves, 265⅔-inning workhorse Pat Hentgen of the Blue Jays and Randy Johnson of the Mariners, who has gone 55–16 since 1993, are anachronisms. They are pitchers who have the heat to dominate games consistently. They matter in a sport in which the owners, in their quest to grab the attention and disposable income of the casual, give-me-action fan, have turned the pitcher into a prop.

"What it takes to succeed as a pitcher now is so much more refined than it was 10 years ago," says Cardinals pitching coach Dave Duncan. That explains why young pitchers, in particular, are getting their lunches handed to them. Only one pitcher younger than 27 won more than 15 games last year: Andy Pettitte of the Yankees. Only three younger than 27 kept their ERAs below 3.50: Pedro Astacio and Ismael Valdes of the Dodgers and Steve Trachsel of the Cubs.

These days baseball belongs to the biggest, strongest men ever to have played the game, swinging extremely light bats at baseballs that seem harder and livelier while the dimensions of ballparks and the strike zone grow smaller. Owners have ignored recent suggestions that the pitching mound be raised or that umpires be compelled to expand the strike zone to the dimensions that are called for in the rule book. Instead, the owners have ensured the further escalation of offense by adding two expansion teams—meaning that about 40 more pitchers who don't belong in the big leagues will be on major league rosters—and by planning another wave of retro ballparks designed to minimize foul territory and maximize home runs.

Today's state-of-the-art hitter crowds the plate with such impunity that he needs to wear a protective plastic guard over his lead forearm while his hands hang in the strike zone. He virtually ignores the inside pitch, knowing the umpire is not likely to call one a strike and the pitcher doesn't want to risk inciting a brawl or give up a home run by throwing one. So the batter dives into the pitch—he doesn't simply stride toward the pitcher as in the old days—and is just as likely to pull an outside pitch out of the park as he is to hit it out to the opposite field. Then, as Gary Sheffield of the Marlins did after crushing 42 dingers last year, he goes home to lift weights with a former Mr. Olympia to get bigger and stronger.

The 1990s hitter has a batting cage in his basement and a library of videotapes in his den. Batters, especially designated hitters, watch pitchers on the clubhouse television during games. It's not unusual for a batter to run to the clubhouse VCR after one of his at bats.

The home run, the quickest way to a fat paycheck, is so driving baseball that striking out is no longer taboo for batters, who last year whiffed at a higher rate than ever. The grip-it-and-rip-it school of hitting does not encourage cutting down on one's swing even with two strikes. Mo Vaughn of the Red Sox was the American League MVP in 1995 while striking out 150 times, the most by an MVP in either league. Sixty-one players belted at least 25 home runs last year, but only seven of them didn't strike out at least 80 times (Barry Larkin, Sheffield, Bobby Higginson, Frank Thomas, Bernie Williams, Barry Bonds and Cal Ripken).

Home runs now occur more frequently than double plays, and nearly half the regular players hit at least 20 dingers (43% of the players with 400 at bats did so last year). For a pitcher to come away from this climate with the level of success achieved by Brown, Smoltz, Hentgen and Johnson is as difficult as coming away from a *Jenny Jones* show appearance with your dignity. Never mind the spotted owl. Who'll save the starting pitcher?

"The best thing you can do is intimidate hitters with your stuff," Smoltz says. "If you don't have really good stuff, I honestly don't know what you do. I believe so much in my stuff that I can dictate the game. I still believe if you make good pitches, it wouldn't matter if they were swinging aluminum bats. But hitters today are so good and so strong that if you don't have good stuff, they'll make you look real bad real quick."

Says Brown, "I don't buy the dilution-of-pitching theory. The offensive explosion has been dictated more by the size of the strike zone and the hitters. They've become stronger, and they have a smaller area to focus on as far as the strike zone is concerned. People say pitchers don't pitch a lot of innings anymore. That's because they have to put more into every pitch. That takes more out of you."

Hitters have raised the standard of what is considered quality pitching. In the mid-1980s, for instance, Dwight Gooden of the Mets dom-

inated the National League with just two pitches: a fastball, which
he usually threw high in the strike zone, and an overhand curveball
with a big break. Davey Johnson, his manager then, thinks more hitters would catch up to pitches of that quality today. "They have more
bat speed now," Johnson says. "It was unheard of then to have a centerfielder who lifted heavy weights. I've noticed a big difference in
the past 10 to 12 years. It's like golf—it's all about clubhead speed
now."

Gooden, too, has had to adjust, adding a changeup and slider to
his repertoire. In one game last year against the Indians, Gooden,
who now pitches for the Yankees, threw nine straight sliders. "There
are some lineups where every guy can take you deep," he says.

The strike zone used to be shaped like a refrigerator, with classic
hard throwers such as Jim Palmer and Sandy Koufax going top-shelf
to get strikes. Now it has become flatter and wider, and it is not only
shaped like a shoe box but also is barely bigger than one. Pitches
about the width of a baseball outside the plate generally are called
strikes, and ones that hit the inside corner are often called balls. Pitches at or above the belt are usually called balls.

Pitchers like to blame umpires for the shrinking strike zone—umpires
say that the zone they call has not changed, despite films of games as
recently as the early 1980s that prove the contrary—but the pitchers are
the ones most responsible. Because it has become harder to throw the
ball past hitters and because mistakes on the inside half of the plate
often become home runs, not just singles and doubles, pitchers nibble
maddeningly off the lower and outside boundaries of the strike zone.
The rare pitch high or inside suddenly looks *too* high or *too* inside
after an umpire sees a continual barrage of pitches down and away.

What, then, do the best pitchers do to thrive in the powerball era?

•**Establish the fastball.** The five toughest pitchers to hit last season in each league (according to opponents' batting average) were all power guys: Al Leiter, Smoltz, Hideo Nomo, Brown and Curt Schilling in the National League and Juan Guzman, Roger Clemens, Hentgen, Kevin Appier and Alex Fernandez in the American League. Johnson, with his 97-mph fastball, is annually among that group when he isn't ailing.

Even finesse pitchers such as Maddux and teammate Tom Glavine work primarily off their fastballs. "If I throw 100 pitches in a game, I'll probably throw as many as 70 fastballs, unless it's a night when I have a great changeup," Glavine says. "Too many guys pitch backward. They throw their breaking ball so much that it's almost like their fastball is their off-speed pitch. What you have to realize is that a breaking ball is tougher to throw for strikes. That means you have more pitchers pitching behind in the count, and that's when you get hit."

Young pitchers in particular tend to stray from the fastball, a habit formed in high school and college where hitters whip 28-ounce aluminum bats. "You can't throw the ball hard enough to get it past someone swinging those bats," Duncan says. "And if you do jam somebody, he can still hit it out. I have two sons whose coaches want them to be pitchers because they have good arms. But they want to hit. I don't blame them."

Pitchers need to be retrained to develop the arm strength to throw with greater velocity. In 1991 the Dodgers drafted a high school pitcher named Rick Gorecki in the 19th round. Gorecki had an outstanding curveball, but his fastball maxed out at only 82 mph. The Dodgers ordered him to throw fastballs 80% of the time at rookie league Great Falls. Gorecki didn't win a game that first season, but his fastball eventually reached 90 mph. Now, at 23, he's one of L.A.'s better prospects. "We did the same thing with a couple of pitchers at [Class A] Bakersfield a number of years ago," says Dodgers pitching coach Dave Wallace. "That team lost 102 games, but we had a couple of young pitchers named Ramon Martinez and John Wetteland."

•**Be aggressive.** "Nowadays too many pitchers go into a self-defense mode," says Braves pitching coach Leo Mazzone. "It's as if they're afraid to throw the ball over the plate."

Pitchers have become so intimidated that hitters see the fear on their faces. Los Angeles catcher Mike Piazza says, "I notice that you don't see young pitchers being aggressive. I don't know if you'd call it cockiness, but you hardly see anyone with a presence on the mound. That's why someone like Pedro Martinez stands out."

Martinez, a 25-year-old Expos righthander, has a natural sailing motion on his fastball that carries the ball toward the hands of righthanded hitters. It's the type of pitch that prompts offended batters to charge the mound. "Hitters disregard the inside corner so much that you can throw a pitch in the strike zone and they'll jackknife out of the way," says one American League All-Star pitcher. "Frank Thomas is the worst one for that, and umpires won't call inside strikes on him."

Pettitte, a lefty, features a cut fastball that bores in on righties. A cutter acts like a hard slider with a smaller, sharper break. Leiter, also a lefthander, held righthanded hitters to a major-league-low .194 average last year employing his cutter.

"The way hitters stand on top of the plate now and dive into the ball, you have to pitch inside to keep them off the plate," Seattle's Johnson says. "You have to come inside so that they don't feel comfortable." In a spring training game Johnson fractured the lower left orbital bone of Giants first baseman J.T. Snow with one of his don't-get-too-comfortable heaters.

•**Emphasize location.** That's what Hentgen did last season on his way to a 20–10 record. "I always knew it was important," Hentgen says, "but last year I really made location my Number 1 priority. That could be the key element in pitching today."

Atlanta's staff is a case in point. Smaller strike zone? Somehow the Braves' pitchers have *expanded* it, especially Maddux. Whereas Jim Palmer once worked "up the ladder"—pitching incrementally higher in the strike zone, an extinct art because of the shrinking zone—Maddux has turned the ladder on its side. With laserlike precision, he pecks away at the outside corner with such regularity that he gets more pitches farther off the plate called strikes than anyone else. It's not unlike Michael Jordan escaping traveling violations that apply to other NBA players. "Maddux pitches to a bigger strike zone than anyone," Duncan says. "If you watch Maddux, the games in which he gets hit are the ones in which he's not getting those pitches called and he has to come in to where the strike zone is for everybody else."

In last year's World Series the Yankees were amazed at how often Atlanta pitchers worked off the outer edge of the plate. The Braves' outfielders shifted to the opposite field on every Yankees hitter because of that pitching style. "My objective with the strike zone is to see how much I can get away with," Glavine says. "I know I get pitches off the plate. You've got to see how far you can go. You start out at a certain spot and see how much more you can get on the outside corner. Every umpire is different and every game is different, so you have to find out."

•**Be creative.** "Varying the speeds of your pitches to throw off the timing of the hitter is much more important than it used to be," Yankees righthander David Cone says. "Teams have charts now that show what pitches you throw and in what location on a 3-and-2 count. So you've got to have at least three pitches, sometimes four."

Says 22-year veteran Dennis Eckersley, the Cardinals' closer, "It's getting to the point where you have to have a trick pitch. You always have to think, What can I do differently? That's one reason Nomo is so effective. It's that twisting delivery. Nobody else pitches like that."

For at least 10 years the trendiest trick pitch has been the split-finger fastball. The splitter looks like a low fastball before it breaks down with a late tumbling action. It rarely results in a called strike because it usually sinks out of the strike zone. Good splitters result in missed swings and ground balls. Smoltz, whose fastball and slider long have been nightmarish for righthanders, reached an elite level last season after he added a splitter to neutralize lefthanders. The pitch, however, has become so common that it has lost some of its effectiveness. "When a few guys first threw it—guys like Bruce Sutter and Mike Scott—they were unhittable," Yankees pitching coach Mel Stottlemyre says. "But it's not a novelty anymore. You can play a three-game series against somebody, and every one of their starters throws a splitter."

Adds Maddux, "The slider was the pitch of the '70s and the splitter was the pitch of the '80s. I think the changeup has become the pitch of the '90s. You've got to have something to mess up a hitter's timing."

Maddux has so much confidence in his changeup that he has been known to intentionally miss the strike zone with a 2-2 pitch so he can shock a hitter with a full-count changeup. Says Johnson, "As hard as I throw, I know everyone sits on my fastball and tries to time it. If

I throw 125 pitches, maybe only five to eight are changeups, but it's enough to throw them off, especially when I mix in my breaking ball."

The changeup, however, can be fickle, especially for young pitchers, because it requires "feel" that can be elusive—like putting in golf as opposed to whaling away with the driver. Pettitte won 12 games as a rookie in 1995 using a changeup as his out pitch. "Last year I hardly threw it," he says. "I didn't have the feel for it. I mostly went with the cutter, fastball and curveball. Maybe the hitters kept waiting for the changeup."

Brown is the rare pitcher who can dominate hitters without a changeup. Everything he throws is hard, but his slider, cutter and sinker all have such movement that he doesn't need much variation in pitch speeds. "There were maybe five times last year where I thought, This would be a good spot for Kevin to throw a changeup," his coach Rothschild says. "That's getting picky." What makes Brown deceptive is that he throws his pitches anywhere from sidearm to overhand, which prevents hitters from quickly recognizing what's coming. "I'll throw from 10 arm angles," he says.

Only three years ago, when he was still with the Rangers, Brown yielded the most hits in the majors and went 7–9. "I'd had a lot of pitching coaches over my career, and I worried so much about my mechanics that I forgot how to pitch," he says. "The last couple of years I just said, The heck with it. I'm just going to go back to what's comfortable."

Brown begins his delivery with his left foot in front of his right, spins his back to the hitter without raising his arms over his head, then slings the ball while untwisting his body. "Kevin rotates his hips more than most anybody," Rothschild says, "and he throws the ball as easily as anybody I've ever been around. You don't see a lot of strain. A lot of that is just natural."

Pitchers with Brown's kind of stuff are increasingly rare in an occupation forced to lower its standards. Only 10 pitchers in the American League had ERAs of less than 4.00 last year. Heck, only 37 in the league—and just 82 among all 28 teams—pitched enough innings (162) to qualify for the ERA title. "I was nearly run out of baseball in 1986 for having a 4.50 ERA," Eckersley says. "Now I see guys with a 5.00 ERA walking around with their heads held high, like they're hot stuff."

The pitching world is populated with hurlers like Wilson Alvarez of the White Sox, who says, "If I go seven innings every time I pitch, I did my job. I gave us a chance to win." And he's considered a pretty good pitcher by today's standards. "People complain that nobody pitches nine innings anymore," Duncan says. "Well, it's really hard to go nine without having so many counts in the hitter's favor. What the small strike zone does more than anything is change the count. Something needs to be done. The game is out of balance."

Short of a telethon or action from the White House, the greatest benefit to needy pitchers would be a return to the strike zone as it's defined in the rule book. However, that is the least likely form of aid because it is the most controversial. Umpires and hitters don't want the grief involved in retooling their judgment of what is a ball and a strike. "The least controversial thing to do," Cone says, "is to change the slope and height of the mound and see where that takes us. It's the fairest change to make."

Without a fundamental change, the downward spiral of pitching is likely to continue. Those who can do what Brown did last year will become all the more phenomenal. "What you're going to see is relief pitchers getting more and more decisions," Glavine says. "You're going to see pitchers with ERAs under four considered to be having a great year. And because teams are so careful about protecting young pitchers as they come through the minors, you're going to see pitchers who can't work beyond 100 pitches in a game, which means they'll be done after four or five innings. What happens then?"

The hiss of a nasty fastball blowing past the thick barrel of a weightlifter's thin-handled bat grows fainter. Is anyone listening?

Postscript: I've always enjoyed talking with pitchers because they need to be more cerebral than hitters. Hitters react. Pitchers think. I once asked Mike Mussina, who is a very good athlete, why he was a pitcher. He said, "Because on that day he works, the pitcher can control the outcome more than anybody else." And that was still true even when this story ran, during an era when it was obvious that virtually every change in the game favored the hitter.

A Farewell to
Skinny Arms

You want finesse, join a bridge club. The Boys of Summer are now beefy,
pumped-up maulers ready to tear down the fences.
Welcome to Extreme Baseball, where too much is never enough

E VERY DAY THIS SPRING A BATTALION OF PROTEIN drinks spiked with the muscle-enhancing supplement creatine awaited the New York Yankees after they ended their workouts in Tampa. The white Styrofoam cups with red straws poking through the lids were lined up on a table in the clubhouse like soldiers awaiting inspection. One afternoon, as his players snatched up all the cups, the most powerful of Yankees sucked on his shake while admonishing a clubhouse attendant. "Next time make sure you have a few more made up," said owner George Steinbrenner, dressed in his own uniform of blue blazer and white turtleneck. "Better to have too much than not enough."

So there you have it. The perfect metaphor (albeit a mixed one) for what has happened to baseball near the end of this millennium: The owner of the game's richest team is downing souped-up shakes that promise to make him even bigger. Steinbrenner knows that baseball has become a big man's game—as surely as it belongs to men named Piazza (240 pounds), McGwire (250 pounds), Bichette (260 pounds) and Thomas (270 pounds), it belongs to men named Jacobs ($62 million payroll), Turner ($65 million), Angelos ($67 million) and, yes, Steinbrenner (more than $70 million). Like never before, baseball is about being buff. Anybody hoping to get to the World Series had better come to play with plenty of muscle and plenty of money. Better to have too much than not enough.

Dodgers catcher Mike Piazza gained 20 pounds over the winter lifting weights at a gym in Venice Beach, Calif. Orioles DH Harold Baines added creatine to his diet as well as a supplement containing fish oil to lubricate his creaking 39-year-old knees. Tampa Bay Devil Rays third baseman Wade Boggs, a slap hitter who turns 40 in June, took creatine while bulking up with heavy weights for the first time in his career.

This is an awful time for a team to be short on pitching. We are in the greatest home run era in history—each of the last four years is among the top five seasons for home runs per game. (The other, second on the list, was the freakish '87 season.) This year holds the promise of breaking more records than were shattered on Bill Veeck's Disco Demolition Night, because it's also an expansion year, and the arrival of the Devil Rays and the Diamondbacks has forced into service 22 pitchers who should be either retired or in the minors.

The impact is predictable. In each of the past five expansion years, there were nearly uniform increases in home runs, batting average, walks and ERA, with dingers going up the most on average. The results will be even more dramatic this season, not only because this is the second expansion within six years but also because hitters have never been stronger or more power-conscious. Yankees first baseman Tino

Martinez, who slugged 44 home runs last year, spent November chugging creatine and lifting weights. He added 12 pounds in a month and now looks more like a blacksmith than a baseball player.

The season's defining moment will take place in Denver on July 6, when the home run hitting contest will be held in conjunction with the All-Star Game at Coors Field, the most homer-happy park in baseball. Unless the rules are changed—say, the ball must land in the upper deck to be counted as a home run—that baseball show might drag on longer than *Titanic*.

Coors Field is the perfect backdrop for such excess, because a select group of high-revenue-producing stadiums like it have stratified baseball like never before. What division you're in doesn't matter much anymore, not with wild cards creating open competition for playoff spots and three rounds of postseason play guaranteeing the occasional Cinderella team a date with a big, ugly large-revenue club. All that matters is a team's willingness to spend money, which is what really separates the contenders from the rest of the pack. Talk about radical realignment: Forget about East, Central and West, and check out the payrolls instead.

The five biggest spenders last year all made the postseason, leaving just three playoff spots for the remaining 23 teams. The three clubs who got those spots each spent at least $33 million—and each was gone from the postseason quicker than footprints in the sand at high tide. The exemplar of this trend is Wayne Huizenga, the owner of the Florida Marlins, who bought himself a world championship last year and then decided that he'd paid too high a price.

"It may not seem that long ago that Oakland, Minnesota and Kansas City were World Series teams," says Athletics president Sandy Alderson. "But that's ancient history. The dynamics of the game are drastically different from what they were 10 years ago—even five years ago. The change is easily explained: It was the construction of stadiums with public money coupled with the drop in TV money." Almost overnight, the poor got poorer, and the rich got a lot richer.

As the gap between the haves and have-nots widens, those clubs in between are the most foolhardy. They are the ones spending enough money to dream of a pennant but not enough to compete with the big-revenue clubs. They might as well drop the money on lottery tickets. "If you're not spending $50 million, then you probably ought to cut way back," says Expos general manager Jim Beattie. "That middle ground is quicksand. I'm not sure why anyone would want to be there."

Over the past decade Major League Baseball has tried to prop up its low-revenue franchises with innovations such as the luxury tax, interleague play and the wild-card spots, but these changes haven't been nearly enough to compensate for the unprecedented revenue of the elite clubs. A radical realignment along geographical lines will almost certainly be the next bold effort to bolster the small-market teams. One American League general manager says the next logical move will be to split the season into halves. "The small-revenue clubs stand a better chance of hanging in" for 81 games than for 162, he explains.

In that scheme, statistics would still be tabulated over the entire season (and even baseball owners understand the historical importance of those numbers). To say only "61" or ".400" is to be nearly poetic—and to anticipate what this season holds in store. Expansion is the El Nino of baseball. It causes extreme conditions.

The 61 came in '61, an expansion year. Not only did Roger Maris hit a major league record number of home runs that season, but Norm

Cash of the Tigers also had one of the most anomalous batting averages in history, .361—78 points higher than any other season in which he batted 400 times. In '62, another expansion year, Tommy Davis of the Dodgers drove in 153 runs, 64 more than in his next-best season.

Maris's mark is more likely than ever to fall this season. Before 1990 only 10 players had hit 50 home runs in a season; five players reached that plateau in the past eight years. "I think 61 is the one record that is almost certainly going to go," says Padres 16-year-veteran Tony Gwynn, who has won the last four National League batting titles and eight in his 16-year career. "I used to think no one would ever come close, but the way guys are today it seems like it's going to go. Last year you had 12 guys hit 40 or more home runs. It's not just one or two guys who could do it. There are five to eight guys capable of hitting 61.

"Expansion definitely helps. By the time you get to the third or fourth game of a series, you'll be facing a pitcher who doesn't have a lot of experience and doesn't have real good command, and you know you're going to get pitches to hit."

Among the many players with a shot at surpassing 61, three stand out as most likely to succeed: in order, the Mariners' Ken Griffey Jr., who hit 56 last season and only now, at 28, is hitting his power prime; the Cardinals' Mark McGwire, who slugged 58 last year despite having one horrible month; and the Rangers' Juan Gonzalez, who has four 40-home-run seasons even though he has played in as many as 150 games only once.

"I like Junior's chances as much as anybody's," says his manager, Lou Piniella. "I've watched him get much stronger the last couple of years. He's not a line drive hitter anymore, even though he likes to say he is.

He's a home run hitter, and if only he could be a *little* more selective. . . . Well, I won't even finish that thought."

Expansion during a power hitter's era makes it possible for baseball fans to imagine—perhaps to even expect—feats that were once considered unthinkable. Among them:

• **.400 Batting Average** In expansion years Rod Carew of the Minnesota Twins (1977) and Andres Galarraga of the Rockies ('93) made lengthy runs at .400, which hasn't been reached since Ted Williams did it in '41. Says Gwynn, who hit .372 last year, "I still think it's possible. What helps me is I think pitchers now see so many guys who can hit the ball out that with a guy like me they figure, 'If I make a mistake, it's only a single. I can live with that.' I'm a throwback. There aren't too many guys left like me."

• **67 Doubles** This is the 67th year since Earl Webb of the Red Sox had 67 two-baggers. The Expos' Mark Grudzielanek and Edgar Martinez and Alex Rodriguez of the Mariners are only a magic carpet ride away. "It can be broken," says Rodriguez, who bashed 54 doubles in '96, "but it's going to take a guy who plays home games on artificial turf."

• **189 Strikeouts** The love affair with power has a downside. The Mariners' Jay Buhner, the Reds' Melvin Nieves and the Cubs' Henry Rodriguez and Sammy Sosa figure to be within whiffing distance of the Giants' Bobby Bonds's 1970 mark.

• **5.04 League ERA** The worst earned run average for a season was the American League's in 1936. That could easily be outdone, considering that league's pitchers ballooned to 4.99 two years ago. The Devil Rays are sure to play a huge role in any run at this record.

"AS A PITCHER, what can you do?" says Yankees righthander David Cone. "You can make your legs stronger, create better balance and make yourself less likely to break down. But lifting weights is not going to translate into having better stuff, not the way getting stronger can make someone a better hitter."

In 1994 the career of shortstop Kevin Elster was in decline when Yankees general manager Gene Michael told him, "You're too soft. You can't play with that body. You've got to get a new body." Shortstops—like Michael himself—regularly hung 15-year careers on thin frames. Not anymore. Elster began a weight-training program. In '96 he cranked 24 homers and drove in 99 runs for the Rangers.

The effect of size on baseball is profound—what was big is now small. The cleanup-hitting outfielder is now a middle infielder. The Braves' Tony Graffanino (6' 1", 195 pounds) is the same height and is 12 pounds heavier than the weight at which Frank Robinson played. The Royals' Jose Offerman (six feet, 190) is just a bit bigger than Stan Musial was in 1948, the year he led the National League in batting (.376) and RBIs (131). Dale Sveum (6' 2", 212) of the Yankees is almost as big as Johnny (Big Cat) Mize, and McGwire (6' 5", 250) is as big as NFL defensive star Bryce Paup.

At 35, Mickey Mantle was virtually finished. At 35, Duke Snider was a part-time player, and Ralph Kiner was in his third year of retirement. At 35, Paul O'Neill of the Yankees is coming off a career year (.324, 21 homers, 117 RBIs) and is more fit than ever, his 6' 4", 215-pound frame chiseled by weights and creatine.

In the clubhouse of the Mariners, who last year hit more home runs than any club in history (264), fat canisters of creatine are piled above lockers like cords of wood. Creatine monohydrate is a naturally occurring compound consisting of three amino acids. In nontechnical terms, it's fuel for muscles. A study by Penn State's Center for Sports

Medicine found that members of a control group taking creatine grew stronger after just seven days.

"Three or four years ago, the nutritional supplement market for baseball players didn't even exist," says Dave Rose, a manager with Champion Nutrition of Concord, Calif., which supplies several major league teams with a variety of nutritional additives. "Now it's gone crazy. The market for baseball is bigger than for football or basketball."

"Let's face it, guys get paid for home runs," Piazza says. "If you hit 30 home runs, nobody cares if you hit .250 doing it. That extra strength may be the difference of five to 10 feet—the difference between a ball being caught or going over the wall. Why wouldn't you lift and take supplements? You've got one time in your life to get it right. I want to get it right."

Piazza is the prototypical player of this new power generation. He was born 10 days before Denny McLain won his 30th game in 1968, the Year of the Pitcher. Only three major league players drove in 100 runs that season; in '97, Piazza was one of 35 players with at least 100 RBIs. No catcher has ever caught as many games (139) and batted higher than Piazza did last year, when he hit .362 (along with 40 home runs). Then he spent the off-season lifting weights with bronzed bodybuilders while his personal shopper-chef-nutritionist whipped up six meals a day for him: omelettes, pancakes, tuna, chicken, steak and, daily, a creatine shake. He reported to camp at 240 pounds, expecting the rigors of catching to wear him down to 225 by the end of the season. He says, "I want to go out and top last season."

Piazza is also a potential free agent seeking the richest contract in baseball history. Meanwhile, the Dodgers are expected to be sold by their longtime family proprietors, the O'Malleys, to a new owner, global media baron Rupert Murdoch. Just another sign of the times. So gather up your fish oil and your amino acids, and fire up your blender. The stakes have never been higher for hitting it big.

Postscript: As predicted, Roger Maris's record of 61 home runs was indeed broken in 1998—twice—by Mark McGwire and Sammy Sosa. Expansion had less to do with the barrage of homers than what had become the accepted culture of getting big, often by any means necessary.

Nasty Stuff

That's what made Kevin Brown worth $105 million to the Dodgers. His nasty disposition was thrown in for free

WITH HIS SEVENTH PITCH OF THIS SEASON Kevin Brown will have earned more than the median household income of the 10,797 folks of Wilkinson County, Ga. The first of Brown's twice-monthly paychecks will bring him $1.25 million, as much as a median wage earner in Wilkinson County makes in 46 years, a lifetime of work. Still, while Brown may rest his head at night in a Beverly Hills mansion after earning about four grand per pitch from the Dodgers, he is never far from Wilkinson County. "I'm afraid we'll be the Beverly Hillbillies," says his wife, Candace, laughing. " 'Here come the Clampetts' " Candace was 13 when she met Kevin, who is three years older, and 19 when they were married.

Wilkinson County is smack in the center of Georgia. The middle of nowhere. There, in the town of McIntyre (pop. 552), Kevin Brown grew up. The county, which begins about 20 miles east of Macon, is a haunting sepia photograph come to life, though barely. A somber stain of umber blots the landscape, as if reddish-brown ink had spilled from the sky. Rusted metal roofs hang heavily over the dark wood planks of tottering houses, and long-dead autos lie like toppled gravestones in dirt the color of a fresh scab. This is a place where collarless dogs chase cars down country roads, where one out of every eight families lives below the poverty level, where there is no obvious sign of the 30 households that, according to the last census, earn $100,000 or more per year, and where there are some 38 churches to offer reminders that everyone is destined for a better place.

"Got a cellphone with you?" Kevin's mother, Carolyn, asks a visitor who is about to drive from Macon to McIntyre. "That's the *country* country over there, you know."

BUSINESS DISTRICT reads the green sign with the white arrow pointing to Main Street in McIntyre, a single block that begins at a salvage yard and ends at a filling station, with a hardware store, a police station and an unmarked convenience store in between. At 5 p.m. on a weekday in February you could play a chess match in the middle of Main Street without vehicular interruption. The police station is locked shut. No one is inside.

An old-timer remembers having no indoor plumbing or electricity in his home in McIntyre as recently as 1948, when he was 19 years old. He remembers the gaps in the floorboards of his old house, through which you could see the earth; the three meals of cornmeal each day; the patched pants he wore to school, which so embarrassed him that many times he just wouldn't go; and the 60 cents per hour he made as a teenager mining kaolin, the fine white clay that is the only reason McIntyre is inhabited at all.

That old-timer is Gerald Brown, who by the grace of his son Kevin's freakish right arm is sipping coffee in a leather chair in a spacious four-bedroom brick house in Macon—out of Wilkinson County. From his front steps Gerald can see the 15,000-square-foot mansion Kevin is building, the brick fortress that sits on 70-plus acres of land and makes Gerald and Carolyn's spread look like one of those plastic Monopoly houses. Kevin grew up in a family of five in a 1,300-square-foot house with one bathroom, where no one knew the luxury of a long shower. His new estate will be flush with 10 bathrooms.

In the reddish-brown dirt of McIntyre and especially in the creases of Gerald's square face are clues as to why Kevin throws a baseball with a fury like that of no other man alive. In those same places are also clues as to why, unless you saw Kevin playing with his own two sons or flying one of his remote-control airplanes or watching one of the 89 episodes of *Star Trek* and *Star Trek: The Next Generation* he keeps in his video library, you might never have seen him smile.

"There were teammates who hated his guts," says Tom House, Brown's pitching coach during his first six major league seasons, with the Rangers. "People who have Kevin's makeup are pretty much oblivious to other people's feelings. There's not a lot of empathy in Kevin. Like a lot of athletes, he is a narcissistic individual who's paid a lot of money to be that way. He's a hard-ass, all right. But I'd like to think that, at heart, he's a great kid."

"I guess that comes naturally," Gerald says of his son's brutish single-mindedness. "I was the same way. I thought I had to be perfect in everything I did." Gerald is a short, stocky man who even in winter wears short-sleeved shirts, which bare his muscular tattooed arms. He has a twinkle in his eyes of the Jimmy Cagney tough-guy sort. Carolyn says that if he were a ballplayer—both she and Gerald played softball—he would be Chuck Knoblauch, the Yankees' hard-nosed second baseman.

"I always worked as hard as I could," Gerald says. "For someone with a seventh-grade education to become the foreman for heavy equipment [for a company that mines kaolin], I did all right by myself. With Kevin, I told him if he wanted to do something, the only way was to do it to the best of his ability. I remember one time before a game he got into a scrap with another boy and he said, 'I ain't goin' to play.' I said, 'Boy, you go get your butt on that dadgum field.' If you want to do something, do it right or quit."

Gerald takes a sip of coffee. On the mug is a picture of Kevin in the uniform of the Padres, for whom he played last year. Carolyn spotted a stack of the mugs in an airport shop in San Diego and bought out the supply. Of course her son is not smiling on the ceramic; he's giving his usual chilly, do-not-disturb look.

ONE DAY in 1997, when Kevin Brown was playing for the Marlins, a radio reporter asked him for a sound bite. It was one of the first days of spring training, when baseball players are usually in a good mood. "One usable sound bite, huh?" Brown replied. "It would probably be, 'Bite me.' " Later in the season, when another reporter asked him about the possible sale of the Marlins, Brown said, "I'm ignoring the issue, just like I'm ignoring you." And that fall he welcomed the national media into the Marlins' clubhouse on the eve of the franchise's first World Series appearance by shouting, "Get these f---s out of here. We can't get any work done." On occasion he has telephoned the press box while watching a game on the clubhouse TV to ream out his team's broadcaster for a mistake—such as misidentifying a pitch that was just thrown.

When Brown was with Texas in '94, he and the other Rangers were obliged to wear baggy, old-fashioned uniforms one night as part of

a promotion. Brown saw Rangers president Tom Schieffer and another team executive on the field before the game and spat out, "You're
the f---s who make us wear these things."

Brown tears up clubhouses in fits of rage so regularly that his teams
have kept running tabs. He has smashed at least two televisions,
ripped an oversized wooden Padres logo from a wall, left scores of
divots in clubhouse drywall, put his fist through one glass door and
kicked in another. After one of those tantrums, when someone asked
Brown what he had been trying to do, he replied icily, "Cut my tendon." Just two weeks ago at Dodgertown he pulverized a toilet with a
baseball bat after he was scalded in the shower when someone flushed
the commode.

Toronto assistant G.M. Dave Stewart, who was San Diego's pitching
coach last year, has compared Brown's game-day visage to that of a se-
rial killer. Brown still gets so agitated on the mound when he makes
a mistake or is stung by a bit of bad fortune that Candace can see
from the stands that he's about to explode. She says, "He gets this
look in his eyes, and he starts twitching, and it's like, Uh-oh." No one
dares to sit near him or talk to him between innings. He has been
heard to curse himself after throwing a 1-2-3 inning.

He has also been known to shoot dagger-sharp looks at fielders
who have dared to make mistakes behind him. "When he played
here," says a Rangers official, "the infielders were uptight because he
had this way of looking right through them." (Texas wanted no part
of the pitcher this winter when he was a free agent.)

Brown has been equally hostile to coaches who have visited him on
the mound. "There were a couple of cases when he said things I didn't
like," says Stewart. "In a different situation I would have settled it in
a different way."

Says House, "You could not have programmed someone to say the absolute wrong thing at the absolute wrong time any better than Kevin did it." There is still truth in that. Before Brown decided on his place in Beverly Hills, he complained about the "sticker shock" he suffered when shopping for Southern California real estate—this from a man who will be paid $105 million over the next seven years. And when he is asked about the Padres' being swept in the '98 World Series by the Yankees, the winningest team in the history of baseball, he asserts that the outcome would have been different if a 2–2 pitch by San Diego reliever Mark Langston to Yankees first baseman Tino Martinez in the seventh inning of Game 1 had been called a strike. "That stands out as a big turning point," says Brown, who couldn't hold a 5–2 lead earlier in the same inning. Martinez hit Langston's 3–2 pitch for a grand slam. "They had the talent *and* the breaks," Brown says of the Yankees. "The Series looked bad on paper, but we really should have won three of those games." Brown spent at least an hour before Game 1 covered in blankets on a training table, warding off chills from the flu. He didn't tell Stewart or Padres manager Bruce Bochy about his condition. Stewart still seethes over that.

Brown is disbelieving when told of his reputation among teammates, foes and the media as a spring-loaded pitcher ready to go off at any moment. "No one's ever told me that," he says. "I think [the reputation in the media] started because a beat writer in Texas continually took shots at me, and I wouldn't let him get away with it. I got in his face several times. But since then—with Baltimore, Florida, San Diego—I haven't had any problems. Listen, I'm my own worst critic, but sometimes guys try to tell me what I'm thinking without asking me. I hate that. And I won't kiss anybody's ass."

"I'm one of the guys who gets along with him," says Mets pitcher Al

Leiter, who played with Brown in Florida. "He's so stressed out that it's real tough to get Kevin to have a belly laugh. But sometimes I think his tough-guy facade is just that—a facade. He's actually hiding a dweeby, nerdy kind of guy. What I tried to do with him, like I do with [Mets catcher Mike] Piazza, was get in his face. They take themselves way too seriously, and I tell them to lighten up.

"Kevin's the most dominant pitcher I've ever played with. But is he the kind of guy to have an influence in the clubhouse and make [everyone else] play better? No, Brownie can't do that."

"YOU CAN hear the ball as soon as it leaves his hand," says Devil Rays manager Larry Rothschild, Brown's pitching coach with the '97 Marlins. Brown's ball spins so fast that it hisses as the seams cut through the air. No other active pitcher—maybe none ever—can make the ball sink as viciously as Brown can while throwing it so hard. He is unique: a power sinkerball pitcher. One of his first catchers in Texas, Mike Stanley, called him Chainsaw because of the way his pitches chewed up bats and hitters' and catchers' hands. Another Texas catcher, former Gold Glove winner Jim Sundberg, spent most of 1989, his last year in the big leagues, with a pack of ice on his left thumb; Brown's dancing bricks repeatedly bent the thumb back.

Brown has won 20 games only once—for the Rangers in 1992, the season after he began seeing a sports psychologist (with whom he still talks)—and has never won the Cy Young Award. He is pitching for his fifth team in six years. He has fewer World Series wins than Jay Powell, having failed to win any of his four starts. His career record (139–99, for a .584 winning percentage) approximates that of the Cubs' unspectacular Kevin Tapani (120–87, .580). So why did the

Dodgers give Brown baseball's first nine-figure contract? That's easy: Brown is one of the rare players who, by himself, can make the difference in getting a team to the World Series. And at 34, an age at which Hall of Famer Don Drysdale, another Dodgers righthander with a mean streak, was retired, Brown confoundingly is in his prime.

Brown was examined by Dr. Frank Jobe, the renowned orthopedic surgeon, before his contract with the Dodgers was made official. At the end of the exam Jobe shook his head and told Brown, "Well, I think the Dodgers got themselves a bargain."

"What do you mean?" Brown asked.

"I mean," Jobe said, "they should have signed you for 10 years, not seven. With the shape your arm is in, I don't see any reason why you can't pitch that long."

Over the past three seasons Brown has gone 51–26 with a 2.33 ERA—little more than half the ERA of all National League pitchers combined in that span (4.22). Last year he threw the ball harder than he ever had (97 mph tops) while striking out 257 batters, 25% more than he had in any other season. In 452 at bats with any count that included two strikes, batters got only 62 hits off him (.137) and not a single home run.

There are physiological reasons that Brown is such a pitching oddity. At 6' 4" and 200 pounds, he has the wingspan and wiry strength of a basketball player. "He can scratch his knees without bending over," House says. Though Brown's windup is unorthodox—he has an exaggerated hip turn, leading with his butt, and can throw any pitch from any arm angle—he maintains flawless balance, and his amazing extension maximizes the whip effect of his long arm. Other pitchers "reach back" for something extra; Brown reaches forward. "The first time I saw him up close," Rothschild says, "was his first day throwing in spring training. After a long winter he gets up on the mound and just starts airing it out. It looked like the middle of the season. I couldn't believe it."

Most pitchers throw once between starts, usually at three-quarters speed, just to maintain the feel of their pitches. Brown throws twice between starts, going full bore. Stewart says such a workload alarmed him. "Not just how much he throws, but the intensity," Stewart says. "Your arm only has so many throws in it. We talked a little bit about it. You know what he told me? 'I'll taper it *if* I can.' "

Brown never has mastered a finesse pitch, nor has he needed one. Everything about him is hard. "He's such a maximum-effort guy without a real nice, fluid delivery, and he's wound so tight, that you wonder if one day his elbow is just going to go," says one American League general manager. Of course, Brown has heard that sort of talk, heard it for years. Mechanics be damned, he knows what is best for him. "If you listen to your body, it will tell you whether you are doing too much or not enough," Brown says. "I don't believe you have only so many throws. This is how I stay sharp: The more time my hand is on the ball, the more comfortable I am."

Outside of his 21–11 breakout year in Texas, Brown was 57–53 with the Rangers, not including a 1–11 nightmare for three minor league teams in 1987. In what would be a recurring struggle in his nine years in the Rangers organization, Brown could not synchronize his natural ability with the mechanics being taught him. Carolyn says, "One day Gerald and I went to have breakfast with Kevin in Mississippi [where he was with the Double A Tulsa Drillers]. We knew he was trying so hard to please them with his mechanics. Gerald said, 'Well, you've tried their way, now maybe you should go back to pitching the way you did at Georgia Tech.' Kevin was probably thinking that anyway. All he needed was his daddy to give him permission to do it. That night he just threw so hard and so well." The battle over mechanics, however, continued throughout Brown's tenure with the Rangers. Brown thinks the team's emphasis on technique stymied his progress, but he says, "Tom House is such a nice guy that I was willing to try anything. If he was a jerk, it would have been easy not to listen to him."

In '95 Brown signed with the Orioles as a free agent without so much as a phone call from the Rangers, who were pleased to be rid of him. He went 10–9 that season despite a 3.60 ERA. "Mike Mussina won 19 games with almost the same ERA [3.29]," Brown says of his Baltimore teammate. Brown was miserable. Mixing the incendiary Georgian with the cool, cliquish veterans on the Orioles went over about as well as a heavy-metal band at a Republican fund-raiser. "It was a quiet team, just put it that way," Brown says.

In December he moved on to Florida as a free agent and figured on a long career there, until owner Wayne Huizenga gutted the Marlins after their world championship. Brown was traded to the Padres in the purge. After helping San Diego get to the World Series—he went 18–7 with a 2.38 ERA and finished third in the Cy Young voting—he turned away offers from the Padres, Orioles and Rockies to take the Dodgers' dough. "It blew my mind," Carolyn says of the $105 million, "and I believe it blew Kevin's mind. I always told him no athlete was worth $1 million a year. But I said, 'If they're going to give it to somebody, I'm glad they gave it to you.' "

KEVIN BROWN was finished with baseball in 1983, of that he was fairly certain. At 6' 2" and 160 pounds, he hadn't even been the top starting pitcher at Wilkinson County High. It's unlikely, Brown says, that any scout saw him play. "It's a remote place," he says, "and my junior and senior years were the first years my coach ever coached. He didn't know much of anything about baseball."

As a boy he had dreamed of being a marine biologist, but later, when he learned that the profession would take him far from Wilkinson County, for low pay, he decided on being an engineer like Candace's dad, Roy Ethridge. Gerald Brown never wanted Kevin to follow him into the mines. Kevin was a brilliant student who enrolled at Georgia Tech to study chemical engineering. The summer before college began he took a job in a lab of Engelhard Corporation, the kaolin-mining company for which his father worked. Kaolin is so important to central Georgia that *The Wilkinson County News* proudly declares each week atop Page One, CIRCULATING IN THE HEART OF THE RICHEST KAOLIN TERRITORY IN THE WHOLE WORLD. Processed kaolin looks like flour and is used in the manufacture of porcelain, brick cement and high-grade white paper, and it is also a filler in paints, plastics and rubber. "That's all there is around here," says Danny Williams, who worked in the lab with Brown. "If the kaolin ever dried up, McIntyre would dry up with it."

During lunch breaks Brown, Williams and the other guys in the lab would play baseball with a wad of aluminum foil and a spatula. It was the only sort of baseball Brown was playing that summer when Kenny Walters, who worked in the same plant in McIntyre, came to visit him in the lab. Walters was the captain of a mostly black semipro team from a nearby town that was playing in a Labor Day weekend tournament in Valdosta, Ga. He needed a pitcher and had heard about Brown from Williams. Brown said no thanks, he wasn't interested. Walters came back "three or four times," Williams says, "until we all said, 'Why don't you just go play ball with that guy?' Kevin finally said yes."

In Valdosta, Brown relieved Walters, who also pitched, in the Saturday game, and on Labor Day he threw a complete-game victory. Brown went back to work on Tuesday. The phone rang in the lab. Someone answered it and shouted to Kevin, "It's a scout for the New York Mets!"

After Brown hung up, Williams asked, "What did they want?"

"Well, they want *me*," Brown said.

"Want you for *what*?"

Until that call, Candace says, Kevin "never thought he was that good." Kevin told the scout, Julian Morgan—who had been in Valdosta and had seen some of Brown's performance—that he was committed to attending Georgia Tech. Morgan telephoned the Tech baseball coach, Jim Morris, to tell him about the kid and make sure he went out for the team. So Brown tried out. He was so raw that he had never pitched in a pair of metal spikes, and had always put his right foot on top of the rubber instead of pushing off the side of the slab from a hole in front of it. "After the first day I pitched, they brought me inside, gave me a locker and said, 'Congratulations. You're on the team,' " Brown says. Three years later, having added 8 mph to his fastball, he was the fourth player picked in the draft, by the Rangers.

"If he hadn't gone to Valdosta, he'd probably still be here," says Williams, who still works for Engelhard as a lab technician in nearby Gordon. "And he'd probably be my boss."

MCINTYRE IS such a nondescript spot that it used to be known simply as Station No. 16. The town's most famous product—other than kaolin, of course—is not celebrated as a hero. At his old high school, with its rusting backstop out back, a secretary answers a knock on the front door after classes have ended. The visitor asks if there is an acknowledgment in the school of its famous alumnus. A plaque? A trophy? A picture?

"Kevin Brown?" the secretary says warily. "No, there's nothing. Nothing at all." Then she closes the door and turns away.

About a quarter mile down the road, behind the elementary school, the Wilkinson County High baseball team is practicing on the current varsity diamond. "Kevin Brown?" says one of the players. "Don't mention that name around here. He's a jerk. The guy gives $1 million to Los Angeles high schools [actually, an inner-city baseball program], and we have to buy our own uniforms. He doesn't even care about his own school."

Told of this, Brown says, "I have given money to the school in the past, and I may in the future."

People in McIntyre are also mad at Brown "because he doesn't say he's from McIntyre," says the father of one player. "He gets to the World Series, and all of a sudden he's from Macon."

In Macon, a Kevin Brown that hitters will never see is laughing as he chases his four-year-old son, Grayson, around the modest house he has lived in for the past nine years. His family is so important to him that he persuaded the Dodgers to give him 12 round-trips a year between Macon and Los Angeles on a private jet, which will cost the team about $480,000 annually. Brown splurged on a two-acre Beverly Hills lot because he wanted Grayson and his eight-year-old brother, Ridge, to have a backyard in which to play. "He's like his father, a country boy who likes to have space around him," Carolyn says. And, yes, she adds, "Kevin smiles a lot. He's really still a kid. I tell Candace all the time, 'You don't have two boys. You have three of them.' "

"I know his reputation, and that's not the Kevin Brown I know," says Sandy Johnson, the Rangers scouting director who signed him and is now an assistant general manager for the Diamondbacks. "He's always been very cordial, a real Southern gentleman. I like him. And with the way he takes care of himself and the arm he has, he can probably pitch into his 40s, like Nolan."

Brown played five seasons with Nolan Ryan in Texas without getting close to him. He did not seek Ryan's counsel. He is blunt about identifying his mentor: "No one."

"Kevin is a product of a very conditional environment," House says. "He had extraordinary expectations placed on him and had to meet those conditions to get acceptance. Lots of athletes grow up with that conditional acceptance. The makeups of Nolan Ryan and Kevin are very similar. The difference is, Nolan was more adept at communicating. I think now you'll see Kevin begin to blossom. There is affirmation that he is among the elite pitchers in the game. By the time he's done, he's going to be revered by everyone. I'm not saying he's going to be as revered as Nolan Ryan or Tom Seaver. But it'll be close."

Gerald used to go to almost all of Kevin's high school games and even most of his practices. He and Carolyn saw all of Kevin's college games that were within a day's drive of McIntyre. Carolyn still enjoys traveling to watch her son, though Gerald, who had a heart attack in 1994, now prefers sitting at home in front of the TV.

In the winter days without baseball, Carolyn and Gerald pass the time watching tapes of Kevin's games. One day they choose a game from May 11, 1998, because it is a duel against Leiter, Kevin's friend. The camera keeps zooming in on the face of the baddest dude in baseball. It is contorted by the maximum effort Kevin's father demanded—

the flared nostrils, the deeply furrowed brow, the quivering lower lip thrust forward and the huffing and puffing behind a three-day beard, and at times it appears as if Brown can blow a baseball past a hitter on sheer will.

Postscript: For his $105 million from the Dodgers and Yankees, Brown averaged 10 wins per season and went on the disabled list 10 times, once after punching a clubhouse wall in a fit of anger. Barring dramatic—and unlikely—developments, the enduring memory of his years in New York will be his horrible start in Game 7 of the 2004 ALCS against Boston, when he was charged with five runs while getting only four outs.

Aces High

Baseball's most precious commodity is the true No. 1 starter, the rare pitcher who can elevate a team single-handedly

BEFORE EACH GAME EARLY IN THE 1997 SEASON THE bearer of the opposing team's lineup card would also deliver condolences to Terry Francona, the Phillies' manager. "Hang in there" or "It'll get better," the rival would say in a solemn bedside manner, as if the team's stumbling start was some sort of illness. But once every five days Francona could fix his counterpart with a devilish look, like a schoolboy with a laser pointer in his pocket, and say, "Don't feel sorry for me tonight."

Every fifth day the Phillies were as good as any team in baseball. Every fifth day they wielded one of the rarest and most potent weapons in the sport. Every fifth day they featured an honest-to-goodness, certified No. 1 starting pitcher. They had righthander Curt Schilling. The real deal. "One night we could be losing 6–0 and look just terrible," Francona says. "Then the next night maybe we still hadn't scored—it's 0–0 or 1–0 in the seventh inning—but we've got Schill out there, and we look sharp. Every fifth day, it doesn't matter who we play or who he's matched up against, we feel like we're going to win. So can you imagine how the Braves feel? They get that feeling almost every night of the week."

With the possible exception of a hot goaltender in hockey, no position in team sports controls the tempo, tenor and outcome of a game as thoroughly as a premier starting pitcher. He is the sun of the baseball universe; the game revolves around him.

Come Opening Day, every team will have a so-called No. 1 starter. After all, *somebody* has to take the ball first—and increasingly, that's all he is: somebody. But we speak here not of the Scott Karls of the world. Rather, we pay tribute to the few virtuosos who can make opposing hitters rest uneasy the night before a game they pitch; the ones who eliminate the need for middle relievers, the weakest link in just about any staff; the ones who take pressure off their rotation mates. Like jazz to Miles Davis or pornography to Justice Potter Stewart, true No. 1's are so obvious that they need no definition.

"To me, naming the Number 1's is like naming the days of the week," Schilling says. "Everybody knows who they are. If you have to stop and think if somebody is a Number 1, he's not."

Here is the A list: Schilling; Kevin Brown of the Dodgers; Roger Clemens of the Yankees; Tom Glavine, Greg Maddux and John Smoltz of the Braves; Randy Johnson of the Diamondbacks; Pedro Martinez of the Red Sox; and Mike Mussina of the Orioles. That's it. Our Starting Nine. End of discussion. That means 23 of the 30 teams in baseball, by our reckoning, don't have a No. 1 pitcher.

David Wells of the Blue Jays, 18–4 in '98, including a perfect game? Three words: Do it again. The Yankees' David Cone? These days the 36-year-old righthander frightens HMOs as much as he does hitters. Even Mussina's inclusion in the club is an indication of how elite pitching standards have declined in this age of powerball and bullpen specialists. Mussina has never won 20 games or pitched 250 innings, the latter being a plateau even journeymen such as Rick Mahler used to reach as recently as the '80s. Over the past two seasons the Orioles righthander has won four fewer games and thrown only eight more innings than peripatetic Mariners lefty Jamie Moyer. Mussina, though, gets the nod here because his ordinary 13–10 season last year was marred by freak injuries (a wart on his pitching hand and a line drive off his face), because he has consistently proved that he can dominate a game (especially in the postseason) and because he has the best winning percentage (.667, 118–59) of any active pitcher with at least 25 victories.

Maddux, Glavine and Smoltz also deserve the smallest of asterisks because each has the insulation of the other two. Each would be a No. 1 on virtually any team in baseball. With Atlanta, though, the pressure to stop losing streaks is both rare and shared. It's self-evident that two of them don't have to face the other team's best pitcher in any given series. For example, Maddux had a loss and a no-decision against Schilling in the first 11 days of last season. The Philadelphia pitcher that Glavine faced was Garrett Stephenson, who finished the season 0–2 with a 9.00 ERA.

"There are two things that make a pitcher a Number 1," Cardinals manager Tony La Russa says. "When it's his turn to pitch, you can see guys on the team get excited because they know they have a real good chance to win. The other thing is, he takes the ball knowing his day to pitch affects the other four days. That guy knows that if we lose tonight, the club is not going to be as confident the next four nights. He allows the bullpen to rest, and he allows all the other starters to fit in slots behind him. They know they don't have to win 18 to 20 games."

Winning 18 games now has roughly the same degree of difficulty as slamming 40 home runs, except it carries greater value. Thirteen players hit at least 40 dingers last year, two more than won at least 18 games. Only six of those power hitters did so for a playoff team; all but one of the 18-game winners—Clemens, the American League Cy Young Award winner then with the Blue Jays—pitched for a team that made the postseason.

BASEBALL LEGEND credits Asa Brainard with being the George Washington of No. 1's. Brainard won 56 of the Cincinnati Red Stockings' 57 games in 1869, thereby eliminating the pressure on—in fact, the relevance of—the rest of the staff. According to baseball folklore, people later began calling great starting pitchers "ace" in honor of Asa, though *The New Dickson Baseball Dictionary* dates the first reference of the term to 1902, and the importance of the ace in many card games would seem a logical part of the etymology.

Ace. Stud. No. 1. The Big Guy. The Big Kahuna. The Big Unit. Whatever you call him, his importance is approaching an alltime high. "That's because expansion has diluted pitching in general, so these guys really stand out and become more valuable," says Dodgers general manager Kevin Malone, who in the off-season put his money where his mouth was, making the winning seven-year, $105 million bid for free-agent Brown.

As recently as 1996 no starting pitcher ranked among the eight highest-paid players in the game. Maddux, who was ninth, was the only one among the top 11. Now four of them rank in the top eight: Brown (first, at $15 million a year), Johnson (third, $13.1 million), Martinez (sixth, $12.5 million) and Maddux (eighth, 11.5 million).

Four members of our Starting Nine have switched teams in the past 18 months. You won't find such frenzied shopping anywhere else this side of eBay. Martinez, who was traded from the Expos to Boston after the '97 season, and Brown, who spent last season with San Diego after helping the Marlins win the '97 World Series, immediately turned awful teams into playoff clubs with no other significant changes to their casts. This winter second-year franchise Arizona signed Johnson, a free-agent lefthander who split last season with the Mariners and the Astros, in hopes of playing into October. The Yankees, who were 125–50, added Clemens in a trade.

No wonder Phillies general manager Ed Wade, whose team is the only noncontender in possession of a stud starter, is at the top of many general managers' speed-dial lists. The drooling over Schilling in the front offices of the Cardinals, Angels, Indians and Rangers is almost embarrassing to watch. "Oh, they *will* trade him," says one National League general manager.

"They'd be crazy not to trade him," says another. "They're not going to win with him, so they might as well not win without him and get some good players to build with."

THE PHILLIES say they need Schilling because they don't even have a bona fide No. 2 starter. (The designee, by default, is righthander Chad Ogea, who was not even a No. 5 in Cleveland last year.) Schilling's impact on the Phillies is so great that their chances of winning improve by 30% whenever he figures in a decision: He is 32–25 (.561) over the past two seasons, and Philadelphia is 111–156 (.432) in all other games in that span. Moreover, he is a throwback to the days when pitchers didn't punch out of games after six innings and boast, "I did my job"—you know, way back when, in the old days of 1988. Schilling threw the most pitches in baseball last year (4,213), went into the eighth inning more than anyone else (30 times in 35 starts), threw the most innings (268⅔) and completed the most games (15).

Eleven years ago, with four fewer clubs in the majors, 10 pitchers threw at least 250 innings. Last year only four did so, with Brown, Maddux and Baltimore's Scott Erickson joining Schilling. Erickson led the American League with 251⅓ innings. Also in '88, major league pitchers averaged a complete game once every seven starts. Last year the frequency dropped to once every 16 starts. Managers have become slaves to the specialized bullpen, mimicking La Russa's model with the Athletics of the late '80s, and to pitch counts, too. Virtually every dugout now has a coach with a handheld clicker, which too often serves the same purpose as an egg timer. Hit the arbitrary pitch-count number, and time's up. You're cooked.

"Pitchers are like rottweilers," Schilling says. "Everyone thinks they're mean dogs. Well, they'll be whatever you train them to be. It's the same with pitchers. Look at [the Cubs' phenom] Kerry Wood. They kept him on a 100-pitch leash in the minors, and then he gets to the majors and he throws more pitches and more innings than he ever has before, and he gets hurt. It's crazy." (Last week Wood was declared out for the season—and maybe beyond—after suffering damage to his right ulnar collateral ligament during a spring training game.)

"The only way you get to be a Number 1 is to earn it," Cubs general manager Ed Lynch says. "Consistency and durability are the most important ingredients. I'd say you'd have to be effective and stay off the disabled list at least two or three years in a row."

The making of a No. 1 starter cannot be rushed. Martinez, 27, is the only member of our Starting Nine younger than 30. Even before the Cardinals' best pitcher, 24-year-old righthander Matt Morris, suffered an elbow sprain last week, La Russa had decided against giving him the Opening Day assignment. "It's only his third year," La Russa says. "For someone to say, 'You're the Number 1 guy, pitch your day and affect the other ones,' that's not fair."

While the Cardinals wait to see what becomes of Schilling, St. Louis general manager Walt Jocketty says his team is sitting on three potential No. 1's: Morris and prospects Rick Ankiel, 19, and Chad Hutchinson, 22, to whom the Cardinals gave a combined $5.8 million in signing bonuses. "To me it makes more sense to spend money like that on young guys with a big upside than a middling veteran, who is going to cost you $8 million, and you only have him for two years," says Jocketty. "Sometimes you have to take the risk."

Ankiel, a lefthander, is considered the best pitching prospect in baseball. He was not selected out of high school until the 72nd pick of the 1997 draft because clubs feared the asking price of his agent, Scott Boras. Ankiel received a $2.5 million signing bonus. "I expect to see Ankiel and [Jose] Jimenez by August," says Reds general manager Jim Bowden, referring to another St. Louis prospect. "And that could have a big impact on our division. Ankiel is that good."

If he is, Ankiel could make the other Cardinals pitchers good, too. Martinez, for instance, helped the Red Sox improve by 14 games last year not only by winning 19 games but also by lightening the load on the rest of the rotation. Bret Saberhagen, for example, won 15 games while averaging only 88 pitches a start, the lowest output of any American League pitcher who made at least 30 starts. "My nine innings are seven now," says the 34-year-old righthander, who has come back from major rotator-cuff surgery. His job was made easier because Martinez usually matched up with the best starting pitchers from other teams and because the bullpen was sharper thanks to Martinez's throwing at least seven innings in 23 of his 33 starts. "It's simple," Martinez says. "You take a bat up there, you're my enemy. I will try to beat you."

That kind of attitude is infectious. Similarly, the Dodgers are hoping the hardworking Brown lifts the rest of their rotation—Chan Ho Park, Ismael Valdes, Carlos Perez and Darren Dreifort—a group with extraordinary stuff that hasn't lived up to expectations. New manager Davey Johnson assigned those pitchers to the same spring workout groups as Brown so they'd learn from his work habits. In past Dodgers camps the starting pitchers completed drills in different groups on different fields.

Yankees pitchers are getting the same drafting effect from being slotted behind Clemens. Manager Joe Torre says Cone will be the most obvious beneficiary. "Now if he needs to take an extra day or two because he's not feeling right, he can do it," Torre explains. Moreover, New York hopes Clemens's portly next-door-locker mate, righthander Hideki Irabu, whose effectiveness waned in the second half last season, will emulate his new teammate. In spring training Clemens often was the first Yankee to arrive and had completed a long session of running before Irabu rolled in rubbing the sleep from his eyes. Clemens always kept watch on Irabu when pitchers ran during workouts, doubling back "just like a dog herding sheep" to get Irabu to pick up his pace, Cone says.

Whither the 23 teams without such a stud at the top of the rotation? Is it worth it to sell the farm to get Schilling from Philadelphia? "I'd say it's a lot harder without one, especially in the postseason," Davey Johnson says. "When you've got that one guy who can dominate two or three games in a short series, you have a huge advantage."

The data on studs in October, though, are inconclusive. On one hand, only one of the past 15 world champions lacked a true No. 1: the 1993 Blue Jays, a tremendous offensive club with no pitcher among the top 10 in the American League in innings or ERA. More recently Cleveland has underscored the value of an ace by trying to get by without one. The Indians have lost Game 1 of eight straight postseason series while giving the ball to five starters in those openers. As a group Cleveland's starters are 15–14 in the past four postseasons, none of which have ended with a world championship. The franchise hasn't had an ace in his prime since Gaylord Perry in '74.

Then again, the impact of No. 1's often is less in October than it is during the regular season. Our nine current No. 1's are a modest 40–35 in 104 combined postseason games, including a 9–10 mark in 26 World Series starts. Randy Johnson has lost five straight postseason games, contributing to his team's defeat in its past three postseason series. Brown hasn't won any of his four World Series starts, the most recent being the pivotal Game 1 last year when he left with two runners on in the seventh and San Diego leading the Yankees 5–2.

Still, most managers would gladly take the security of giving the ball to that special breed of starter who can exert more influence on a game than anyone else on the field. No better example exists than what righthander Jack Morris did for the Twins in Game 7 of the 1991 World Series. Morris threw 10 shutout innings in the 1–0 win, all the while giving the impression that he would still be out there chucking today if the game were still tied. Morris's singular performance actually began with his appearance at a postgame news conference the previous night, following Game 6. Asked if he was ready for his start, Morris leaned into a microphone and announced with the strongest possible timbre, "In the words of the late, great Marvin Gaye, 'Let's get it on!' " In those two nights Morris came as close to a definition of a No. 1 starter as you'll ever see.

Postscript: In 2000 the Phillies traded Curt Schilling to the Diamondbacks, who won the world championship in his first full season there; Arizona then traded him to the Red Sox, who won the world championship in his first season in Boston. The fate of would-be ace Rick Ankiel only underscored the precariousness of that rare commodity; incurable wildness forced him to abandon his pitching aspirations and try to make it as an outfielder.

The Left Arm
Of God

He was a consummate artist on the mound, the most dominant
player of his time, yet he shunned fame and always put team above self.
On the field or off, Sandy Koufax was pitcher perfect

H E SAT IN THE SAME BOOTH EVERY TIME. IT WAS always the one in back, farthest from the door. The trim, darkly handsome man would come alone, without his wife, nearly every morning at six o'clock for breakfast at Dick's Diner in Ellsworth, Maine, about 14 miles from their home. He often wore one of those red-and-black-checkered shirts you expect to see in Maine, though he wasn't a hunter. He might not have shaved that morning. He would walk past the long counter up front, the one with the swivel stools that, good Lord, gave complete strangers license to strike up a conversation. He preferred the clearly delineated no-trespassing zone of a booth. He would rest those famously large hands on the Formica tabletop, one of those mini-jukeboxes to his left and give his order to Annette, the waitress, in a voice as soft and smooth as honey.

He came so often that the family who ran the diner quickly stopped thinking of him as Sandy Koufax, one of the greatest pitchers who ever lived. They thought of him the way Koufax strived all his life to be thought of, as something better even than a famous athlete: He was a regular.

Dick Anderson and his son Richard, better known as Bub, might glance up from their chores when Koufax walked in, but that was usually all. One time Bub got him to autograph a napkin but never talked baseball with him. Annette, Bub's sister, always worked the section with that back booth. For three years Koufax came to the diner and not once did he volunteer information to her about his life or his career. It was always polite small talk. Neighborly. Regular.

Koufax was 35, five years since his last pitch, in 1966, when he came eagerly, even dreamily, to Maine, the back booth of America. He had seen a photo spread in *Look* about the Down East country homestead of a man named Blakely Babcock, a 350-pound Burpee Seed salesman, gentleman farmer and gadfly whom everybody called Tiny. Tiny would invite neighbors and friends over for cookouts and dinner parties, during which he liked to consume great quantities of food and then, laughing, rub his huge belly and bellow to his wife, "So, what's for dinner, Alberta?" Tiny's North Ellsworth farmhouse caught Koufax's fancy at just about the same time one of his wife's friends was renovating her farmhouse in Maine. Wouldn't it be perfect, Koufax thought, to live quietly, almost anonymously, in an old farmhouse just like Tiny's?

Alberta Babcock was pulling a hot tin of sweet-smelling blueberry muffins from the oven when Koufax first saw the place in person, and the old Cape-style house was filled with so many flowers that it looked like a watercolor come to life. Koufax was sold, and on Oct. 4, 1971, Sanford and Anne Koufax of Los Angeles (as they signed the deed), took out a 15-year, $15,000 mortgage from Penobscot Savings Bank and bought what was known as Winkumpaugh Farm from Blakely and Alberta Babcock for about $30,000. A cord was cut. The rest of Sandy Koufax's life had begun.

The Babcocks had lived in the farmhouse since 1962, but no one was exactly sure how old the place was. Property records were lost to a fire at Ellsworth City Hall in 1933, and records from 1944 list the farmhouse's age even then only as "old." Nestled on the side of a small mountain off a dusty dirt road called Happytown Road and around the corner from another called Winkumpaugh Road, the farmhouse was the perfect setting for a man hoping to drop out of sight, even if that man was a beloved American icon who had mastered the art of pitching as well as anyone who ever threw a baseball. A man so fiercely modest and private that while at the University of Cincinnati on a basketball scholarship, he didn't tell his parents back in Brooklyn that he was also on the baseball team. The man whose mother requested one of the first copies of his 1966 autobiography, *Koufax*, so she could find out something about her son. ("You never told me anything," she said to him.) The man who in 1968, two years after retiring with three Cy Young Awards, four no-hitters and five ERA titles, mentioned nothing of his baseball career upon meeting a pretty young woman named Anne who was redecorating her parents' Malibu beach house. Koufax did offer to help her paint, though. It wasn't until several days later that she learned his identity—and he learned hers: She was the daughter of actor Richard Widmark. They were married six months later, in front of about a dozen people, in her father's West Los Angeles home.

The last two years that Anne and Sandy Koufax lived at Winkumpaugh Farm were the first in his life when he was bound by neither school nor work. After commuting from Maine during the summer of 1972 for his sixth season as a television commentator for NBC, he quit with four years left on his contract. He loathed the work. He could tell you every pitch thrown by every pitcher in a game without having written anything down, but there was a problem: He didn't like to talk about himself. At a meeting before Game 5 of the 1970 World Series, fellow announcer Joe Garagiola noted that Cincinnati's starting pitcher, Jim Merritt, had an injured arm. "I said, 'Sandy, what a perfect thing to talk about. That's what you had, too.' " Garagiola says. "But he said he didn't want to talk about himself. He wouldn't do it."

"Every time he had to leave Maine to work one of those games, it broke his heart," says MaJo Keleshian, a friend and former neighbor who attended Sarah Lawrence College with Anne. She still lives without a television on land she and her husband bought from Koufax. "He was very happy here. He came here to be left alone."

Since then only his address has changed—and many times, at that. Joe DiMaggio, baseball's other legendary protector of privacy, was practically Rodmanesque compared with Koufax. DiMaggio was regal, having acquired even the stiff-handed wave of royalty. We watched the graying of DiMaggio as he played TV pitchman and public icon. Koufax is a living James Dean, the aura of his youth frozen in time; he has grayed without our even knowing it. He is a sphinx, except that he doesn't want anyone to try to solve his riddle.

Koufax was the kind of man boys idolized, men envied, women swooned over and rabbis thanked, especially when he refused to pitch Game 1 of the 1965 World Series because it fell on Yom Kippur. And when he was suddenly, tragically, done with baseball, he slipped into a life nearly monastic in its privacy.

One question comes to mind: Why? Why did he turn his back on Fame and Fortune, the twin sirens of celebrity? Why did the most beloved athlete of his time carve out a quiet life—the very antithesis of the American dream at the close of the century? For the answer I will go searching for the soul of Sandy Koufax, which seems as mysterious as the deepest Maine woods on a moonless night.

BOB BALLARD is a retiree in Vero Beach, Fla., who works part time as a security guard at Dodgertown, the sleepiest spring training site in all of baseball. Sometime around 1987 he told the secretary for Peter O'Malley, then the owner of the Dodgers, how much he would enjoy getting an autograph from Koufax for his birthday. A few days later Koufax, working for the Dodgers as a roving pitching instructor, handed Ballard an autographed ball and said, "Happy birthday."

Every year since then, on or about Ballard's birthday, Koufax has brought the old man an autographed ball. Koufax delivered on schedule this year for Ballard's 79th birthday. "He's a super, super guy," says Ballard. "Very courteous. A real gentleman. A lot nicer than these players today."

It is a lovely day for golf. I am standing in the tiny pro shop of the Bucksport (Maine) Golf Club, a rustic, nine-hole track. The parking lot is gravel. Even the rates are quaint: $15 to play nine holes, $22 for 18, and you are instructed to play the white tees as the front nine, then the blue tees as the back nine. There is no valet parking, no tiny pyramids of Titleists on the scrubby range, no MEMBERS ONLY signs, no attitude. This is Koufax's kind of place. I am standing in the imprint of his golf spikes, a quarter-century removed. He was a member of the Bucksport Golf Club, one of its more enthusiastic members.

It wasn't enough that he play golf, he wanted to be good enough to win amateur tournaments. Koufax was working on the engine of a tractor one day when a thought came to him about a certain kind of grip for a golf club. He dropped his tools, dashed into his machine shop, fiddled with a club and then raced off to the Bucksport range. He was still wearing dungaree shorts and a grease-splattered shirt when he arrived. "That's how dedicated to the game he was," says Gene Bowden, one of his old playing partners.

Koufax diligently whittled his handicap to a six and entered the 1973 Maine State Amateur. He advanced to the championship flights by draining a 30-foot putt on the 18th hole. He missed the next cut, though, losing on the last hole of a playoff.

Koufax is exacting in every pursuit. Ron Fairly, one of his Dodgers roommates, would watch with exasperation as Koufax, dressed suavely for dinner in glossy alligator shoes, crisply pressed slacks and a fruit-colored alpaca sweater, would fuss over each hair in his sideburns. "Reservation's in 15 minutes, and it's a 20-minute ride," Fairly would announce, and Koufax would go right on trimming until his sideburns were in perfect alignment.

He brought that same meticulousness to Maine. It wasn't enough to dabble in carpentry and home electronics—he built and installed a sound system throughout the house. It wasn't enough to cook—he became a gourmet cook, whipping up dishes not by following recipes but by substituting ingredients and improvising by *feel*. Later in life it wasn't enough to jog; he ran a marathon. He didn't just take up fishing, he moved to Idaho for some of the best salmon fishing in the world. He defines himself by the fullness of his life and the excellence he seeks in every corner of it, not the way the rest of the word defines him: through the narrow prism of his career as a pitcher. "I think he pitched for the excellence of it," Keleshian says. "He didn't set out to beat someone or make anyone look bad. He used himself as his only measure of excellence. And he was that way in everything he did. He was a fabulous cook, but he was almost never quite satisfied. He'd say, 'Ah, it needs a little salt or a little oregano, or something.' Once in a great while he'd say, 'Ah-ha! That's it!' "

Walt Disney, John Wayne, Kirk Douglas, Darryl Zanuck and all the other Hollywood stars who held Dodgers season tickets when Koufax was the biggest star in America never came to Winkumpaugh Farm. The fans never came, either, though a fat sack of fan mail arrived every week, even seven years after he last threw a pitch. The place was perfect, all right. He could move about without fuss, without having to talk about his least favorite subject: himself. "He did say once that he'd rather not talk baseball and his career," Bowden says. "And we never did."

"WHEN HIDEO NOMO was getting really, really big, Sandy told me, 'He'd better learn to like room service,' " O'Malley says. "That's how Sandy handled the attention." Koufax almost never left his hotel room in his final two seasons for the Dodgers. It wasn't enough that he move to a creaky, charmingly flawed farmhouse in Maine with a leaky basement, he quickly bought up almost 300 acres adjacent to it.

Not even the serenity of Maine, though, could quell Koufax's wanderlust. After three years he decided the winters were too long and too cold. The farmhouse needed constant work. His stepfather took ill in California. Koufax sold Winkumpaugh Farm on July 22, 1974, leaving for the warmer but still rural setting of Templeton, Calif., in San Luis Obispo County.

Koufax is 63, in terrific shape and, thanks to shoulder surgery a few years back, probably still able to get hitters out. (In his 50s Koufax was pitching in a fantasy camp when a camper scoffed after one of his pitches, "Is that all you've got?" Koufax's lips tightened and his eyes narrowed—just about all the emotion he would ever show on the mound—and he unleashed a heater that flew damn near 90 mph.)

The romance with Anne ended with a divorce in the early '80s. He remarried a few years later, this time to a fitness enthusiast who, like Anne, had a passion for the arts. That marriage ended in divorce last winter. Friends say Koufax is delighted to be on his own again. Says Lou Johnson, a former Dodgers teammate, "He has an inner peace that's really deep-rooted. I wish I had that."

He is the child of a broken marriage who rejected everything associated with his father, including his name. Sanford Braun was three years old when Jack and Evelyn Braun divorced, and his contact with Jack all but ended about six years later when Jack remarried and stopped sending alimony payments. Evelyn, an accountant, married Irving Koufax, an attorney, a short time later. "When I speak of my father," he wrote in his autobiography, "I speak of Irving Koufax, for he has been to me everything a father could be." Koufax rarely spoke to Jack Braun, and not at all during his playing days. When the Dodgers played at Shea Stadium, Jack would sit a few rows behind the visitors' dugout and cheer for the son who neither knew nor cared that he was there.

Now there is but one Koufax bearing that name. He has no children, no immediate family—both his mother and stepfather are deceased. The death of his only sibling, a sister, in 1997, had a profound impact on a man who has struggled to deal with the deaths of friends and other players from his era. "People react to death differently," O'-Malley says. "Sandy takes a death very, very, very hard."

He has a small circle of close friends, and many other buddies who always seem to be one or two phone numbers behind him. "It sounds odd, but he's very home-oriented," Keleshian says, "yet very nomadic."

His list of home addresses since he stopped playing baseball reads like a KOA campground directory: North Ellsworth, Maine; Templeton and Santa Barbara, Calif.; Idaho; Oregon (where his second wife ran a gallery); North Carolina (where he and his second wife kept horses); and Vero Beach—not to mention extensive trips to Hawaii, New Zealand and Europe. This spring he was looking for a new place to spend the summer and once again had his eye on rural New England. "He doesn't say much about what he's up to," says Bobby McCarthy, a friend who owns a Vero Beach restaurant that Koufax prefers to frequent when it's closed. "We'll be sitting in the restaurant in the morning, and that night I'll see he's at a Mets game in New York. And he hadn't said anything that morning about going there. But that's Sandy."

At 8:30 on a lovely Sunday morning in March, I attend a chapel service in the Sandy Koufax Room at Dodgertown. Players and coaches in their fabulously white Dodgers uniforms are there, but not Koufax. The Dodgers give glory to Jesus Christ every Sunday in a conference room named for the greatest Jewish ballplayer who ever lived. Outside the room is a picture of a young Koufax, smiling, as if he is in on the joke.

DON SUTTON is a native of Clio, Ala., who reached the big leagues at age 21 in 1966, which is to say he got there just in time. His first season in the majors was Koufax's last. Says Sutton, "I saw how he dressed, how he tipped, how he carried himself and knew that's how a big leaguer was supposed to act. He was a star who didn't feel he was a star. That's a gift not many people have."

Tommy Hutton, who grew up in Los Angeles, also made his big league debut for the Dodgers in '66, entering the game in the ninth inning at first base as Koufax finished off the Pirates 5–1 on Sept. 16. Says Hutton, now a broadcaster for the Marlins, "I'll never forget this. After the game he came up to me and said, 'Congratulations.' Ever since then, I've always made it a point to congratulate a guy when he gets into his first game."

I AM STANDING in a tunnel under the stands behind home plate at Dodger Stadium on a clear summer night in 1998. Koufax is about 75 feet in front of me, seated on a folding chair on the infield while the Dodgers honor Sutton with the retirement of his number before a game against the Braves. When the program ends, Sutton and all his guests—former Dodgers Ron Cey and Steve Garvey among them—march past me toward an elevator that will take them to a stadium suite. All except Koufax. He is gone. Vanished. I find out later that as soon as the ceremony was over, he arose from his chair, walked briskly into the Dodgers dugout and kept right on going, into the team parking lot and off into the night. "That's Sandy," said one team official. "We call him the Ghost."

I am searching for an apparition. I never saw Koufax pitch, never felt the spell he held over America. I had just turned six when Koufax walked into the Sansui room of the Regent Beverly Wilshire Hotel on Nov. 18, 1966, to announce his retirement from baseball. To have missed his brilliance heightens the fascination. For me he is black-and-white newsreel footage shot from high behind home plate, and an inexhaustible supply of statistics that border on the absurd. A favorite: Every time he took the mound, Koufax was twice as likely to throw a shutout as he was to hit a batter.

Koufax was 30 years old when he quit. Women at the press conference cried. Reporters applauded him, then lined up for his autograph. The world, including his teammates, was shocked. In the last 26 days of his career, including a loss in the 1966 World Series, Koufax started seven times, threw five complete-game wins and had a 1.07 ERA. He clinched the pennant for Los Angeles for the second straight year with a complete game on two days rest. Everyone knew he was pitching with traumatic arthritis in his left elbow, but how bad could it be when he pitched like that?

It was this bad: Koufax couldn't straighten his left arm—it was curved like a parenthesis. He had to have a tailor shorten the left sleeve on all his coats. Use of his left arm was severely limited when he wasn't pitching. On bad days he'd have to bend his neck to get his face closer to his left hand so that he could shave. And on the worst days he had to shave with his right hand. He still held his fork in his left hand, but sometimes he had to bend closer to the plate to get the food into his mouth.

His elbow was shot full of cortisone several times a season. His stomach was always queasy from the cocktail of anti-inflammatories he swallowed before and after games, which he once said made him "half-high on the mound." He soaked his elbow in an ice bath for 30 minutes after each game, his arm encased in an inner tube to protect against frostbite. And even then his arm would swell an inch. He couldn't go on like this, not when his doctors could not rule out the possibility that he was risking permanent damage to his arm.

Not everyone was shocked when Koufax quit. In August 1965 he told Phil Collier, a writer for *The San Diego Union-Tribune* to meet him in a room off the Dodgers' clubhouse. Koufax and Collier often sat next to each other on the team's charter flights, yapping about politics, the economy or literature. "Next year's going to be my last year," Koufax told Collier. "The damn thing's all swelled up. And I hate taking the pills. They slow my reactions. I'm afraid someone's going to hit a line drive that hits me in the head."

Koufax didn't tell anyone else, and he made Collier promise not to write the story. So they shared that little secret throughout the 1966 season. When the Dodgers went to Atlanta, Collier whispered to Koufax, "Last time here for you." And that is exactly how Koufax pitched that season, as if he would never pass this way again. He won a career-high 27 games, pushing his record in his final six seasons to 129–47. He was 11–3 in his career in 1–0 games. In 1965 and '66 he was 53–17 for the club that scored fewer runs than all but two National League teams.

"He's the greatest pitcher I ever saw," says Hall of Famer Ernie Banks. "I can still see that big curveball. It had a great arc on it, and he never bounced it in the dirt. Sandy's curve had a lot more spin than anybody else's—it spun like a fastball coming out of his hand—and he had the fastball of a pure strikeout pitcher. It jumped up at the end. The batter would swing half a foot under it. Most of the time we knew what was coming, because he held his hands closer to his head when he threw a curveball, but it didn't matter. Even though he was tipping off his pitches, you still couldn't hit him."

Koufax was so good, he once taped a postgame radio show with Vin Scully *before* the game. He was so good, the relief pitchers treated the night before his starts the way a sailor treats shore leave. On one rare occasion in which Koufax struggled to go his usual nine innings—he averaged 7.64 per start from '61 to '66—manager Walter Alston visited his pitcher while a hungover Bob Miller warmed in the bullpen.

"How do you feel, Sandy?" Alston asked.

"I'll be honest with you, Skip," Koufax said. "I feel a hell of a lot better than the guy you've got warming up."

On Nov. 17, 1966, Collier came home from watching the Ice Capades and was greeted with this message from his babysitter: "Mr. Koufax has been trying to call you for a couple of hours." Collier knew exactly what it was about. He called Koufax.

"I'm calling the wire services in the morning," Koufax told him. "Is there anything you need from me now?"

"Sandy," Collier said, "I wrote that story months ago. It's in my desk drawer. All I have to do is make a call and tell them to run it."

Says Collier, "It was the biggest story I'll ever write. They ran it across the top of Page One with a big headline like it was the end of World War II."

I HAVE GOTTEN ahold of Koufax's home telephone number in Vero Beach, but I do not dare dial it. Even from afar I can feel the strength of this force field he has put around himself. To puncture it with a surprise phone call means certain disaster. I have read that Koufax so hated the intrusions of the telephone during his playing days that he once took to stashing it in his oven. Buzzie Bavasi, the Dodgers' general manager, would have to send telegrams to his house saying, "Please call."

I don't call. I am an archeologist—dig I must, but with the delicate touch of brushes and hand tools. I enlist the help of Koufax's friends. Now I understand why people I talk to about Koufax are apprehensive. They ask, Does Sandy know you're doing this story? (Yes.) It's as if speaking about him is itself a violation of his code of honor.

There is a 58-year-old health-care worker in Port Chester, N.Y., named David Saks who attended Camp Chi-Wan-Da in Kingston, N.Y., in the summer of 1954. Koufax, who is from Brooklyn, was his counselor. "He was this handsome, strapping guy, a great athlete who had professional scouts trying to sign him," Saks says. "I was 13. He was 18. We all were in awe of him. But even then there were signs that he wanted people to avoid fussing about him to the nth degree."

Saks needed a day to think before agreeing to share two photographs he has from Camp Chi-Wan-Da that include the teenage Koufax. "Knowing how he is . . . ," Saks explains. Saks has neither seen nor spoken to Koufax in 45 years. He does, however, have recurring dreams about happy reunions with him.

In Vero Beach, where Koufax spends much of his time now, the townsfolk choose not to speak his name when they come upon him in public. They will say, "Hello, Mr. K.," when they run into him at the post office or, "Hello, my good friend," rather than tip off a tourist and risk creating one of those moments Koufax detests.

"Sandy has a quiet, productive way about him," says Garagiola, president of the Baseball Assistance Team (BAT), a charity that helps former players in medical or financial straits. Garagiola sometimes calls Koufax to ask him to speak with former players who are particularly hurting. "He can't really understand that," Garagiola says. "He's got a great streak of modesty. He'll say, 'What do they want to talk to me for?' He is a Hall of Famer in every way. He'll make an impact. You won't know it and I won't know it, but the guy he's helping will know it. Above anything else, I'll remember him for his feelings for fellow players."

There was an outfielder named Jim Barbieri who joined the Dodgers during the 1966 pennant race. He was so nervous that he would talk to himself in the shower, and the pressure so knotted his stomach that he once threw up in the locker room. One day Koufax motioned toward Barbieri in the dugout and said to Fairly, "I have a responsibility to guys like him. If I pitch well from here on out, I can double that man's income." Koufax, who was referring to World Series bonus money, went 8–2 the rest of the season. From 1963 to '66 he was 14–2 in September, with a 1.55 ERA.

Earlier in that 1966 season a television network offered Koufax $25,000 to allow their cameras to trail him on and off the field. Koufax said he would do it for $35,000, and only if that money was divided so that every Dodgers player, coach and trainer received $1,000.

Koufax attends Garagiola's BAT dinner in New York City every winter, and always draws the biggest crowd among the many Hall of Famers who sign autographs during the cocktail hour. "I grew up in Brooklyn," says Lester Marks of Ernst and Young, which secured the Koufax table this year. "I went to Ebbets Field all the time. I'm 52. I thought seeing Sandy Koufax pitch was the thrill of a lifetime, but meeting him as an adult was an even bigger thrill. My guests were shocked at what a down-to-earth gentleman he is."

After this year's dinner I walked through the crowded ballroom toward Koufax's table, only to see him hustle to a secured area on the dais. He posed for pictures with the Toms River, N.J., Little League world champions. Then he was gone, this time for a night of refreshments in Manhattan with pitcher Al Leiter, as close to a protégé as Koufax has in baseball.

I should mention that I did meet Sandy Koufax a few years ago, before I embarked on this quest to find out what makes him run. I was at Dodgertown, standing next to the row of six pitching mounds adjacent to the Dodgers' clubhouse. "Sacred ground," as former Dodgers pitcher Claude Osteen calls it, seeing as it was here that Branch Rickey hung his famous strings, forming the borders of a strike zone at which every Dodgers pitcher from Don Newcombe to Koufax to Sutton to Orel Hershiser took aim. (Koufax was so wild as a rookie that pitching coach Joe Becker took him to a mound behind the clubhouse so he would not embarrass himself in front of teammates and fans.) Tan and lean, Koufax looked as if he had just come in from the boardwalk to watch the Los Angeles pitchers throw. He was dressed in sandals, a short pair of shorts and a polo shirt. I said something to him about the extinction of the high strike. Koufax said that he hadn't needed to have that pitch called a strike in order to get batters to swing at his high heater. When I followed up with a question about whether baseball should enforce the high strike in today's strike zone, Koufax's face tightened. I could almost hear the alarms sounding in his head, his warning system announcing, This is an interview! He smiled in a polite but pained way and said in almost a whisper, "I'd rather not," and walked away.

When chatty reporters aren't around, that lonely pedestal called a pitching mound still gives Koufax great pleasure. He is the James Bond of pitching coaches. His work is quick, clean, stylish in its understatement and usually done in top-secret fashion. He has tutored Cleveland's Dwight Gooden and L.A.'s Chan Ho Park on their curveballs and Houston's Mike Hampton on his confidence; convinced L.A.'s Kevin Brown that it was O.K. to lead his delivery with his butt; and taught former Dodger Hershiser to push off the rubber with the ball of his foot on the dirt and the heel of his foot on the rubber. Hershiser removed some spikes from the back of his right shoe so that he could be more comfortable with Koufax's style of pushing off.

Koufax has tried since 1982 to teach his curveball technique to Mets closer John Franco. "I can't do it," Franco says. "My fingers aren't big enough to get that kind of snap." Koufax was God's template for a pitcher: a prizefighter's back muscles for strength, long arms for leverage and long fingers for extra spin on his fastball and curveball. The baseball was as low as the top of his left ankle when he reached back to throw in that last calm moment of his delivery—like a freight train cresting a hill—just before he flung the weight and force of his body toward the plate.

His overhand curveball was vicious because his long fingers allowed him to spin the ball faster than anybody else. Most pitchers use their thumb to generate spin, pushing with it from the bottom of the ball and up the back side. Koufax could place his thumb on the top of the ball, as a guide—similar to the way a basketball player shooting a jumper uses his off-hand on the side of the ball—because his long fingers did all the work, pulling down on the baseball with a wicked snap. On the days he wasn't pitching Koufax liked to hold a ball with his fastball and curveball grips because he believed it would strengthen the muscles and tendons in his left hand by just the tiniest bit.

Koufax may be the best pitching coach alive, though he wants no part of that job's high visibility or demands on his time. He cannot be pinned down any easier than a tuft of a dandelion blown free by the wind. After quitting NBC in February 1973, Koufax didn't take another job until 1979, when he explained that his return to the Dodgers as a roving minor league pitching coach was partly due to financial concerns. Koufax pitched 12 years in the majors and made only $430,500 in salary. He has steadfastly rejected endorsement offers and supplements his income with perhaps two card shows a year.

In the '80s Koufax enjoyed staying under the big league radar by doing his coaching for the Dodgers at the minor league level, in places such as San Antonio, Albuquerque and Great Falls, Mont., where he liked to stay up late talking pitching with the players and staff. He likes helping young players. In Great Falls he saw the potential of a righthander the organization was down on for being too hot-tempered.

"He's got the best arm on the staff," Koufax said. "Stay with this guy." He was right about John Wetteland, the Rangers' closer, now in his 11th season as one of the most reliable short relievers in baseball.

Koufax abruptly quit the Dodgers in February 1990. O'Malley had thought he was doing Koufax a favor by ordering the farm director to cut back on Koufax's assignments in 1989, but Koufax told O'-Malley, "I just don't think I'm earning what you're paying me." He also was ticked off when one of the Dodgers bean counters bounced back an expense report to him over a trivial matter. Since then Koufax has worked on an ad hoc basis, ready to help his friends. Fox baseball analyst Kevin Kennedy, who carries a handwritten note from Koufax in his wallet, invited him to spring training in 1993 when Kennedy was managing the Rangers. Koufax stayed one week, insisting that he wear an unmarked jersey with a plain blue cap rather than the team's official uniform. "He really enjoyed it," says Osteen, who was Kennedy's pitching coach. "Every night we'd go out to dinner and just talk baseball deep into the night. At the end of the week he said, 'You know, I've really had a good time.' I was floored. For him to acknowledge how he felt was a major, major thing. Believe me. I could tell he had missed the game. But at the same time, after a week of it he was ready to go back to his own life. One week was enough."

Last year Koufax visited the Mets' camp in Port St. Lucie, Fla., as a favor to owner Fred Wilpon, a former teammate at Lafayette High School in Brooklyn, and Dave Wallace, the Mets' pitching coach who befriended Koufax when Wallace was working in the Dodgers' minor league system. Koufax sat in front of the row of lockers assigned to the Mets' pitchers and began talking. A crowd grew, pulling into a tight circle like Boy Scouts around a campfire. Koufax looked at Leiter—also a lefthander—and said, "Al, you've had a nice career. Pitched in the World Series. But you can be better."

"I know," Leiter said. "Can you help me?"

Koufax liked that. He showed Leiter how he used to push off the rubber. He asked Leiter about where he aimed a certain pitch, and when Leiter said, "I'm thinking outer half—" Koufax cut him off. "Stop!" he said. "You never think outer half. You think a spot on the outside corner. Think about throwing the ball through the back corner of the plate, not to it."

What Koufax stressed most was that Leiter needed to pitch away more to righthanded hitters. Koufax lived on fastballs on the outside corner. Leiter, who says that many hitters today dive into the ball, prefers to pound cut fastballs on their fists. But Koufax showed Leiter how to make the ball run away from righthanders by changing the landing spot of his right foot by one inch and by letting his fingers come off slightly to the inside half of the ball. And Koufax shared the lesson that saved his career, the lesson it took him six years in the big leagues to learn: A fastball will behave better, with just as much life and better control, if you throttle back a little. "Taking the grunt out of it," is how Koufax put it.

In 1961 Koufax was a career 36–40 pitcher with awful control problems. He was scheduled to throw five innings in the Dodgers spring training B game against the Twins in Orlando, but the other pitcher missed the flight, and Koufax said he'd try to go seven. His catcher and roommate, Norm Sherry, urged him to ease up slightly on his fastball, throw his curve and hit his spots. Koufax had nothing to lose; manager Walter Alston and the front office were at the A game. Cue the chorus of angels and dramatic lighting. Koufax got it. He threw seven no-hit innings and, as he wrote in his book, "I came home a different pitcher from the one who had left."

A few weeks after Koufax spoke to the Mets' staff, an excited Wilpon approached Leiter in the clubhouse and said, "I don't know what you did with Sandy, but he wants you to have his home number. I've never known him to do this before with any player. If you ever want to talk with him, just give him a call."

Leiter says he rang the dial-a-legend line three or four times. "I wasn't sure what to do," he says. "I didn't want to call so much where he would think I was taking advantage of our friendship. On the other hand, I didn't want to *not* call, and he'd think, 'That guy is blowing me off.' It's kind of delicate, you know what I mean? But Sandy's cool. Real cool." At 32, Leiter had the best season of his career (17–6, 2.47). "I accepted the idea of throwing outside more," he says. "The times when I did it fairly often were the three or four most dominating games I had all year."

Koufax likes to slip into Dodgertown during spring training unnoticed, parking in a back lot, visiting with O'Malley if he sees the shades open at Villa 162 and watching pitchers throw on the sacred ground of the practice mounds. He has noticed that there are a lot more microphones and cameras at Dodgertown since Rupert Murdoch bought the team last year. He is not happy about that.

I am chatting with Bobby McCarthy, Koufax's friend from Vero Beach, during an exhibition game at Dodgertown when Dave Stewart, a former Koufax pupil (who himself coached the pennant-winning Padres pitching staff last year), stops by. "We were talking about Sandy," McCarthy says.

"Oh, yeah?" Stewart says. "I just saw him in the clubhouse."

I bolt, but when I get to the clubhouse, the Ghost has vanished. I can practically smell the ethereal contrails.

A few days later I get the official word from a member of Koufax's inner circle: "He doesn't want to talk. He's at the point where he doesn't care what people write; he just doesn't want to say anything. Sorry."

I fire my last bullet. The home phone number. I haven't needed to muster this kind of courage to dial a telephone since I asked my date to our high school prom. The phone rings. I remember the code: The answering machine is on if he's in town, off if he's not. The phone just keeps ringing.

IT IS Opening Day of the 1999 season. I am standing before the house at Winkumpaugh Farm. Or what is left of it. It burned to the ground 22 days ago.

I am staring at a cement hole in the ground filled with ash and garbage and the stump of a chimney. Standing with me is Dean Harrison, a 45-year-old intensive-care nurse who grew up in West Orange, N.J., rooting for Koufax. He bought the property last year and lives in a house farther up the hill. When his power goes out during a winter storm, he calls the utility company and says, "The Koufax line is out." And they know exactly where the problem is. He knows the history of the place.

Koufax sold Winkumpaugh Farm to Herbert Haynes of Winn, Maine, who sold it three months later to John and Kay Cox of Mare Island, Calif. Cox was an absentee landlord, renting it when he could. Young people used it as a party house. Necessary repairs were left undone. By the time Henderson bought it last fall, Winkumpaugh Farm was in awful shape. "I wanted to save it," he says. "I was about 30 years too late." He finally decided to donate the farmhouse to the Ellsworth Fire Department.

When the fire company went out to the house on March 14, patches of ground were showing through what was left of winter's last snowfall. The first thing the firemen did was grab pieces of Sandy Koufax's life for themselves. They pulled up floorboards and planks of clapboard siding. A policeman tossed some switch plates, two faucet handles and a small pile of bricks into the back of his squad car.

After this bit of scavenging, the firefighters practiced a few rescues with a controlled fire, then they scattered hay on Winkumpaugh Farm's old wood floors and torched it. The old place went up quick as kindling, gone before a tear could fall to the snow.

After the fire burned out, Keleshian reached into the smoldering ruin and took some ancient square-headed nails. She also took some of the farmhouse's charcoaled remains, with which she plans to sketch from memory two drawings of Winkumpaugh Farm—one for Anne and one for Sandy.

The early spring sun holds me in its warmth as it begins to sink behind the mountain beyond the valley. The quiet of North Ellsworth is profound, disturbed only by the gentle whisper of the wind through the pines and the bare branches of the oak, beech, birch and apple trees.

The farmhouse is gone, and yet I see it clearly. I see the weather vane atop the tiny cupola, the second-floor dormers, the screened-in porch and the white sign under the eaves that says WINKUMPAUGH FARM in black letters. I can hear classical music playing through homemade speakers. I can smell dinner wafting through the cozy house. Without the recipe in front of him, Sandy is making his grandmother's stuffed cabbage. He is surrounded by friends, laughter, the glow of a wood-burning stove and the warmth of walls lined with hardbound books. He is home.

Sandy Koufax always hated it when people described him as a recluse, and I have come to understand how wrong that label is. A recluse doesn't touch so many people with lifelong lessons of generosity, humility and the Zen of the curveball.

I have rebuilt his farmhouse in my mind, and it is sturdier and more beautiful this way. Why shouldn't I do the same when taking the measure of the man who once lived there? Must every blank be filled in, leaving us no room to construct parts of him as we wish? What we don't see can help us keep him forever young, unflinchingly true to himself, forever an inspiration.

Looking at the ruins of Winkumpaugh Farm at my feet, I realize that I no longer need that Vero Beach phone number. I have found Sandy Koufax.

Postscript: Sandy Koufax called me after I wrote this piece but before it ran in SI. We talked for a long time, mostly about college basketball. He politely explained that he did not want to be interviewed or quoted. I was oddly happy about that. I had enjoyed the challenge of finding the essence of a man through the people he touched and the places he had been. Fascinated by his career and impressed by his integrity, I had wanted to write this story for years, and it's still one of my favorites.

A Game for
Unlikely Heroes

*One out away from the indignity of a World Series no-hitter
at the hands of the Yankees, the Dodgers sent a little-used
infielder named Cookie Lavagetto to the plate*

TONIGHT, MY SONS, I WILL TELL YOU MY FAVORITE bedtime story. It happened back when your grandfather was a young man, before he was a father himself. So, of course, I was not there. But whenever I want to think about the essence of baseball—the equity of its possibilities—I *am* there, inside that little snow globe of a ballpark in Brooklyn, amid the fading light and encroaching shadows of late afternoon on Oct. 3, 1947.

Someday you will learn how a snapshot can capture not just an image but something much larger. A sailor kissing a woman in Times Square. A girl wailing beside a student felled by a National Guardsman's bullet. A line drive ricocheting off the rightfield wall at Ebbets Field in the fourth game of the 1947 World Series.

This was the first Series to feature a black player, the courageous rookie Jackie Robinson, at first base for the Brooklyn Dodgers against the New York Yankees. It was also the first World Series to be televised. Robinson was but one of five future Hall of Famers on the field that day—and one of those was the great DiMaggio, the player whose picture hangs right there above your bed, Adam. But none of them had anything to do with what I am about to tell you. And that is among the many ways in which baseball the fairest of sports.

It was the bottom of the ninth, and Bill Bevens, an otherwise unremarkable Yankees righthander with a 40–36 career record, was one out away from the first no-hitter in World Series history. The Yankees led the game, and the Series, 2–1. Pinch-hitting for Brooklyn with two runners aboard on walks was Cookie Lavagetto, a lifetime .269 hitter who had batted just 69 times that season with only four extra-base hits.

The Yankees could not kill the clock. They could not sit on the ball. The Dodgers could not call timeout. They could not design a play to put the game in the hands of their best player. At its most critical moments, baseball chooses its heroes and goats with the randomness of a carnival barker's rickety spinning wheel. Where she stops nobody knows.

The strapping Bevens blew his first pitch, a fastball, past Lavagetto. Then, with his 137th and last offering, he tried another. Lavagetto struck a liner that caromed off the rightfield wall and then off the chest of Yankees rightfielder Tommy Henrich, who retrieved the ball and began a vain relay to the plate. By the time Eddie Miksis came home with Brooklyn's winning run, Bevens was trudging off the field toward the third base dugout, his head bowed in mourning at having been beaten by just one hit, Lavagetto's double.

I suppose I should mention, almost parenthetically, that the Yankees would go on to win the Series in seven games, that Bevens, 18 days short of his 31st birthday when he threw that final fastball, would never start another major league game, ruined by a sore arm.

Lavagetto, finished at 34, would never get another major league hit.

Delirious Brooklyn fans stormed the mottled grass and dusty dirt of Ebbets Field after Lavagetto's blow. A few of them tore at his shirt, and one snatched the cap from his head. Whenever I picture myself at that game, I am standing along the first base line with a more reverential cluster of fans, many of them topped by brushed wool fedoras, staring in awe at the rightfield wall as big-muscled Buicks and Fords honk like a flock of happy geese down Bedford Avenue on the other side. Many of the fans are pointing to the spot where Lavagetto's hit clanked off the Burma Shave sign, about 12 feet above the ground, as if, like Thomas probing Jesus' wounds, to make the miracle real.

My gaze, however, is drawn to the advertisement below that one. It is for a movie starring Danny Kaye. I smile at the perfection of its placement in the composition of this snapshot: *The Secret Life of Walter Mitty*. Anything is possible.

Sweet dreams, my boys. Sweet dreams.

Postscript: I chose to write about this game when SI asked its staffers to contribute to a 20th century retrospective called "I Wish I'd Been There." I intended it to be a valentine not just to baseball, but also to my sons.

The Power
Of Pedro

*Godlike in the eyes of Red Sox fans, Pedro Martinez used
an astonishing mastery of four pitches and a ferocious
will to fuel Boston's fever for a World Series title*

O N A BASEBALL DIAMOND SO SCRAGGLY THAT AN
impoverished goat would find it unappetizing, a
schoolboy and the master cross paths while running sprints in centerfield. They are just two of a
hundred or so professional and amateur ballplayers who have come
to a rubble-strewn public park smack in the midst of the heat, grime and
grit of Santo Domingo, capital of the Dominican Republic. The park,
Centro Olimpico, is ground zero of the last place in the free world
where baseball is the unchallenged national pastime. They are here to
train.

The boy catches the master's eye and bows his head respectfully, dip-
ping the bill of his threadbare cap. He speaks in the worshipful manner of a peasant addressing a king. *El Duro* is all the boy dares say.

Pedro Martinez returns a nod and a smile. *El Duro* is the loose equiv-
alent of that obsequious Americanism, the Man. Its literal translation
is more apt. *El Duro* means "the Hard One." When a baseball flies from

the long, grotesquely concave fingers of the Red Sox righthander, Martinez seems to possess the properties of misch metal, an alloy of iron and rare earth elements. Scratch it, as happens in a cigarette lighter, and sparks fly.

"Look at this," says Martinez to a visitor. He offers up his right hand, the very hand of God, as it were, if you happen to be among an extremist sect of Web-based Red Sox zealots, such as those who commune on www.redsoxdiehard.com. (The rest of the faithful, including Dan Duquette, the otherwise reserved Boston general manager, place him merely between sainthood and Providence. "He is a gift from God," Duquette gushes.)

Martinez points to the tips of the index and middle fingers of his right hand. Each one is calloused, even now, in January, three months removed from his last pitch of '99. But the calluses are not where you expect them to be, on the lower part of the fingertip, the contact points of a pitcher's grip. No, the slivers of hardened skin are at the very top of the fingers, almost beneath the edge of the fingernails. But . . . how could this be? "The longer the ball stays on your fingers, the more spin you get," Martinez says. Spin is the DNA of a fastball, its very code of life. Martinez's heater is a 97-mph double helix of hell for a hitter.

His fingers curve backward so easily that the baseball stays on his fingers longer than on most pitchers'. The last part of his fingers to touch the ball is not the part you would use to dribble a basketball, but the part you would use to push a doorbell. As a few of the baseball's furiously spinning 108 stitches of waxed red thread scratch the skin of his fingertips . . . sparks fly. "I can feel a burning sensation from the seams," he says. "That's what it feels like—a burn."

That's El Duro, the pyrophoric pitcher. Human flint. The effort to imbue each pitch with fire and brimstone contorts his face so harshly that even he cannot stand the sight of it. "I hate signing action pictures," he tells autograph-seeking fans. "That is one ugly face."

Martinez possesses the power of Randy Johnson, the precision of Greg Maddux, the mound intellect of Mike Mussina and, at 5' 11", 175 pounds, the body of Bud Selig. Baseball has never seen anything quite like him. In 1997 he became the shortest and lightest pitcher ever to strike out 300 batters in a season. Last year Martinez became the greatest combination of power and control in the history of the game.

Until last year Curt Schilling and Sandy Koufax had been the only pitchers in history to whiff 300 batters in a season while striking out more than five times as many batters as they walked. Schilling's strike-out-to-walk ratio was 5.5:1 in 1997; Koufax's was 5.38:1 in '65 and 5.28:1 in '63. In '99 Martinez went where no man had ever gone before—8.46:1. His totals of 313 strikeouts and 37 walks seem implausible by any manner of achievement other than by joystick. "I'm not afraid of hitting anyone," he says, "because I can put the ball where I want to. I only hit nine guys last year. When I do hit them, it's usually just a nibble. I can nibble their jersey with the ball. That's how much I can control the ball."

Martinez already has two Cy Young Awards (the National League's, in 1997 with the Expos, and the American League's last year), and he doesn't turn 29 until October. He put up more impressive figures in '99 than a Miss America pageant. He went 23–4 with a 2.07 ERA, won the pitching triple crown (wins, ERA and strikeouts), set a major league record with 13.2 strikeouts per nine innings, did not allow a home run in any of the 293 at bats against him with a runner on, permitted only three leadoff walks to score (he walked the first batter only six times in 213⅓ innings) and struck out 37% of all batters he faced. That was not enough.

"Every day in Boston somebody will tell me, 'My father—or grandfather—wants to see the Red Sox win the World Series, just once. You are the one who can do it,'" Martinez says. "I tell them I will try, but I cannot do it by myself. It takes a team, and I think the team we have now is as good as any in the big leagues."

Martinez climbs the crude, cratered mound on one of Centro Olimpico's diamonds. He peers into the plate and smiles knowingly, even wickedly. He has no ball or glove. But even so, even here, as you watch him on that mound, you sense what it must feel like to know you can play tic-tac-toe with a baseball at 20 paces without ever using the center square . . . this is what it feels like to hold 5.19 ounces of absolute superiority in your hands . . . this is what it feels like to be El Duro.

"The plate," he says. "It looks so close. There are days when I first get out to the mound and it feels like the plate is closer than it's supposed to be. Then I know right away. It's over. You are f-----."

At that moment you can feel his fire, wavelets of passion and supreme confidence radiating from him. "I am a pitcher because I like the challenge of being responsible for the game, of being in charge of the action," Martinez says. "If the shortstop makes an error, I am responsible. I let the batter hit the ball."

Yes, standing in the wake of his fire, you understand perfectly that this is a man who can use a baseball to snip the button from a hitter's shirt, who is the last great hope of geriatric New Englanders and who sent the Indians home for the winter, despite an injured arm he could barely lift above his head and with little more of his usual weaponry than the look of a lion tamer in his eyes.

This also is a man who wears jeans with Linus embroidered on the back pocket. A man who prepares for his starts by tending to flowers in his garden. A man who melts around children. A man who gave his $6,500 signing bonus in 1988 to his big brother, Ramon. A man who has built a church and three houses—with an elementary school, a playground, a ball field and more houses to come—for the impoverished people of Manoguayabo, his hometown in the Dominican.

This is also a man who, as a skinny boy, loved to climb the old mango tree in his backyard. Alone, the boy would study his school lessons high in the branches. Sometimes in that tree he would remember his parents' yelling and screaming in his house, and it could still make him cry years later. He would explain it—this ache he felt in his heart—many times to many doctors and psychiatrists in Santo Domingo, who told him he had a heart murmur but could do nothing for the sadness he kept inside.

All that is part of the fire, too. That, too, is El Duro.

THE DOCTORS examined the strained muscle running from his right shoulder down his back and said Martinez might be able to throw 40 pitches, absolute max. Jimy Williams, the Boston manager, decided that if his club was tied or had a small lead in the eighth inning, Martinez would pitch that inning and, the good Lord willing, the ninth too. If the Red Sox could beat Cleveland at Jacobs Field in Game 5 of the 1999 Division Series, they would play the Yankees for a spot in the World Series. If the Red Sox lost, they went home.

Williams's plan blew up early. Boston and Cleveland slugged away at each other with a ferocity that made Ali-Frazier look like a church cotillion. It was 8–8 in the fourth inning when Williams reached for a tourniquet. He needed those one or two innings out of Martinez, and he needed them right now.

"I put my career in jeopardy that game," Martinez says. "I knew that. Why? We had to win the game."

With every pitch Martinez felt a stabbing sensation behind his shoulder. His fastball couldn't break 90 mph. It wasn't until he saw a video later that he realized he couldn't raise his arm high enough to throw the ball from his usual three-quarters delivery. None of that mattered, except to burnish a newly minted legend.

"I've always said that you could take five, six, seven, eight miles an hour off his fastball, and he'd still be a great pitcher," Red Sox pitching coach Joe Kerrigan says. "That game proved it."

Says Martinez, "I can change the way I pitch in 10 seconds—in the middle of a game, in the middle of an at bat. No problem. I know myself. I know my body. If I have to get you out a different way, I will do it."

The Indians were finished, and they knew it. One at bat in the fifth inning made it official. First baseman Jim Thome, who already had walloped two home runs, foolishly salivated at the opportunity to bat with a 3-and-0 count against Martinez. "I'm looking to hit the ball out of the stadium," Thome will explain later. "I'm in high-gear mode. Grip it and rip it, basically."

But Thome is momentarily unnerved when he sees Martinez studying him. It's like getting one of those little pink WHILE YOU WERE OUT slips scribbled with "IRS called." Says Thome, "What makes Pedro so great is that he's so intelligent. You watch Pedro and it's like a cat-and-mouse game, and he's the cat, studying you. He's watching you, watching your feet to see if they've moved, watching your body language. He's looking at you all around and up and down. He's trying to figure out what *I'm* trying to figure out about him."

During the home-run-hitting contest at the All-Star Game, which most players treated as kindergartners would recess, Martinez watched Mark McGwire closely. "I watch and learn," Martinez says. "I noticed all those balls he hit out were in the same place. Middle [of the plate], up a little. I said, O.K., I'm not stupid. I know where he likes it."

This is what McGwire saw from Martinez the next night in the All-Star Game at Fenway Park: changeup away for a ball, changeup down for strike one, fastball down for strike two and fastball up—just enough out of McGwire's happy zone—for strike three swinging. Martinez struck out five of the six batters he faced that night, the home run king and four MVPs: Barry Larkin, Larry Walker, Sammy Sosa and Jeff Bagwell. The bricks and mortar of Boston's antique ballpark threatened to split wide open from the din of the home crowd. In Martinez's real backyard proud Dominicans tied any sort of junked metal to their bicycles—pieces of iron fencing, broken washing machines, various car parts—and dragged them through the narrow, darkened, dusty streets of Manoguayabo. Homemade fireworks—what better tribute to El Duro than sparks dancing in the night?

When Martinez went about reading Thome at 3 and 0, he found all the challenge of the Sunday comics. Martinez is adept at exploiting big-swinging sluggers. The eight top home run hitters over the past five years—McGwire, Sosa, Albert Belle, Vinny Castilla, Juan Gonzalez, Ken Griffey Jr., Rafael Palmeiro and Mo Vaughn—have a combined career average of .107 against Martinez, with just one home run (by Gonzalez) in 84 times at bat. Thome is 2 for 14 with seven punchouts.

"I knew he'd be swinging," Martinez says. "The Indians are aggressive. I told [fellow Boston starter] Bret Saberhagen before the game, 'Sabes, you've got to bounce some changeups to these guys.

Bounce 'em.' He didn't do it. He has great control. Too good. The Indians swing at everything. It was a bad matchup. So I knew Thome was looking to hit it out."

Martinez flips a 3-and-0 changeup into the strike zone. Stunned, Thome doesn't dare swing. "I can't go up there looking for a 3-and-0 change," Thome says. "That's not good hitting."

Now Martinez spins a backdoor curveball that catches the outside corner. Thome does not—cannot—swing. A 3-and-1 hook? It's like seeing snow in August.

O.K., Thome thinks, now just try to hit the ball. But what's coming? He can't be certain. This predicament is why Yankees manager Joe Torre will say one week later—after Martinez has dealt New York its only loss of the postseason, a 12-strikeout, 13–1 laugher in Game 3 of the American League Championship Series—that trying to hit Martinez is "like trying to hit in a dark room." (It was the second time in five weeks that Torre had witnessed such frustration at the plate. On Sept. 10 Martinez had one-hit the Yankees, whiffing 12 of the final 15 batters to finish with 17 strikeouts.)

Martinez decides on a fastball. Of course, it is not just any fastball. It is a smart bomb laser-guided to skirt the inside corner of the plate. After the camouflage of a flirtatious changeup and a looping curveball, the fastball has the illusion of traveling faster than it actually is. "Put it this way," Thome says. "It had some hair on it."

Thome swings at it. He is too late. The pitch is past him. He's been eviscerated like a flounder. The Indians are finished. The most prolific scoring team in the second half of the 20th century cannot get a single hit off the wounded Martinez, who winds up chucking 97 pitches over six innings. Heroic? It was Kirk Gibson limping off the bench to hit his home run—and doing it five more times.

THE DODGERS' Dominican training complex in Campo Las Palmas is a remote, pastoral pleasure of lush green fields, swaying palm trees and fresh paint—that is, once you get past the entrance gate with the guard carrying the semiautomatic assault weapon. The face of baseball is being changed at this academy, at others like it run by other organizations and on just about any available expanse of grass in the Dominican. One out of every five players now under contract to major league organizations was born in the Dominican, a country with the approximate population (7.5 million) of North Carolina. More are coming. The three fields of Centro Olimpico are busy every day with players training on their own. Three pickup teams fill each field on weekends, two playing and one, on the sidelines, that has winners. The basketball courts are virtually abandoned.

In May 1988 a kid from Manoguayabo came to Campo Las Palmas for a tryout. He was so skinny he could have slipped through the iron bars of the entrance gate if he wished, maybe without turning sideways. Pedro Martinez was 16 years old, weighed 137 pounds and threw his fastball no better than 82 mph. The Dodgers knew him as the younger brother of Ramon, a rising pitching star in their organization who would make his big league debut later that year. "He wasn't impressive to look at, physically," says Eleodoro Arias, the academy's pitching instructor. "But looking into the eyes of Pedro, I could see he had *el corazón*. Heart. Guts. I recommended he not be signed at the moment, but that we work with him, and with some added nourishment he could be signed."

The Dodgers did sign him about four weeks and many meals later. Pedro turned over his bonus money to Ramon as a gesture of thanks for serving as his pitching mentor. It was Ramon who had taught him how to throw a curve and a changeup and counseled him on the tenets of pitching, such as, "Remember, in baseball you have no friends." Teammates with the Dodgers in 1992 and '93, the brothers Martinez were reunited late last season with the Red Sox after Ramon recovered from rotator cuff surgery. When Ramon presented Pedro with his second Cy Young Award at a dinner in Boston in January, Pedro said to his brother, "There is more of you in this trophy than there is of me."

"It's funny," says Pedro, who gave his first Cy Young to Dominican pitching legend Juan Marichal, "I like to think I am a man who knows what I want. But to this day, no matter what I want to do, first I must have Ramon next to me to ask him what he thinks. I will always look up to him. That will never change."

Pedro came to be known around the academy, where he spent 1988 and '89, as Chichilito, a pet name for a child. He was, however, so ferociously driven to win that after games he had lost, even those in which he had pitched splendidly, Arias would find him alone, crying. "I thought Pedro could be somebody," Arias says, "but I never thought Pedro would be as special as Pedro is now."

Every good pitcher has a strikeout pitch, the kind that should be marked IN CASE OF EMERGENCY, BREAK GLASS. The great pitchers have two. Martinez is the only one today who has three equally lethal options. He commands them with near-equal precision. Last year he threw 67% of his fastballs for strikes, 67% of his changeups for strikes and 62% of his curveballs for strikes.

What makes him all the more treacherous is that Martinez offers no clue as to what's coming. Every pitch is thrown with his hand in the same release slot and with the same arm speed. What you think is a 97-mph heater leaving his fingertips may be an 83-mph curveball that can turn the bravest hitter's knees into gelatin, or it may be a

77-mph changeup that breaks like a hyperactive screwball. The spin of each pitch has its own DNA, and you'd better be quick to decode it. The changeup is particularly perplexing. Martinez varies the speed and break of the pitch—he can make it wiggle six to eight inches, generally saving the biggest break for two-strike situations—by adjusting the pressure on the ball from his fingers. "It's a Bugs Bunny changeup; it moves so much," Saberhagen says. "Bugs Bunny is the only one with a changeup that can move like that, and he has the help of animators."

It is Martinez's fastball, though, that measures his growth as a pitcher. Five months after signing, in November 1988, Martinez was throwing 89 mph. Two months after that, he was clocked at 93. He attributes much of that gain to playing long toss, which he still regularly employs, in which he plays catch at distances up to 250 feet. "That's his holy grail," Kerrigan says.

In 1990 the Dodgers assigned him to their rookie league team in Great Falls, Mont. Great Falls advanced to a playoff series against Salt Lake City, an independent club stocked with older players, many of whom had played Double A ball. Martinez, scheduled to start Game 2, charted pitches in Game 1 from the stands next to Dodgers roving instructor Dave Wallace. "Tomorrow," he promised Wallace, "I will take care of these guys."

The next night the Salt Lake City leadoff batter dug his spikes confidently into the dirt as he stepped into the batter's box. Little 18-year-old Chichilito whizzed his very first pitch past the hitter's chin. Salt Lake City didn't score that night. "Right then I thought he was something special," Wallace says.

The Dodgers, though, never did give Martinez much of a chance. He made 67 appearances for them, all but three in relief, before L.A.

traded him to the Expos after the 1993 season for second baseman Delino DeShields. The Dodgers had decided that someone that small who threw that hard could never hold up in the big leagues. Dodgers physician Frank Jobe, who the year before had performed an anterior capsolaral reconstruction on Martinez's left shoulder, cautioned that his small frame left him injury-prone.

"Tommy Lasorda never told me, but he thought I couldn't be a starter," Martinez says of his Los Angeles manager. "He pitched me five days in a row out of the bullpen, but thought I'm not strong enough to pitch once every five days? That makes no sense."

Martinez blossomed into a star in Montreal, going 55–33 in four years without missing a start for manager (and fellow Dominican) Felipe Alou, who believed in him as a starter and whom Martinez still quotes as a priest does scripture. To become a true master, though, Martinez had to harness his fastball. That 82-mph floater from Campo Las Palmas had grown up to be the most hazardous pitch in the majors. Martinez threw it with his index and middle fingers along two seams and slung it in such a way that it broke by as much as nine inches toward the hands and heads of righthanded hitters. That's the way Martinez and the Expos explained it, anyway. Hitters regarded him as a headhunter. "He pitched inside aggressively and hit people for the effect," says Mets first baseman Todd Zeile. "He'd hit you or put the ball right under your chin, and he'd stare right at you, not like most guys, who'll look away."

In 1995 Kerrigan, his pitching coach in Montreal, changed Martinez's grip to a four-seam fastball. Martinez gradually gained control of the pitch, trading that erratic, sideways-riding movement for a late, explosive giddyup that appears to make the ball hop as it nears the plate. In the past two years Martinez has also learned how to cut his fastball, making it bore in on the hands of lefthanded hitters. "Since 1994 I don't think anybody else has gotten better and better the way I have," Martinez says. "Every year I know more and more about the hitters and how they react to me. There are some guys I know how to get out every single time, and I'll keep doing it unless they make an adjustment—and then I'll adjust. If my ability remains the same as I continue to get experience, I'll have a bunch of Cy Youngs."

Martinez threw the ball with his usual zing this spring training and pronounced himself fully recovered from his shoulder injury last October. Then again, his durability will always be a question. Only one pitcher under six feet tall born after 1900 has made the Hall of Fame: 5' 10" Whitey Ford. In 1998 Martinez was physically unable to pitch on short rest in a win-or-go-home Division Series game against Cleveland. (Boston lost.) He missed two starts last July because of soreness in his right shoulder. He doesn't throw off a mound between starts, choosing to conserve his candlepower by long tossing and lightly spinning his off-speed pitches on flat ground. The Red Sox dare not use him as a traditional workhorse at the top of a rotation. They give him an extra day of rest between starts whenever possible. He was 13–0 in 15 such starts last year. "We'll do it again this year," Kerrigan says. "As Felipe used to always say, 'We've got to take care of the little man.' "

WITH EACH passing hour of the afternoon the air above four-lane Avenida George Washington in Santo Domingo, hard by the Caribbean Sea, turns bluer. It is the noxious, hazy blue of fossil fuels being burned often and inefficiently. The boulevard is a cacophonous conga of compact rattletraps enmeshed with brazenly driven scooters that clatter like an army of power saws and leaf blowers. In the middle of this mayhem Martinez drives a . . . spaceship.

Well, it is not exactly a spaceship. But the black Mercedes convertible might as well be an alien craft to judge by the way everyone ogles it. Virgin steel and paint! Gleaming chrome and glass! Former Reds pitcher Jose Rijo used to drive his Bentley deep into the Dominican countryside, where children would gaze into the automobile's hubcaps, mesmerized. Twenty percent of the country lives below the poverty line.

"It's uncomfortable sometimes," Martinez says of the attention he gets driving his luxury car, "but I like having the top down." He is wearing jeans and a short-sleeve, button-down orange oxford shirt. Three years into a six-year deal that pays him $75 million (that's 1.196 billion pesos), he still lives in the modest fourth-floor apartment he's kept for five years. He gives away money, baseball equipment, houses and his time without ever an accompanying press release.

Martinez is driving the hour or so to Manoguayabo after one of his daily four-hour workouts at Centro Olimpico, sessions devoid of weights or baseballs. (He uses medicine balls and rubber tubing for strength training.) Of course, if you factored out all the time he spent laughing, yapping and needling, and boogying to the salsa blasted out of speakers the size of steamer trunks in another of his vehicles, a Lexus SUV, the workout would take about 2½ hours. But then it would not be a Pedro Martinez workout.

One day a seven-year-old boy carrying a tennis ball approached Martinez as he worked under the concrete stands of the park's track and field stadium. "*Soy el segundo Pedro,*" said the boy. ("I am the second Pedro.") Martinez hugged him, then played ball with the kid for

10 minutes, the two taking turns trying to strike each other out with the tennis ball.

"Pedro," Duquette says, "has natural charisma. He's comfortable being a star. He loves it."

No one in the pantheon of Red Sox icons has ever appealed to a more diverse audience than this slight man with a child's smile and an assassin's pulmonary system. At an autograph event in Boston in January, people began queuing up at seven in the morning to see him four hours later. One of the first in line was 69-year-old, Irish-born Margaret Flynn, a Red Sox fan since 1953. "Pedro's the one," she says. "He's going to get us there."

Here's how Martinez greeted Flynn upon meeting her for the first time: "Mommy!"

Parents handed their babies to Pedro for pictures—he didn't just hold them like sacks of groceries, he snuggled them and cooed—Latin kids shouted to him in Spanish, and women swooned and shrieked girlishly, including one who asked him to marry her. "I'm a nurse," she purred. "I can take real good care of you."

REPLIED MARTINEZ, "I'm not ready yet. I'm having too much fun."

When he blows the horn of his Mercedes at an iron gate in Manoguayabo, one of his nephews slides it open. This is where he grew up, though the tiny house he shared with three brothers, two sisters and two foster boys raised as brothers is no longer standing. In fact, no house stands in this compound, a place that serves as an informal gathering spot for the extended Martinez family. There is a small clubhouse attached to a four-car garage, and a two-story pavilion built expressly to host family parties. Between the two buildings there is a gravel parking area that overlooks a grassy ravine. As boys

Pedro, Ramon and Jesus, the youngest brother, who is a pitcher in the Red Sox organization, would throw rocks across the ravine toward an abandoned house tucked behind trees and bushes. Then they'd listen for the triumphant tinkle of glass breaking. Even now the brothers will sling rocks across the ravine to see who can throw the farthest. The rocks always land out of sight, enabling each hurler to claim superiority.

Sometimes Pedro comes alone. The old mango tree is still here, though now he prefers to do his thinking on a brick wall at the end of the gravel parking area. What he does not like to think about is how his parents, Paulino and Leopoldina, used to fight before their divorce, when Pedro was six. The bouts of utter silence between them that hung over the house like a stalled front of Arctic air were bad enough. The arguments were much worse. Even now when he recalls their straining voices, he winces. "No, no, enough. Ugh!" he says, shaking his head as if it were an Etch-A-Sketch, making the picture go away.

After his father left, Pedro would work in the garden with his mother, developing a love for flowers that he still has today. The garden and the mango tree and a diary he kept under lock and key provided respite. At 16, when he signed with the Dodgers, the crying subsided a bit. But two years later, during spring training, he could not pitch for a week because of the heart murmur, which doctors had long ago related to the stress of his youth.

Around the same time Ramon blossomed into an established big leaguer and principal wage earner in the family, and he found the confidence to bring his mother and father together on friendly terms. By 1993 Pedro, too, was a confident professional who encouraged Paulino and Leopoldina to share moments together. His heart murmur disappeared. He burned the diary. "Looking back, I have to say [the family strife] made me stronger," he says. "It forced me to become a man at a young age."

The little boy in the mango tree is all grown up. This gift he has for throwing a baseball has helped transform him. So, too, has he transformed baseball. "There is a time in baseball before Pedro and a time after Pedro," Arias says. "Before, no one wanted to sign a pitcher as small as Pedro. After, now they begin to think, He could be another Pedro."

One afternoon at Centro Olimpico an American asked Martinez to ask a teenage minor league prospect what Martinez meant to him and his country. The youth gave a lengthy, measured answer. Martinez turned his eyes away and said nothing. It wasn't until that night, about eight hours later, that Martinez translated the prospect's response. "I'm sorry I didn't say anything then, but it felt strange to ask about myself and hear the answer," he says. "What he said was that I am a great example for the young people and that I show what can be done through hard work. Wow. It makes you feel good. And if you think you can ever run away from that responsibility, you can't. It pushes you every day."

Nineteen ninety-nine, the year Martinez owned baseball, ended for him under a yellow-and-white striped party tent behind a two-story concrete building on Avenida George Washington. The tent serves as a church for a Catholic orphanage. Martinez had heard about the orphanage from a friend, watched a video about its mission and was moved to help with more than just pesos. He decided to welcome the millennium in this makeshift church, at a New Year's Eve service with one hundred or so orphaned children. Most had been rescued off the street, including one infant girl who had been plucked from a trash can. Many wore the nice new dress clothes he had bought them for Christmas.

It had been a year worthy of its own time capsule: Martinez had won the All-Star MVP award, smothered the Yankees with the one-hitter, beaten Cleveland with his head and his heart, whipped New York in the League Championship Series and won the Cy Young. Time after time home plate had looked ridiculously close to him.

Those moments, though, were no more meaningful than when the last seconds of the year fell away. At the stroke of midnight, surrounded by children who felt like his own flesh and blood, he prayed. He prayed for peace, he prayed for his family, he prayed for his health, and he prayed for the children. He knew right then that this was one of the best moments of his life. El Duro felt sure about that, as sure as he could feel the tears falling down his face.

Postscript: The night I arrived in the Dominican Republic, Pedro said he'd pick me up at my hotel at six for dinner. Sometime near 11 p.m., after I had eaten room service and gone to sleep with no word from him, I was awakened by the telephone. "Ready to go?" It was Pedro, and the first sign that this would be a most interesting week. I worked out with him, toured some of the country with him and, under a beautiful starry sky and amid the fragrance of flowers, shared a homemade meal under the mango tree that was his refuge as a boy. With that kind of time and access, a writer stands a pretty good chance of understanding his subject.

High-Wire Act

There's no safety net for major league closers, who put it all on the line each time they work, saving the day . . . or squandering their teams' best efforts

AIRPLANE PILOT, TIGHTROPE WALKER, SWORD swallower, bomb-squad member, skydiver, closer. Success or failure in these jobs is absolute: You either do the job or you don't. The closer's job is the most clearly delineated one in sports. Most times he either gets a *save*—you need not dig too deep to hit the religious or heroic bedrock of the word—or a *blown save*, the cruelest, most negative stat ever invented. There is no middle ground. No safety net. Closers are the Flying Wallendas of baseball.

Trevor Hoffman fell off the high wire on May 27. Hoffman, 33, is the Padres' closer. He is the only active pitcher to have saved 30 games in each of the past six years. That afternoon the Padres gave the righthander a 4–2 lead to protect in the ninth inning against a division rival, the Diamondbacks. The game took a total of two hours and 47 minutes, but Hoffman lost it in an eye blink: single, home run, flyout, single, home run. Good night. Drive home safely.

What Hoffman did in the wake of that defeat, when utter failure is a virus that attacks the immune system of confidence, would reveal more about his staying power than his National League-record-tying 53 saves in 1998. "To last in this job," Hoffman says, "you have to learn to take the good and the bad equally."

The results are brutally self-evident: You do or you don't. Many closers do (44 pitchers saved at least 30 games in a season over the past five years), but most don't for long. (Four current closers have saved 30 or more in each of the past three years.) Just about any pitcher with good stuff, given the liberal nature of the save rule and the programmed use of closers by robotic managers, can save 30 games once. Mel Rojas, Heathcliff Slocumb and Billy Taylor proved as much in recent years—before they disappeared as quickly as they'd arrived among the brethren of closers.

Hoffman, one of the rare closers who endures, fought the virus after the Arizona defeat. He has developed an emergency routine for such cases. First, while sitting alone in the dugout, he reflects on what just happened; then, even after his worst outings, he goes to the clubhouse and fields questions from the media. "The people asking the questions are not responsible for the ball flying out of the park," he explains. Finally, alone, he finds something positive amid the despair. He won't leave the stadium until he is sure the virus is under control. This time Hoffman began the cleansing process at about 4:50 in the afternoon. He did not leave until nine o'clock that night.

"That's not normal, believe me—not that long," Hoffman says. "There were a lot of issues with that one. Some games have a lasting impact, and that was one of them. I didn't do a whole lot, just kind of sat around, watched the Coca-Cola 600, drank Coca-Colas. The first home run ran through my mind. A 2-and-2 pitch. I threw a fastball.

When I get to two strikes in that situation, it's easy to think, I ought to have thrown a changeup. But if he pops up a fastball to leftfield, you don't think twice.

"Confidence is everything," Hoffman adds. "If you start second-guessing yourself, you're bound to run into more bad [outings]. It took a while, but I got through it. It's a cliché, but it's true: It's better to have competed and lost than not to have competed at all. That's what I told myself. I battled. And I knew I'd be out there again."

ARMANDO BENITEZ fell off the high wire on May 11. Benitez, 28, is the Mets' closer. He is, with only one 30-save season on his resume, a work in progress. Whether he turns out to be a Trevor Hoffman or a Mel Rojas will depend on nights like this, when he surrendered the game-winning hit to the Giants. The righthander's response, with the help of at least one other Met, was to demolish parts of the visiting dugout and clubhouse at Pacific Bell Park. The Giants sent the Mets a bill for $4,000 to cover repairs.

What was it that Hoffman said? Treat the good and the bad equally? How can any closer do that when, as Cardinals manager Tony La Russa put it, he has to endure "a maximum amount of pressure in a minimum amount of time"? How can he do it when success is so intoxicating and failure so debilitating?

Stacey O'Neill heard about Benitez's rage in San Francisco and winced. Three months earlier O'Neill, Benitez's former girlfriend, had dropped domestic-abuse charges against the reliever only after he agreed to seek anger-management counseling. She had recognized a pattern of postgame behavior by Benitez that was linked to success or failure on the mound. "He either didn't get counseling or he ignored it," O'Neill says of the Pac Bell Park incident. "[If he did get therapy,] it obviously didn't do him any good. I guess what I'm worried about is whether the Mets really want him to be able to manage his anger. I think they encourage that in him. He was supposed to be intimidating on the mound, so I would think they wouldn't want his mentality to change. The other team is supposed to fear him. That's what a closer is about. He told me he was supposed to scare people. I told him not to scare me. Be intimidating at work but not at home. Be like an actor and leave it behind. He couldn't do that. He was Armando the Intimidator all the time. That's part of what he said made him successful."

When asked about O'Neill's description of his difficulty accepting failure, Benitez cuts off the question with a wave of his hand and says, "I don't want to say anything bad about the woman. I wish her well. My mind is clear, and I am happy. All my troubles are gone."

Benitez does say he appreciates the support of his teammates, especially that of bullpen mate John Franco, manager Bobby Valentine and equipment manager Charlie Samuels. With their assistance, he says, he is learning to recover quickly from defeat. "It's tough because nobody likes to lose," he says. "But the important thing is to forget about it and come back tomorrow."

When asked how he puts bad games behind him now, Benitez says, "I sit around and watch cartoons to relax."

Jay Horwitz, the Mets' vice president of media relations, says O'Neill's concern that the club facilitated Benitez's anger "couldn't be further from the truth. We're concerned about Armando as a person first and as a ballplayer second. We don't encourage being 'on edge.' "

Benitez is 6' 4" and listed at 229 pounds. He is a large man with the shoulders of a linebacker and the scowl of a prison guard way too long on the job. He throws 96 mph worth of wicked fury on a pitching mound. The sensation of burying his heater past the best hitters in baseball to lock down a victory for New York—the fans standing, cheering and pleading, with the knowledge that he alone, not some scoreboard clock clicking off seconds, has the power to suck the last breath of life out of the opposition—that sensation has been known to make this bear of a man dance with joy like a pixie. He might quickly lift one knee, as if he had stepped barefoot on a hot sidewalk, or give a dismissive wave with his right hand. He knows that Franco, his mentor, hates it when he reacts like that ("Never give the other guy extra incentive to beat your ass," Franco likes to tell him), but such is the overwhelming power of the moment.

After those triumphs O'Neill knew exactly what Benitez wanted to do first when he returned home in Queens, N.Y. Armando Benitez would click on the TV to surf for highlights, so he could watch Armando Benitez close the game all over again. "Almost like he had to see it again to believe it," O'Neill says.

On the bad nights, when the crowd did not cheer and the bear did not dance, the television stayed off. O'Neill says that Benitez might pour himself a glass of Grand Marnier and retreat to another room in the apartment, his only companions the drink and a poisonous feeling he wanted to be rid of. Says O'Neill, whose three-year relationship with Benitez ended last November, "I feared for myself after a loss, because stupid things could send him over the edge." After a succession of poor outings, O'Neill adds, Benitez might perform a Santerian ritual in which he would bathe by candlelight in a mixture of water, milk, alcohol, herbs and flowers to rid himself of bad luck.

Benitez did convert all nine of his save chances through the first 10 weeks of this season. But he has run into trouble in other situations, such as the one on May 28 when he yielded a home run to the Phillies' Pat Burrell that broke a tie. Benitez refused to speak with the media after that game. Is he Hoffman or Rojas? It is too soon to know. This much is certain: There is only one active closer who saved even one game before 1991, the Cubs' Tom Gordon.

"Closers have a short shelf life because it takes an awful lot out of you," says Giants pitching coach Dave Righetti, who saved 252 games. "It's the only job where you're not allowed to go into a slump. Some guys can't get over the bad games, and that's why they don't become full-time closers. Some guys put up a facade to protect themselves from the demons, but that usually doesn't last long. If you don't have the stomach for it, you'll be discovered before too long. You just have to be mentally tough and shrug it off no matter how much it hurts."

ONE NIGHT in 1978 Yankees catcher Thurman Munson waited for Rich Gossage on the mound at Yankee Stadium. Gossage had been summoned from the bullpen to save a game. He was in a terrible slump. This was his first season with New York after the club had signed him as a free agent, displacing the reigning Cy Young Award winner, Sparky Lyle, as the team's closer. Yankees fans booed him. Things were going so badly for Gossage that when he reached the mound Munson said, "So, how are you going to blow this one?"

"I don't know," Gossage barked back. "Get your ass behind the plate, and we'll find out."

Gossage lasted 22 seasons in the big leagues, most of them as a closer, and rang up 310 saves. The closer "is only one pitch from disaster all the time," he says. Like Benitez, he forged a gunslinger's reputation with an imposing physical bearing and a fastball that looked as angry as he did.

"I joke about it now," Gossage says. "People go, 'God, Goose, you looked so mean!' I was scared to death. Fear of failure is a big motivator. When you're a closer, every game is huge. You're out there on the mound s------- down your leg, the game is on the line, you've got all this adrenaline running through your body, and somehow you've got to get ahold of your emotions.

"When you fail, it's awful. Sometimes I drank. Sometimes I just sat around the clubhouse. You go home, you have trouble sleeping. First thing when you wake up, you feel that sinking feeling in your stomach. It's like waking up to a disaster, almost like a sickness in your family. It's almost too much to take. Sometimes the pressure did get to me. Sometimes I'd be short with my family. They suffered."

The physical demands of the closer's job have eased since pitchers like Gossage were asked to put out fires in the seventh inning and finish the game. Today's closers might throw little more than half the innings of their counterparts of 20 or 30 years ago, who often did more than 100 innings of heavy lifting in a season. The evolution of specialized layers of relief pitching also has turned the closer's job into such a well-insulated one that the term *fireman* has disappeared from baseball vernacular. The typical closer doesn't answer distress calls anymore. He usually enters a game with no one on base and is asked to pitch no more than one inning. For instance, Antonio Alfonseca of the Marlins led the majors with 45 saves last season and never entered a game with the tying run on base. Ryan Kohlmeier of the Orioles, who is 23 years old and has 19 career saves, is treated like a sultan; he hadn't worked more than one inning at a time until last Saturday, when he pitched 1⅓ against the Expos. Jeff Shaw of the Dodgers pitched exactly one inning in 28 of his first 30 appearances this season.

As closers have moved more deeply into the realm of highly specialized labor, the mental toll has become greater than the physical one. A closer will pitch only about 5% of his team's innings over the course of a season—and spend the other 95% of the time waiting, like a storm chaser, for the confluence of events that requires him to go to work. Surviving the nightly anxiety, and those inevitable episodes of abject failure, are the most difficult parts of the job.

There is an old saying among closers that the most important qualification for the job is a short memory. "I learned from Lee Smith," Angels closer Troy Percival says of the alltime saves leader, whose major league career ended in 1997. "I've seen him give up a game-winning grand slam, and 10 minutes later in the clubhouse you'd never know it. He'd be his usual self."

"I get over the bad games right away," says the Yankees' Mariano Rivera, who shows as little emotion as any closer in baseball. "Sometimes I've let it go even before I've left the mound. That quick. Why? Because it's over. What can you do about it? Nothing. The only thing you can do is fight if you're still in the game. After that you can do nothing."

Closers like Benitez and John Rocker of the Braves, whose engines always redline, are increasingly rare. Baseball executives fear that those emotional, maximum-effort pitchers will flame out the way Rob Dibble did. The former hard-throwing Reds righthander blew out his arm and was finished as a closer at 29. He saved 20 games in a season only twice.

Rivera, lean, perpetually calm and clean-shaven, is the cutting-edge übercloser. There is nothing intimidating about him, other than a hellacious cut fastball and a 0.38 postseason ERA. "The best there is," Percival says. Like Rivera, Hoffman, Percival and Robb Nen of the Giants all project an even temperament. All four served apprenticeships as setup men before proving they had the fortitude to close games—and they are the only active pitchers who have saved 30 games in each of the past three seasons.

"Some guys don't have the stomach for pitching the ninth inning," Twins manager Tom Kelly says. "They're great in the eighth but don't want anything to do with the ninth. You have to find out. It might take a while, but you'll find out."

The jury is still out on Kelly's 28-year-old closer, LaTroy Hawkins. The righthander failed as a starter for all or parts of five seasons with the Twins. Last year he was shunted to the bullpen and, around the All-Star break, auditioned as a closer. Suddenly he'd found his niche, converting 30 of the 32 save opportunities that followed. Easy, right? Somebody named Matt Karchner tied a White Sox record by converting 20 consecutive save chances over the 1997 and '98 seasons. He was traded to the Cubs on July 29, 1998, but didn't record a single save during the parts of three seasons he spent with them and disappeared from the majors. Hawkins, like any aspiring closer, won't know if he's fit for the job until he slumps.

Red Sox reliever Rod Beck, who has 263 career saves, tried to make that point to the team's emerging closer Derek Lowe, while Lowe was converting 42 of 47 save chances last year. "I told Derek, 'Listen, I don't expect you to understand this, but you have no idea what this job is about.' " Lowe wound up pitching in 74 games and went 4–4. "I thought it was the greatest job in the world," Lowe says. "This year I was 1–5 after 11 games! Self-doubt began to creep into my mind. I got beat three times on curveballs. I got beat on pitches in the hittable zone, whereas last year they were sinking out of the hittable zone. It hurt. Your team works all game long to get you the ball, and then you lose it. I've learned you have to push away that doubt. Now I'm trying to go out there and just pitch, and whatever happens, happens. I don't want to feel as if it's life or death."

The Rangers promoted setup man Tim Crabtree to closer after John Wetteland retired at the end of last season. The 31-year-old Crabtree is a six-year veteran with a live fastball and a hard slider, the kind of pitches that baseball people like to call "closer's stuff" because managers typically like strikeout pitchers to throw the last inning. (The theory is that the less often the ball is put in play, the less can go wrong.) After six weeks—including three on the DL with lower-back pain—and two blown saves, Crabtree lost his job closing. "You think you're ready, but it's something you're not going to understand until you go through it," Crabtree says. "As a setup man I pretty much knew when I was pitching. Jeff Zimmerman and I knew it was one guy on and the other guy off every night.

"What I found with closing is you have to recharge yourself every night," Crabtree continues. "Every day you're on call for that ninth inning. Mentally, that gets tiring. The other difference is when you blow a game. You feel like you let down 24 guys and seven coaches and management. It's tough to look your teammates in the eye after they worked so hard to get a lead for eight innings over three hours and you lose it just like that. When you don't get it done, it's more frustrating than just having a bad outing as a setup man."

In the 1992 draft the Indians used their first pick on righthander Paul Shuey with the intent of grooming him as a closer. Shuey is 30 and has still never been a full-time closer in the big leagues. The Indians have converted a succession of former starters and setup men—Jose Mesa, Mike Jackson and Steve Karsay—into closers in that time, and last year they traded a rising star slugger, Richie Sexson, to get another closer, Bob Wickman, but Shuey still has not graduated from pitching the seventh and eighth innings. "Shuey has power stuff, three 'plus' pitches that give him closer's stuff," Cleveland assistant general manager Mark Shapiro says. "But closing is not just stuff. Strike-throwing consistency is huge. He's had problems repeating his delivery. That's not unusual for pitchers who have violence in their delivery."

Rivera has an easy motion, and his ability to throw strikes is yet another element that sets him apart. He is so efficient with his pitches that Yankees manager Joe Torre often uses him in the eighth inning, knowing Rivera can throw more than one inning and still pitch the next day. Through the first 10 weeks of this season he had pitched more than one inning to get a save six times, the most in the majors. Over the same period 17 closers, including Alfonseca, Benitez, Hawkins and Wickman, had yet to work more than one inning for a save.

The closer isn't a modern invention, only a modern convention. Firpo Marberry saved 22 games for the 1926 Washington Senators without starting a trend. (The save rule was established in '69; previous totals have been derived by researchers from box scores and game accounts.) Marberry's "record" stood for 23 years, during which complete games were common and most teams used their starting pitchers out of the bullpen between starts. The success of the Yankees' Joe Page, a mediocre starter, as a relief pitcher from '47 through '49 prompted other teams to employ a specialist who was summoned in close games, regardless of which team was winning. Roy Face won a record 18 games in relief for the '59 Pirates in that manner.

Then, in 1979, Cubs manager Herman Franks came up with a novel way to use Bruce Sutter, his relief specialist, who was on the DL with a pulled muscle in '77 and was arm weary in the second half of '78.

Franks lightened Sutter's load by using him only if the Cubs were winning. Franks was ahead of his time (though he did resign before the end of that season and never managed again). In the late '80s La Russa, then the A's manager, refined the job further with Dennis Eckersley, who was used mostly when the A's had a lead and only to start the ninth inning.

Today, in a game so rich in strategic possibilities that half the fun is kicking around the what-would-you-have-dones, every manager agrees in Stepford-like fashion exactly how to run a bullpen. No manager dares use his best reliever to pitch to the middle of the order in the seventh inning—and seldom in the eighth—of a close game. No manager dares *not* to use his closer with a lead of three runs or less in the ninth, the main requirement for a save. Percival, in fact, will start warming for those situations without Angels manager Mike Scioscia's even calling the bullpen. No other statistic dictates actual strategic decisions the way the save does. Indeed, if a home team adds a fourth run to its lead in the eighth inning, the closer will stop warming. Someone else will pitch the ninth.

"A good strategy is to try to build on a good year," La Russa says about the three-run gimme save. "How does he get a good year going? By piling up saves, like a hitter hits .300 or a starting pitcher gets wins. So, if you have a three-run lead and your closer is available, you ought to get him that one because he's going to have plenty of one-run leads."

Bobby Thigpen of the White Sox set the single-season save record with 57 in 1990. Still, in this Age of the Specialized Bullpen, the irony is that, despite the "advances" made in establishing layers of relief pitchers, teams are no more successful at protecting late leads now than they were 10 or 20 years ago—in fact, they are slightly worse.

According to the Elias Sports Bureau, teams taking a one-run lead into the ninth inning last season won 83.9% of the time. Given a one- or two-run lead heading into the ninth, they won 88.7% of the time. In 1990 those conversion rates were 86.4% and 90.7%, respectively. If you go back to 1980, a year in which only three pitchers saved 30 or more games (15 did so last year) and the idea of paying a setup man $4 million was absurd, teams cashed in 84.7% and 89.6% of such opportunities, a better rate than they do today.

Get the ball to the closer has become the unchallenged strategy. No starting pitcher has ended a World Series with a complete game since Jack Morris of the Twins did it in 1991. No team that played a full season has won a world championship without a closer getting 30 saves since the '88 Dodgers, who split the job primarily among Jay Howell, Jesse Orosco and Alejandro Pena. (They combined for 42.) "You want a guy who creates the feeling when he comes in that the game's over," says Scioscia, the catcher for that '88 L.A. team. "You have to use your closer carefully, because you don't want to burn him out, but you can't be afraid to use him when a save situation comes up. You worry most about the mental grind with a closer, and that's why you look for a guy with the mental makeup to handle the job."

The ones who survive the anxiety and the failure usually forge their own kind of mental armor, tricks of their trade that become as unique as a family crest. "You have to treat every day the same," Beck says, "until it feels like *Groundhog Day*." Smith would nap on a training table for the first six innings. Percival would gulp down a six-pack of cola and a dozen cups of coffee every night—until a biochemist told him last winter that his body was grossly dehydrated because of all the caffeine. (Percival has cut his coffee intake to five cups, maybe three of which are decaffeinated, while drinking a gallon of water daily.)

When Tom Gordon saved 46 games in 47 opportunities for Boston in 1998, he spent the early innings of every game chomping fried chicken in the office of manager Jimy Williams.

Hoffman spends most of the game in the clubhouse "developing a little quiet zone" while watching television, stretching and getting a massage. "If I time it right, I'll get to the bullpen five or 10 minutes before I come into the game," he says. Billy Wagner of the Astros throws four warmup pitches—and four pitches only, rather than the customary eight—when he enters a game "because I want everybody to know I mean business and I'm ready to go." For three years Billy Koch of the Blue Jays has carried a stuffed goat, a gift from his sister in homage to his wispy goatee.

Facial hair, in fact, is to closers what masks were to Greek thespians. From Hall of Famer Rollie Fingers (handlebar mustache) to Gossage (Fu Manchu) to Al Hrabosky (horseshoe mustache) to Eckersley (swarthy mustache) to Doug Jones (push-broom-style mustache) to Kerry Ligtenberg (Edwardian sideburns) to Koch, closers have a long history of assuming an identity through the creative growth of facial hair, whether intimidation is their motivation or not. "Hey, I waited 27 years to grow anything on my face," says Wagner, who sports a mustache and goatee. "I was trying to get out of that Billy the Kid phase."

Says Gossage, "People think I grew the Fu Manchu to intimidate people. That wasn't it at all. I grew it to piss off [George] Steinbrenner."

Some of the worst emotional meltdowns in baseball history involve closers. Dibble ripped off his jersey—buttons popping—as he walked off the mound at Shea Stadium after a blown save. Righetti heaved a baseball from the mound over the right centerfield wall of Exhibition Stadium in Toronto. A depressed Donnie Moore killed himself in 1989, and many acquaintances believe he did it in part because he never got over losing the '86 American League Championship Series game that would have put the Angels in the World Series.

As a rookie with the Reds in 1984 John Franco watched how closers Tom Hume and Ted Power never seemed to change their demeanor, whether they saved a game or lost it. Still, when his time came to close games, Franco, flush with the raw emotions of youth, "busted up my share of locker rooms in my early years." The more games he saved, though, the more Franco learned that those failures would be temporary. He learned, too, how to act like a closer. There was a certain way you had to stand and walk and carry yourself on the mound so that every bit of body language announced to the hitter, "I am supremely confident!"—especially during those times when Franco knew in his gut that it was a lie. Hitters are like dogs, he figured, who can sniff the slightest bit of fear in a person. If he thought his face gave off a faint hint of doubt, Franco would walk down the back of the mound and keep his back to home plate until, like an actor finding the soul of his character, he had fixed the most cocksure look he could muster.

"Never, ever let them see you sweat," Franco says. That is the motto that has helped Franco, a 5' 10" sinkerballer who couldn't make it as a starter because he would tire by the fifth or sixth inning, to 421 saves. That is also another bit of advice he has passed on to Benitez.

The education of Benitez continues, though Franco knows his successor as the Mets' closer must figure out for himself how to handle the bad nights as well as the good. Even Franco, in his last years as the Mets' closer, struggled sometimes with this core truth. As he drove from Shea Stadium to his Staten Island home after blowing a game, Franco would tune his car's radio to the sports talk show station. He would listen to fans call in with pronouncements that Franco was finished. He was torturing himself. "I'd get so angry I'd want to drive off the Verrazano Bridge," he says. "It's bad enough that the game stays in your mind. Then you hear this stuff on the radio and think, Hey, so-and-so from Stony Brook, what the hell do you do for a living? What do you know?"

These days, as Franco drives over the Verrazano Bridge in the late hours of the night, he doesn't think about busting through a guardrail. The radio is off. He pops in a CD of *The Three Tenors* or, perhaps, Andrea Bocelli. He has moved on to soothing music. He is a setup man now. The ninth inning, and all of its good and all of its bad, belongs to Benitez.

Postscript: No job in baseball (and few jobs in sports) generates as much mental stress as closing games, and no job so clearly inflicts torment in inverse proportion to the accompanying physical stress. Four months after this story ran, the baseball season ended on a blown save by the best in the business, Mariano Rivera. He stood at his locker immediately afterward and answered every question with grace and not the slightest sign of distress. It's one reason why he's prospered so long in a job that burns up so many.

Totally Juiced

With this groundbreaking story, SI documented how the use of steroids and other performance enhancers had become rampant in baseball, and how players—and their reliance on drugs—had grown to alarming proportions

D IAMONDBACKS RIGHTHANDER CURT SCHILLING thinks twice before giving a teammate the traditional slap on the butt for a job well-done. "I'll pat guys on the ass, and they'll look at me and say, 'Don't hit me there, man. It hurts,' " Schilling says. "That's because that's where they shoot the steroid needles."

The Rangers were packing their gear after the final game of a road series last year when a player accidentally knocked over a small carry bag by his locker. Several vials of steroids spilled out and rolled on the carpet. The player, hardly embarrassed or concerned, gave a slight chuckle and scooped them up. No one else in the room showed any surprise.

STEROID USE, which a decade ago was considered a taboo violated only by a few renegade sluggers, is now so rampant in baseball that even pitchers and wispy outfielders are juicing up—and talking openly among themselves about it. According to players, trainers and executives interviewed by SPORTS ILLUSTRATED over the last three months, the game has become a pharmacological trade show. What emerges from dozens of interviews is a portrait of baseball's intensifying reliance on steroids and other performance-enhancing drugs. These drugs include not only human growth hormone (hGH) but also an array of legal and illegal stimulants, ranging from amphetamines to Ritalin to ephedrine-laced dietary supplements, that many big leaguers pop to get a jolt of pregame energy and sharpen their focus. But it is the use of illegal steroids that is growing fastest and having a profound impact on the game.

The surest sign that steroids are gaining acceptance in baseball: the first public admission of steroid use—without remorse—by a prominent former player. Ken Caminiti, whose 15-year big league career ended after a stint with the Braves last season, revealed to SI that he won the 1996 National League Most Valuable Player award while on steroids he purchased from a pharmacy in Tijuana, Mexico. Spurred to try the drugs by concern over a shoulder injury in early '96, Caminiti said that his steroid use improved his performance noticeably and became more sophisticated over the next five seasons. He told SI that he used steroids so heavily in '96 that by the end of that season, his testicles shrank and retracted; doctors found that his body had virtually stopped producing its own testosterone and that his level of the hormone had fallen to 20% of normal. "It took four months to get my nuts to drop on their own," he said of the period after he stopped taking the drugs.

Yet Caminiti, a recovering alcoholic and former drug user, defended his use of steroids and said he would not discourage others from taking them because they have become a widely accepted—even necessary—choice for ballplayers looking for a competitive edge and financial security. "I've made a ton of mistakes," said Caminiti. "I don't think using steroids is one of them.

"It's no secret what's going on in baseball. At least half the guys are using steroids. They talk about it. They joke about it with each other. The guys who want to protect themselves or their image by lying have that right. Me? I'm at the point in my career where I've done just about every bad thing you can do. I try to walk with my head up. I don't have to hold my tongue. I don't want to hurt teammates or friends. But I've got nothing to hide.

"If a young player were to ask me what to do," Caminiti continued, "I'm not going to tell him it's bad. Look at all the money in the game: You have a chance to set your family up, to get your daughter into a better school. . . . So I can't say, 'Don't do it,' not when the guy next to you is as big as a house and he's going to take your job and make the money."

ANABOLIC STEROIDS elevate the body's testosterone level, increasing muscle mass without changes in diet or activity, though their effect is greatly enhanced in conjunction with proper nutrition and strength training. Steroids are illegal in the U.S. unless prescribed by a physician for medical conditions, such as AIDS and hypogonadism (an inability to produce enough testosterone). Studies have shown that the side effects from steroids can include heart and liver damage, persistent endocrine-system imbalance, elevated cholesterol levels, strokes, aggressive behavior and the dysfunction of genitalia. Doctors suspect that steroid use is a major factor in the recent increase in baseball injuries, especially severe injuries such as complete muscle tears.

Unlike the NFL and NBA, both of which ban and test for steroid use— the NHL does neither—Major League Baseball has no steroid policy or testing program for big leaguers. (Baseball does test minor league players, but violators are neither penalized nor required to undergo counseling.) Any such program would have to be collectively bargained with the Major League Baseball Players Association, which traditionally has resisted any form of drug testing but now faces a division in its membership over this issue. "Part of our task is to let a consensus emerge," says Gene Orza, the associate general counsel for the players union.

"No one denies that it is a problem," says commissioner Bud Selig. "It's a problem we can and must deal with now, rather than years from now when the public says, 'Why didn't you do something about it?' I'm very worried about this."

But it is also true that fans have become more accepting of steroids as part of the game. Fourteen years ago the crowd at Fenway Park in Boston chided A's outfielder Jose Canseco during the American League Championship Series with damning chants of "Ster-oids! Ster-oids!" The game had never before seen a physical marvel such as Canseco, a 240-pound hulk who could slug a baseball 500 feet and still be swift enough to steal 40 bases. Upon retiring last month after failing to catch on with a major league team, Canseco, while not admitting steroid use himself, said that steroids have "revolutionized" the game and that he would write a tell-all book blowing the lid off drug use in the majors. Canseco estimated that 85% of major leaguers use steroids.

Heavily muscled bodies like Canseco's have now become so common that they no longer invite scorn. Players even find dark humor in steroid use. One American League outfielder, for instance, was known to be taking a steroid typically given by veterinarians to injured, ill or overworked horses and readily available in Latin America. An opposing player pointed to him and remarked, "He takes so much of that horse stuff that one day we're going to look out in the outfield and he's going to be grazing."

STEROIDS HAVE helped create the greatest extended era of slugging the game has ever seen—and, not coincidentally, the highest rate of strikeouts in history. Power, the eye candy for the casual fan, is a common denominator among pitchers and hitters, as hurlers, too, juice up to boost the velocity of their pitches.

Schilling says that muscle-building drugs have transformed baseball into something of a freak show. "You sit there and look at some of these players and you know what's going on," he says. "Guys out there look like Mr. Potato Head, with a head and arms and six or seven body parts that just don't look right. They don't fit. I'm not sure how [steroid use] snuck in so quickly, but it's become a prominent thing very quietly. It's widely known in the game.

"We're playing in an environment in the last decade that's been tailored to produce offensive numbers anyway, with the smaller ballparks, the smaller strike zone and so forth," Schilling continues. "When you add in steroids and strength training, you're seeing records not just being broken but completely shattered.

"I know guys who use and don't admit it because they think it means they don't work hard. And I know plenty of guys now are mixing steroids with human growth hormone. Those guys are pretty obvious."

If steroids are the cement of body construction, then human growth hormone is the rebar, taken in an attempt to strengthen joints so they can hold the added muscle mass produced by steroids. Human growth hormone can be detected only in specific blood tests, not the standard urine test used for other performance-enhancing drugs. It is prescribed to treat dwarfism in children, but it can also change a mature person's body structure and facial characteristics. Players joke about the swollen heads, protruding brows and lantern jaws of hGH users. "And they talk like this," Caminiti says, pushing his tongue to the front of his mouth and stammering, "because the size of their head changes." One major league executive knows of a star player whose hat size has grown two sizes in his late 30s.

Says Chad Curtis, an outfielder who retired last year after 10 seasons with six clubs, including three (1997 to '99) with the Yankees, "When I was in New York, a player there told me that hGH was the next big thing, that that's the road the game's heading down next. Now you see guys whose facial features, jawbones and cheekbones change after they're 30. Do they think that happens naturally? You say, 'What happened to that guy?' Then you'll hear him say he worked out over the winter and put on 15 pounds of muscle. I'm sorry, working out is not going to change your facial features."

"Here's one easy way to tell," says a veteran American League infielder who asked not to be identified. He grabbed a batting helmet and put it on the top of his head without pushing it down for the proper fit. "They can't get their helmet to go all the way down. It sits up on their heads. You see it all the time. You see this new culture of young players coming in, caught up in the vanity of getting big. They're bloated and ripped, and they shave their chests [to accentuate their physiques]. It's gotten to the point where more guys use [steroids or hGH] than don't use."

The infielder says that last year he asked a star teammate, whom he suspected of steroid use, why he used. The star replied, "It's a personal decision. It's like taking aspirin. Some people choose to take it and some don't. I respect somebody's choice one way or the other."

Clearly, the players who choose to use steroids do so because they believe the drugs work. "It's still a hand-eye coordination game, but the difference [with steroids] is the ball is going to go a little farther," Caminiti says. "Some of the balls that would go to the warning track will go out. That's the difference."

The improvement steroids have made in some players has been striking. Says one veteran National League general manager, "You might expect the B player to become an A player with steroids. But now you see the C player go to an A player. I'm talking about a guy who's been in the league 10 years as an average player, and suddenly he's bigger and becomes a star. That's very troublesome."

Another National League G.M. tells a story about an overweight, lumpy backup player who had kicked around the fringes of the major leagues. "We signed him, and two years later the guy looked like someone in a muscle magazine," he says. The player, by then in his 30s, won a starting job for the first time and, with a decent season, earned a multiyear contract. He subsequently suffered a series of muscle tears and ruptures and was quickly out of baseball. "He was gone that fast," the G.M. says. "But the contract probably set up him for life. Other guys see that."

Says Texas lefthander Kenny Rogers, "Basically, steroids can jump you a level or two. The average player can become a star, and the star player can become a superstar, and the superstar? Forget it. He can do things we've never seen before. You take a guy who already has great hand-eye coordination and make him stronger, and without a doubt he'll be better."

Steroids might even help a player become an MVP.

CAMINITI WAS playing third base for the Padres in a series against the Astros in April 1996 when Derrick May hit a flare into short left-field. Caminiti dived for the ball, landed hard on his left elbow and shoulder, and tore his rotator cuff. "For the next six or seven days I couldn't lift my arm," he says. "I played for a month and a half in pure pain." Finally, he says, he decided to do something "to get me through the season." Caminiti had heard of players taking steroids to help them through injuries. He knew where to go. "When you play in San Diego, it's easy to just drive into Mexico," he says.

Anabolic steroids are readily available in parts of Latin America as an over-the-counter item at *farmacias* that, in Mexican border towns such as Tijuana, cater to an American trade. Caminiti says he purchased a steroid labeled *testosterona* "to get me through the second half of the season." Then 33, he was playing in his 10th big league season. Never had he hit more than 26 home runs. He exceeded that in the second half alone, belting 28 homers after the All-Star break. He finished the year with 40 home runs, 130 RBIs (his previous best was 94) and a .326 batting average (24 points better than his previous high). He won the MVP award unanimously.

"There is a mental edge that comes with the injections, and it's definitely something that gets you more intense," Caminiti says. "The thing is, I didn't do it to make me a better player. I did it because my body broke down.

"At first I felt like a cheater. But I looked around, and everybody was doing it. Now it's not as black market as when I started. Back then you had to go and find it in Mexico or someplace. Now, it's everywhere. It's very easy to get."

Steroids are taken in what users call "cycles"—several weeks of use followed by several weeks of nonuse to allow the body to recover. Caminiti, a novice, never stopped using during the 1996 season. He wound up injecting twice as much steroids as was considered normal for ballplayers at that time. "I was just experimenting on my own," he says. "I did it wrong. My body shut down and stopped producing testosterone."

After a slow start the next season, Caminiti says he returned to steroid use, this time with the help of a friend in California who supplied the drugs. He says he continued using at various times through his career, learning from his supplier how to do cycles. "I felt like a kid," he says. "I'd be running the bases and think, Man, I'm fast! And I had never been fast. Steroids made me like that. The stronger you get, the more relaxed you get. You feel good. You just let it fly.

"If you don't feel good, you try so hard to make something happen. You grip the bat harder and swing harder, and that's when you tighten up. But you get that edge when you feel strong. That's the way I felt, like I could just try to meet the ball and—*wham!*—it's going to go 1,000 mph. Man, I felt good. I'd think, Damn, this pitcher's in trouble, and I'd crush the ball 450 feet with almost no effort. It's all about getting an edge."

Though he kept using steroids—in 1998, he says, "I showed up at spring training as big as an ox"—Caminiti never again approached the statistics he generated in 1996, partly because he never played another season without going on the disabled list. His injuries were mostly muscular, including a strained hamstring, a strained quadriceps, a strained calf muscle and a ruptured tendon sheath in his wrist.

"I got really strong, really quick," he says. "I pulled a lot of muscles. I broke down a lot. I'm still paying for it. My tendons and ligaments got all torn up. My muscles got too strong for my tendons and ligaments."

Caminiti was released twice last season, by the Rangers and the Braves. Upon his second release, Caminiti, who had used cocaine in the past, says he drove into a notorious section of Houston, rolled down his window and asked a man on the street where he could score some coke. Four days later Caminiti woke up in a drug-strewn motel room still wearing the same clothes. Police showed up, and he was arrested for cocaine possession. He pleaded guilty and was sentenced to three years' probation and 200 hours of community service.

Caminiti lives on the outskirts of Houston, where he is tested regularly for drugs, attends support meetings three times a week and meets with his probation officer once a month. He visits often with his estranged wife and three daughters, who live about 45 minutes from him. He spends his time working out, customizing vintage cars and riding his motorcycles. He suffers from bulging disks in his back, underwent surgery last month to remove bone fragments in his right ankle and is scheduled to have surgery on his right ankle and right foot this month. He eats dinner at a pancake house near his home so often that the cooks know just what he likes: 10 egg whites. He still appears close to his playing size of six feet, 200 pounds.

"I don't think this puts an asterisk by my name," he says, referring to his 239 homers and .272 career average. "I worked for everything I've got. I played the game hard, gave it everything I had. Nothing came easy. I could sit here and lie and try to make myself look like a better person, but I'm not going to do that. I take responsibility for what I've done. I'm guilty of some bad behavior. It's embarrassing, some of the things I've done. But like I said, I don't consider steroids to be one of them."

That's not to say that Caminiti hasn't paid a price for his steroid use. He is now legally prescribed weekly shots of testosterone because of his body's continuing inability to make the hormone in sufficient quantity. "My body's not producing testosterone," he says. "You know what that's like? You get lethargic. You get depressed. It's terrible."

HE IS 5' 11" and 190 pounds. He is not a home run hitter. Pete is a speedy minor league outfielder. He is also a steroid user who has been juicing up for five years, hoping all those needles in his buttocks will finally get him to the majors. His wife knows about it. Sometimes she's the one who sticks the needle in.

"I'm not looking for size," says Pete, who asked that his real name not be used. "I do it for my fast-twitch muscles. If I don't feel good that week or if my hands don't feel good, if they're a little slow, I'll

189

take a shot or get on a cycle. It helps immediately. I notice the difference. My hands are quicker, so my bat is quicker."

Pete began his steroid use through a familiar gateway: Latin America. He was playing winter ball in Venezuela in 1997 when, after hearing other players talk about the easy availability of the drugs, he decided to purchase a steroid, Winstrol, at a *farmacia*. A year later he was introduced to a female bodybuilder in California who made steroid runs to Mexico. Pete would place orders with her or an intermediary.

While making contacts in the steroid subculture, Pete eventually found a supplier, his current source, in the U.S. Pete places his orders by telephone with the supplier, who ships the steroids and needles to him in a FedEx package. A user of Winstrol and Sustanon, Pete says 10-week cycles of steroids cost him $300 to $400, or about $12 a shot. He says steroids obtained in Mexico are cheaper, but the quality of the foreign product is not as reliable. "You pay a pretty good price for the U.S. stuff, but it's worth it," Pete says. "The guy I have runs a fair business. He's got the needles, which are not always easy to get. And he cares about his guys. He's not just about making money. He wants you to use the stuff right. He's got just baseball players—a bunch of them."

According to Pete, steroid use is discussed so openly among players that everyone knows who's using and who's not. He says one player can walk up to another in batting practice, bring the subject up, and tell by his answers whether he's using. "There are code words or street names that everybody knows," Pete says. "Listen, this is not my choice. I'd rather not [use]. I discussed it with my wife, and she understands. When you want to get to a higher level of competition, it's pretty obvious that it's worth trying."

Last year Pete tested positive for steroids under the program administered by Major League Baseball. So did several other players on his team. Here's what happened to them: nothing.

Major League Baseball randomly tests minor leaguers during the season. The best prospects, those on the 40-man major league roster, cannot be tested because they fall under the protection of the collective bargaining agreement. (Pete was not a 40-man-roster player.) That exemption explains why players in the Arizona Fall League, which is filled with top prospects, are notorious, one scout says, for driving by the carload into Mexico to stock up on steroids for the winter.

According to two highly placed baseball sources, physicians for Major League Baseball reported at an internal meeting among doctors and trainers last December that 10% to 15% of the minor leaguers tested came up positive for steroids. The sources acknowledged that the number of users is probably significantly higher than that because baseball does not test in the off-season, when many players follow the traditional steroid training regimen: They shoot up in November, December and January, then get off steroids to start a four-week flexibility program before spring training. Two minor leaguers told SI that they attempt to cheat the tests by gulping water and diuretics when a test administrator arrives to take urine samples.

Virtually all of the 20 or so minor leaguers interviewed by SI described the use of steroids and other drugs (including amphetamines and marijuana) as rampant in the minors. They said that testing is spotty. A player in the Royals' system says he wasn't tested at all last season. One former pitcher in the Tigers' system even says, "Two coaches approached me and suggested I *do* steroids." Two players say they easily obtained steroids from contacts at their gyms. "When you were in college, everybody knew someone who could get them pot," says one minor leaguer. "In baseball everyone knows someone who can get them steroids."

Pete says the follow-up to his positive test was familiar to any minor leaguer on steroids: A club employee told him he had tested positive, warned him about the danger of steroids and sent him on his way.

When asked why baseball doesn't crack down on steroid users, Pete replied, "I've got an easy answer for that. I'd say, You've set up a reward system where you're paying people $1 million to put the ball into the seats. Well, I need help doing that."

It may not be so easy in the future. Robert Manfred, baseball's executive vice president for labor relations and human resources, says baseball will suspend and fine repeat minor league offenders this season. The Padres have administered their own three-strikes-and-you're-out steroid policy for the past five years, though they do not test in the off-season, either. "The word's out in our organization, but the trend we're seeing is that most of the players who tested positive were in [Class] A ball," says San Diego general manager Kevin Towers. "That tells me the problem is spreading fast. I think it's prevalent in college and high school—even before we get them."

KENNY ROGERS made his major league pitching debut with the Rangers in 1989. He was taught in the early years of his career that the safest place to throw a pitch was the low-outside part of the plate. Nobody was going to hit that pitch out of the park, coaches told him. "It's not true anymore," Rogers says. "Now you've got 5' 7" guys built like weightlifters taking that down-and-away pitch and hitting it out to the opposite field. No one thinks it's unusual because it happens all the time."

And steroids are not just for sluggers anymore. They're used by everyone, from erstwhile singles hitters to aging pitchers. Says Rogers, "Just look around. You've got guys in their late 30s, almost 40, who are throwing the ball 96 to 99, and they never threw that hard before in their lives. I'm sorry. That's not natural evolution. Steroids are changing the game. You've got players who say, 'All I want to do is hit,' and you have pitchers who say, 'All I want to do is throw 97. I don't care if I walk [everyone].'" Steroids have helped even mediocre pitchers turn up the heat. "The biggest change I've seen in the game," says a veteran major league infielder, "is seeing middle relievers come into the game throwing 91, 92 [mph]. Those guys used to be in the mid-80s or so. Now everybody is throwing gas, including the last guy in the bullpen."

The changes in the game are also evident in the increasingly hulking physiques of the players. The average weight of an All-Star in 1991 was 199 pounds. Last year it was 211. "We're kidding ourselves if we say this is not a problem," says Towers. "Look at the before and after shots, at the size of some of these players from the '90s to now. It's a joke."

Barry Bonds of the Giants is often cited as a player who dramatically altered his size and his game, growing from a lithe, 185-pound lead-off hitter into a 230-pound force who is one of the greatest home run hitters of all time. Bonds's most dramatic size gains have come in the past four years, over which he has doubled his home run rate. Bonds, who insists he added muscle through diet and intense training, has issued several denials of rumors that he uses steroids, including one to a group of reporters in April in which he said, "You can test me and solve that problem [of rumors] real quick."

But there is no testing in baseball, and everyone continues to speculate. What's a little speculation and innuendo these days anyway? Mark McGwire was cheered in every park on his march to 70 home runs in 1998 by fans hardly concerned about his reluctant admission that he'd used androstendione, an over-the-counter supplement that reputedly has the muscle-building effects of steroids.

"If you polled the fans," says former outfielder Curtis, "I think they'd tell you, 'I don't care about illegal steroids. I'd rather see a guy hit the ball a mile or throw it 105 miles an hour.' "

Says Caminiti, "They come to the arena to watch gladiators. Do they want to see a bunch of guys choking up on the bat against pitchers throwing 82 miles an hour or do they want to see the ball go 500 feet? They want to see warriors."

It is a long way from 1988, when Canseco lost a prospective national endorsement deal with a major soft drink company because of unconfirmed suspicions that he used steroids. Many players, too, are showing more acceptance of steroids, especially when users and nonusers alike believe the health risks can be minimized if the drugs are used in proper doses. Today's user, they claim, is more educated about steroid use than Caminiti in 1996 or NFL lineman Lyle Alzado, who died in 1992 at age 43 from brain cancer he believed was caused by grossly excessive steroid use.

Pete, the minor league steroid user, says, "I've talked to doctors. They've studied [steroids], and they know if you don't abuse them, they can help you. As long as you don't go crazy with them, like Alzado, you should be fine."

Says Curtis, who estimates that 40% to 50% of major leaguers use steroids, "There are two things that might stop a person from using steroids: a moral obligation—they're illegal—and a fear of the medical complications. I was 100 percent against the use of steroids. But I must tell you, I would not fear the medical side of it. I fully agree you can take them safely."

Rogers also opposes steroid use on ethical grounds, but understands why it is so tempting. "My belief is that God gave you a certain amount of ability, and I don't want to enhance it by doing something that is not natural and creates an unfair advantage. I'm critical of guys who do it," he says. "On the other hand if I were 22 or 21 and trying to make it in baseball, I can't say for sure that I wouldn't try something when I plainly see the benefits other guys are getting. I can't say I'm 100 percent positive I wouldn't resort to that."

The first generation of ballplayers who have grown up in the steroid culture is only now arriving, biceps bulging, chests shaven and buttocks tender. The acceptance level of steroids in the game may very well continue rising until . . . until what? A labor deal that includes a comprehensive testing plan? Such a plan, unlikely as it is, given the union's resistance, might deter some players, but even baseball officials concede that the minor league testing program in place gives players the green light to shoot up in the off-season. And athletes in other sports subject to testing have stayed one step ahead of enforcement with tactics such as using so-called "designer drugs," steroids that are chemically altered to mask the unique signature of that drug that otherwise would show on a urine test.

So even with testing, will it take something much darker for steroids to fall from favor? Renowned sports orthopedist James Andrews recalled the impact of two prominent deaths on the drug culture in football. "Major League Baseball can't continue to leave this door open," says Andrews. "Steroids became a big deal in football after Lyle Alzado [died] and ephedrine became a big deal after Korey Stringer. You don't want to see it get to that [in baseball] before someone says stop. But, unfortunately, that's what it seems to take to wake people up."

Rogers has a nightmare about how it might end, and that is why he does not always throw his fastball as hard as he can. It is the thought of some beast pumped up on steroids whacking a line drive off his head. "We're the closest ones to the hitter," he says of the men on the mound. "I don't want the ball coming back at me any faster. It's a wonder it hasn't happened already. When one of us is down there dead on the field, then something might happen. Maybe. And if it's me, I've already given very clear instructions to my wife: Sue every one of their asses. Because everybody in baseball knows what's been going on."

Postscript: This story began in 2001, when more and more players were complaining to me (off the record) about the competitive disadvantage of facing an increasing number of opponents using steroids. I told my editors in March, "Somebody's going to write this story, and it better be us." I had been reporting the story for many weeks when I called Ken Caminiti, and he agreed to meet me at his garage in Houston, where he worked on his cars. With no apparent agenda except to tell the truth, Caminiti took responsibility for his steroid use and implicated no one else. That night we ate dinner close by, at his favorite diner. "This is going to be a pretty big story, huh?" he asked me. "Yes," I said. "It is." He looked at me and said, "Well, I've got nothing to hide," and went back to eating his egg whites.

The story ran with sidebars about the high incidence of amphetamine use in baseball, the ease with which steroids could be obtained and the connection between steroids and injuries that were costing owners millions of dollars. I don't believe the package shocked anybody in baseball, but I think it's fair to say that the story changed the terms of the public debate about steroid use in the game.

Within three months of publication, the players association reversed its long-standing policy and agreed to a drug testing program. I do not believe that would have happened without Caminiti's honesty.

Caminiti died Oct. 10, 2004 of a drug overdose.

600 and Counting

After belting his 500th homer only one season earlier, late boomer
Barry Bonds busted another milestone in his run at Hammerin' Hank

O N A PLEASANT SUMMER NIGHT IN SAN FRANCISCO
last Friday, Barry Bonds did something the rest of us
should try. No, hitting the 600th home run of a
major league career is beyond the general popu-
lace, not to mention all but three other ballplayers in history. What's in-
structive is what Bonds did *after* he connected with a fastball from Pirates righthander Kip Wells. Like De Kooning before a drying canvas,
Bonds took a step back and admired the majesty and magnitude of his
work.

A Bonds home run typically leaves nothing to doubt from the vi-
olent, noisy moment of contact. This one screamed for 421 feet before landing among the centerfield loonies of Pacific Bell Park. They
clawed, pummeled and bloodied one another at the chance to own
the five-ounce piece of history, at least until it could be sold to the
highest bidder. And just as Bonds took a long, steady view of the
moment when he joined Hank Aaron, Babe Ruth and Willie Mays

in an exclusive fraternity, so do we need to take a long view of his career.

We need to pause because Bonds is not only a late boomer, but also a mostly unembraceable presence. He has, despite his unsurpassed skills, engendered no simpatico emotions or even a nickname. After blasting 73 home runs last year in one of the greatest seasons of all time, Bonds finished third—*third!*—among outfielders in fan balloting for the All-Star Game this year, drawing less support than Ichiro or Sammy Sosa.

"People don't appreciate him," says teammate Shawon Dunston, an 18-year veteran. "We're playing with arguably the best ever, but he won't get that recognition because people say he's not nice. He's going to break [Aaron's] record. He's going to hit 800."

So step back and behold. On Friday night Bonds was again at that jewel of a ballpark beside the shimmering waters of McCovey Cove. He hit No. 500 there. He hit 71 there. He hit 600 there, as if joining Hammerin' Hank, the Babe and the Say Hey Kid was another return engagement on the tour, like Sinatra at the Mirage or Springsteen at the Garden. You half expected the crowd not only to cheer but also to flick cigarette lighters. "To be in that select group is great," Bonds said after the game, "but nothing's more satisfying than doing it in front of 40,000 fans in San Francisco."

Perspective? Bonds is the only player who broke into the big leagues in the past 47 years to hit 600 homers. If he plays another four seasons with a modest decrease in production, the 38-year-old leftfielder might retire as the alltime leader in home runs, extra-base hits, runs, walks and intentional walks (a mark he already has). Explaining how he arrived at 600 is a lesson in spontaneous combustion.

The alltime greats announce themselves early, like youthful princes born to the throne. Ruth, Ted Williams, Mays, Mickey Mantle all glowed with an unmistakable destiny from their first moments as big leaguers. Outside this regal procession is Bonds, the only man to sneak up on one of baseball's numeric Mount Everests. Ever defiant, Bonds has overturned the game's actuarial tables.

Bonds began his career as a lithe leadoff hitter for the Pittsburgh Pirates in 1986. In determining Bonds's statistical twin after each of his first eight seasons, the comprehensive website Baseball-Reference.com found him to be most similar, in career production by age, to this mixed bag of hitters from throughout major league history: Bob Coluccio, Tom Brunansky (twice), Jack Clark (thrice), Bobby Bonds and, as recently as '93, Greg Luzinski. Two years ago Bonds wasn't even among the 10 outfielders named to major league baseball's All-Century team.

Today he ranks not only among the greatest players of all time, but also as perhaps the most feared hitter ever. Never before have pitchers avoided a batter as much as they do the lefty-swinging Bonds, who, like a supersized Danny Almonte, seems too good for his league. In 2001 pitchers walked Bonds a record 177 times, or 26.7% of his plate appearances. They have been even more careful this year, walking him 31.6% of the time. The respect Bonds gets is most extraordinary with runners in scoring position (47.3%), and with runners on and first base open (67.2%).

That fear factor is a late-career development. Entering this season Bonds had almost the same number of plate appearances as Williams (14 more, or 9,805 to be precise), but he had made 13% more outs and struck out 82% more often. Bonds trailed Williams by wide margins in batting average (.344 to .292), on-base percentage (.483 to

.419) and slugging percentage (.634 to .585). Ruth and Williams were feared throughout their careers—they walked in 20% or more of their plate appearances in nine and 10 seasons, respectively. Bonds has done so only four times.

"When he was younger, you were more concerned about him hitting a line drive in the gap or stealing a base than you were about him hitting a home run," says Atlanta Braves veteran lefthander Tom Glavine, against whom Bonds, at week's end, was 24 for 75 (.320) for his career. "He's a different hitter now. In fact he's a different hitter over the last five years than he was, say, when he first went to San Francisco [in 1993]. He went from a guy who would occasionally hit the mistake pitch for a home run to somebody who hits mistakes out all the time."

No batter ever has made himself this good this late in his career. How did it happen? Most evident, the 6' 2", 228-pound Bonds filled out physically without losing any of the snap to one of the quickest batting strokes in the game. (He has repeatedly denied that he uses steroids and says his growth is attributable to his workout routine and nutritional supplements.) More subtly, Bonds's development as a power hitter accelerated when baseball entered this post-Camden Yards age of long-ball worship and he learned to lift the ball.

His career can be delineated into three stages. In Stage 1, from 1986 through '89, Bonds was a slasher who hit as many ground balls as he did fly balls. In Stage 2, from '90 through '97, Bonds was a consistent run producer who became a better home run hitter by getting the ball in the air more often. In those eight seasons his ground-ball-to-fly-ball ratio fluctuated between 71:100 and 87:100. Not coincidentally, Stage 3 began in '98, an expansion year best remembered for the McGwire-Sosa home run race, when an even bigger, smarter Bonds moved into the company of the alltime power hitters. Over this last stage his ground ball-to-fly ball ratio has decreased every full year: 63:100 (in '98), 62:100, 57:100, 56:100. In other words, he now hits almost two flies for every grounder. This transformation would not be possible without Bonds's putting more arc in his swing—he's *looking* to go deep. With his added strength, many of those fly balls are sailing far beyond the fences of today's cozy retroparks.

Further, in Stage 3 Bonds has crept closer to home plate, enabling him to pull pitches on the outside half of the plate with power rather than hitting line drives to the leftfield gap. The defensive shift most teams employ against him is also a Stage 3 development. "He's so close to the plate, he can take a pitch away and turn on it," Glavine says. "If you hit him on the hands, it's almost a strike. Yet he's so quick that he kills the inside pitch. You have to pitch him inside to keep him honest, but you'd better bury it way in because if you miss [over the plate], it's gone."

In Stage 1 Bonds hit 21 home runs per season; in Stage 2, 36. He is on pace to slug 48 homers this year—his average during Stage 3—which would give him 615 for his career at season's end. With another 48-homer season next year he would pass Mays, who finished with 660. If he continues to maintain his Stage 3 rate, Bonds will pass Ruth (714) and Aaron (755) in 2005, the year he turns 41.

Is it possible for Bonds to maintain this production at such an advanced age? In his final season (1960) Williams, at 41, hit 29 homers—sixth in the American League—in a much less homer-friendly, much less muscular time. In '72 Mays, at 41, hit eight homers and followed that with six the next year, his last. In '75 Aaron, at 41, hit 12 homers and bowed out the next year with 10.

If Bonds has taught us anything, it's that the arc of his career is like no other's—especially not like Bob Coluccio's.

Postscript: Today Bonds's off-the-charts late-career power surge is to be questioned at least as much as it is admired. "How did he do it?" is a more haunting question now than it was then, given his leaked grand jury testimony about his use of steroids (unknowingly, he claimed), charges by a mistress that he used steroids, and a guilty plea by his personal trainer, Greg Anderson, to a charge of steroid distribution.

❖

The Ultimate Gamer

In perhaps the best World Series game ever played, the Twins'
Jack Morris gave us one final glimpse of a dying breed:
a pitcher determined to finish what he started

JACK MORRIS AWOKE ON THE MORNING OF OCT. 27, 1991, without a doubt in his mind. There was only one thing in his life that mattered that day, and he knew how it would turn out. The Minnesota Twins pitcher could not know that an offensive revolution was coming, fueled by the trend-setting coziness of Camden Yards, which would open in six months; the addition of two expansion teams a year after that; and the relentless quest for muscle enhancement, by any means necessary. He could not know that his way of pitching, in which a real ace had no need for a bullpen, was doomed.

No, all that mattered that day was the outcome of the seventh game of the most closely contested World Series ever. The Twins and the Atlanta Braves had played so many cliffhangers so deep into the night that one sleep disorder expert, in a Page One story in *The Atlanta Constitution*, warned of "a rise in car wrecks and work accidents" due to frazzled fans.

As Morris prepared breakfast for himself, his parents and his two boys, he knew exactly how the game would end. What bothered him was that his father, Arvid, and mother, Dona, who flew in from Michigan to stay with him during the Series, were not so certain. His father was too quiet. His eyes betrayed his anxiety.

Didn't he *know*? Arvid was a rock, a left-brain master, a former troubleshooter for 3M labs in St. Paul. He had driven his sons, Tom and Jack, hard, throwing to them when they were two or three years old, much to Dona's consternation. "People used to say, My gosh, how many hours do you spend with the boys?" Arvid says. "They showed a lot of ability, and we were going to work that and see if something might develop." When the boys got a little older, dinner became conditional on how well they played: If they won a Little League game, Arvid bought them steak. If they lost, they got hamburger. Every drive home from the ball field included a lecture on how they could improve.

By the time the boys were in high school, Tom and Jack decided to confront Arvid. "Enough is enough," Tom said to his father. "You need to back off." Arvid eased up after that.

When Jack first earned big money in the game, in 1983, he asked his father, "How would you like to retire?" Arvid was 53. Jack bought his parents a lakeside home and a car.

Now, eight years later, with Game 7 upon them, Arvid was nervous, but Jack smiled and laughed. "Don't worry, Dad," he said. "We're going to win the World Series."

"I was amazed," Arvid says. "He had never done anything like that before. It had always been a 'Let the chips fall . . . ' type thing with him."

Arvid had not seen his son in the clubhouse the night before, after

Twins centerfielder Kirby Puckett hit an 11th-inning home run—yet another traffic-alert game—to make Game 7 necessary. "He had this huge smile on his face," Minnesota pitcher Kevin Tapani says of Morris, "as if he couldn't wait for the next game to start, couldn't wait to pitch that game."

Nor did Arvid see his son plop into a chair in the press interview room that night, grab a microphone and, with a heavyweight's bravado, bellow, "In the immortal words of the late, great Marvin Gaye, Let's get it on!" Morris *knew*.

"I never had as much will to win a game as I did on that day," says Morris. "I was in trouble many times during that game but didn't realize it because I never once had a negative thought."

Morris was right to be so confident. He pitched the game of his life, the game of his *generation*, the game neither his father nor his manager could have imagined. Game 7 became *his* game.

AS LONNIE SMITH, the Braves' leadoff batter, stepped in to hit against Morris, he turned to have a word with catcher Brian Harper. They had played together briefly with the 1985 Cardinals and only four nights earlier had met at home plate in a bone-rattling collision.

"Lonnie looked at me, and I looked at him," Harper says, "and you could tell we were both thinking the same thing: Wow, this is going to be something! These six games have been tremendous. And now one more...."

"Hey, have a good game," Smith said.

"Good luck," Harper said. "God bless you."

"We knew it was going to be a war," Harper says. "It was like two boxers tapping gloves before the fight."

At 7:38 Central time—with 55,118 fans in the Metrodome screaming like a jet engine, the noise bouncing off the white Teflon roof and concrete walls—Morris threw his first pitch, an inside fastball to Smith. Home plate umpire Don Denkinger called it a ball. Morris glared at him. The third pitch, also a ball, brought the same silent, icy protest from Morris.

"I knew Jack," Denkinger says, "and I never found too much that he *did* like. I had the utmost respect for him as a competitor. He was a guy who didn't like to lose. Tim Tschida, another umpire, grew up in St. Paul. Jack played with Tim's brothers, and he told me how Jack brought the ball to play. And if he didn't like how the game was going, he'd go home and take the ball with him. And that would be the end of the game."

Morris wore a mustache in the bushy, droopy style of the stock bad guy in an old Western. His face seemed petrified in a scowl. The press, which he might have hated even more than he did hitters, called him Black Jack and approached him as one would a live grenade. Sparky Anderson, his manager for 12 seasons in Detroit, called him Cactus Jack.

"He was the last of a breed," Anderson says. "Somebody who actually comes to the park with *anger* to beat you. I never went near him when it was his day to pitch."

Says Tapani, "We used to joke that Jack had low blood sugar. It was as if he hadn't eaten in a while and his chemistry would change. If he lost a game, it was the end of the world. But if he was happy, he'd be buying drinks, telling stories and asking, 'What can I do for you?' What you saw was what you got with Jack. He hid nothing. Every once in a while with the media he'd say something that would make you cringe, make you say, 'Did he really say that?' "

Once, in Detroit, a female reporter asked him a question in the

Tigers' clubhouse. "I don't talk to women when I'm naked," Morris snapped, "unless they're on top of me or I'm on top of them."

Morris channeled so much rage on the mound that it lingered with him in the clubhouse, like an engine that stays hot after it's been turned off. "Show me a good loser," Morris would say, "and I'll show you a loser."

Anger was a beast inside him, and baseball provoked the beast in 1986. Morris was a free agent that winter, a 21-game winner, 31 years old and one of the best pitchers in the game. And nobody wanted him. The owners conspired not to sign other teams' free agents. Collusion. Morris wanted to sign with Minnesota, to come home to St. Paul, but learned quickly that that would not happen. "[Twins owner] Carl Pohlad was ready to sign me," says Morris, "and then [G.M.] Andy [MacPhail] came in and said no."

Morris and his agent, Dick Moss, flew to Tampa to meet with Yankees owner George Steinbrenner. Morris loved Steinbrenner's cocksure attitude and was impressed when Steinbrenner asked him about some Yankees, including a young first baseman named Dan Pasqua. "This guy has ungodly power," Morris said. "It's just a matter of him getting it together."

"I'm not sure," Steinbrenner said. "I don't think he's got the heart you do. You're my kind of guy. You're just the kind of guy I need."

Moss seized the opportunity and threw out numbers for a three-year deal. Suddenly Steinbrenner turned cool, saying that he needed to sign his own free agents, but Moss and Morris knew what was happening. "George," Moss said, "you wouldn't be the kind of person to have anybody tell you what to do, would you?"

Steinbrenner replied, "I swear on my mother's grave nobody's telling me what to do."

Morris looked Steinbrenner square in the eyes and said to him, slowly and firmly, "Do not do that to your mom. She hears what you're saying."

"Steinbrenner," Morris says, "lied to my face."

Morris wound up returning to the Tigers, squeezing a $1.85 million one-year deal out of them in arbitration. Five years later, after the owners were found guilty of collusion and Morris was one of several players set free as a "new look" free agent, he knocked again on the doors of Pohlad and MacPhail. This time they signed him.

Arvid's boy at last had come home to the Twin Cities. It was a heartwarming story, unless you knew that Morris's marriage was falling apart and that he would live alone that year, his two sons living with their mother. "It was miserable," Morris says. "I poured all of my focus into baseball."

The first day of spring training he told his new teammates, who had finished last the previous season, "Men, I'm going to get you guys to the World Series. I'm going to throw the most innings on this team, have the best ERA and win the most games. I will lead you."

"The guy was the ultimate competitor," Tapani says. "If we were running wind sprints, he'd try to beat you. Scott Erickson and I would take turns running hard. That way we'd save energy so one of us would always be strong enough to beat him. But Jack would run all 16 sprints hard and beat us every time. He had this attitude, *Whatever* you do, I'm going to beat you."

Morris won 18 games for the Twins. He won both of his starts against Toronto in the American League Championship Series. He won Game 1 of the World Series 5–2. He was ahead 2–1 in Game 4 when manager Tom Kelly pinch-hit for him after six innings. His replacement, Carl Willis, gave up a home run to the third batter he faced, Smith. Minnesota lost 3–2 in the bottom of the ninth.

"T.K. screwed up by taking me out," Morris says. "We would have won it, and I would never have had to pitch Game 7."

That final World Series game was his third start in eight days. He had already logged 273 innings for the year.

The Braves quickly and consistently challenged whatever was left in his reservoir of strength and will. They put a runner on second in the second inning, runners at first and second in the third, a runner at second in the fourth, runners at first and third in the fifth . . . and Morris allowed none of them to score.

"When Kirby hit that [Game 6] home run, a calm came over me that I never had felt in the game," Morris says. "Growing up, I always envisioned being on the mound in Game 7, bottom of the ninth. I had this calm come over me knowing that I had mentally prepared for this game my whole life."

There was, however, something Morris never counted on: an opposing pitcher with the same kind of resolve.

JOHN SMOLTZ grew up in Lansing, Mich., 90 minutes from Tiger Stadium. His father played the accordion at the Tigers' team party after they won the 1968 World Series. Smoltz's grandfather worked at Tiger Stadium for more than 30 years, first on the grounds crew and then as an attendant in the pressroom. He would brag to Bill Campbell, Al Kaline, Bill Lajoie and anybody else in the Detroit front office, "My grandson's going to play for you one day."

John was a huge Tigers fan. "Never missed a game," he says. He made a few trips to Tiger Stadium each year and listened to all the other games on the radio. When the team played on the West Coast, Smoltz would set his alarm clock so he could wake to hear Ernie Harwell call the first pitch. He'd catch a few innings before falling asleep again.

He liked all those Tigers—Kirk Gibson, Alan Trammell, Sweet Lou Whitaker and the rest—but one player stood out above all others: Jack Morris. "He was tough on the mound," Smoltz says. "He had good stuff. And he wasn't one of those pitchers who came out when it was convenient. He pitched a lot of innings, a lot of big games."

In the summer of 1985, just as Grandpa Smoltz had been predicting for years, Detroit drafted his grandson. Smoltz signed too late to play in rookie ball, so the Tigers let him spend two weeks with the major league club. Smoltz would put on a uniform for batting practice, change into his street clothes and watch the game from the stands, then return to the clubhouse upon its conclusion. He was just a kid out of high school, so green that when the team traveled to New York City and the hotel desk clerk gave him a card to open the door to his room, he had no idea what it was.

Smoltz hung out with the bullpen catcher and kept his mouth shut. He sat there in awe as he shared a locker room with the Tigers of Harwell's word pictures, only they were crankier and saltier in real life, veterans playing out the string in a disappointing season.

Morris was there, but Smoltz didn't have the nerve to say hello. Then one day somebody said something funny in the clubhouse, and Smoltz laughed. Morris gave Smoltz one of his icy glares. "Go ahead and laugh, kid," Morris said. "You're trying to take our jobs." Smoltz stopped laughing.

Morris has no memory of Smoltz's being with the team, had no knowledge of him two years later when the Tigers traded Smoltz to Atlanta to get Doyle Alexander, had no idea that his Game 7 opponent grew up idolizing him.

In that game Smoltz, then 24, matched Morris zero for zero, clutch pitch for clutch pitch. After seven innings neither team had scored, the first time that had happened in a final game of a World Series. The tension was excruciating. The noise was so loud that Twins bullpen coach Rick Stelmaszek watched the game with his foot on the bullpen telephone: He had to feel for the vibration if it rang, because he couldn't count on hearing it.

"There was no discussion on the bench of what was going on," Tapani says, "because you had to yell in the ear of the guy next to you if you wanted to be heard. And that gets old real quick. So we just watched."

Smoltz got three ground ball outs to end the seventh then, exhausted, trudged up the four flights of stairs from the dugout to the clubhouse for some rest. He flopped into a chair in front of a television and cried out, "Please, *please* can we score?" They would not. Morris, with some help from Lonnie Smith, would not allow it.

SMITH CHECKED his swing on the second pitch of the eighth inning, sending the ball softly into rightfield for a single. Morris missed with his first pitch to Terry Pendleton, and the bullpen phone vibrated. Pitching coach Dick Such wanted Steve Bedrosian and Mark Guthrie to warm up.

With the count 1 and 2 on what was Morris's 100th pitch, Pendleton crushed a fastball toward the gap in left centerfield. The speedy Smith seemed certain to score. Except there was a problem—Smith had broken toward second on a delayed steal but committed a fundamental mistake by not peeking toward home to pick up the ball when it was hit. Now he was looking to his left, then to his right. Where was it?

The Metrodome is as artificial a ballpark as you will find. The ceiling is a dull white, perfect camouflage for baseballs. Outfielders—who otherwise can check base runners, teammates or the proximity of walls while tracking fly balls—are warned never to take their eyes off the baseball once it is in the air in the Metrodome. Smith knew Pendleton's hit was in play. He just had no clue where.

As Smith took off for second base, Braves jumped off their seats in the dugout. "I remember yelling, 'Go! Go! Go!'" says pitcher Mark Grant. "When the ball was hit we thought, There it is. There's the run that's going to win it."

As Smith searched, Chuck Knoblauch, the second baseman, crouched as if fielding a ground ball, then threw an invisible baseball to shortstop Greg Gagne, who raced to cover second base, finishing the pantomime double play. A legend was born: Knoblauch deked Smith. It may have looked that way on television, especially with broadcaster Tim McCarver telling the world that's what had happened, but it wasn't true.

"In no way was I faked out by Knoblauch," Smith says. "If I did think Knoblauch had the ball, why didn't I slide?"

Leftfielder Dan Gladden, his back to the infield, chased the ball. Smith pulled into second standing up and rounded it, stopping four steps past the bag. He then froze, staring into left centerfield. Puckett, the centerfielder, was nowhere near the ball, but his reputation for the impossible catch—only the night before he had made a leaping grab to take away a home run—made Smith indecisive. "What people don't realize is that I had played in Kansas City," Smith says. "I saw Kirby run down the ball many times."

Up in the clubhouse Smoltz yelled at the television—and at Smith—"*Go! Go! Go!*"

Smith, still staring into the outfield, took two more hop-steps. Jimy Williams, the third base coach, never gave Smith any direction, never moved in the coaching box. Finally, only after the ball had bounced in front of the wall (about 20 feet from Gladden), off the wall, into the air like a little pop-up and eventually into Gladden's glove, Smith took off for third base. Gagne circled into the outfield to take Gladden's throw as Williams finally threw his left hand up and pointed at third base with his right hand, the signal for Smith to stop there. Pendleton easily pulled into second with a double.

Smoltz came running down those four flights of stairs, back to the dugout. "I wanted to watch us score some runs," he says, "because I knew the game was over if we scored. Lonnie's play didn't bother me. It was like, We're going to score. Second and third, no outs, and we've got our boys coming up."

Ron Gant, the number three hitter, failed for the third time that night with two runners on, grounding meekly to first base.

David Justice, a lefthanded hitter, was up next. Kelly came out to the mound, a daring move, according to Harper. "I learned early that you're better off not talking to Jack when he's on the mound."

"When they'd come to the mound, I didn't want to hear nothing," Morris says. "I already knew I was in trouble. You got something to say to me? Tell me between innings on the bench. I'm embarrassed when you're out there. I know I suck. That's why you're out there."

"What do you think?" Kelly said.

"I can get him," Morris said.

Kelly said, "Let's walk him."

Morris, head bowed, replied, "All right."

Justice was intentionally walked. Now the bases were loaded. The tension was too much for Dona. She left Arvid and her grandsons in their press-level box to stand alone in an empty concourse, unable to see the field. "It's unbelievable," Morris says, laughing at the tension he sees on the TV as he watches a tape of the game, "because I realize the importance of [the moment], but I'm still believing that I can get out of this. They are *not* going to score."

Harper had another thought, a horrible one. He suddenly thought of the error Bill Buckner made in the 1986 World Series, an error so huge it blotted out the memory of his prolific hitting career. Harper saw himself throwing the baseball into rightfield, the winning runs scampering home. It was a horrible thought at a horrible time.

Four pitches later Morris hung a forkball to Sid Bream. It was a lousy pitch, the kind of awful pitch that sometimes causes a hitter to jump at it. Bream topped the ball to first baseman Kent Hrbek, who fired a strike to Harper to force Smith at home. Harper took a step, cocked his arm and made a perfect return throw to Hrbek. Double play. Inning over.

"I sat on the bench," Harper says, "and thought, I don't know how much longer I can take this. I was exhausted. My head hurt."

The bottom of the inning was just as wild. Smoltz, pitching with one out and a runner at first, yielded a hit-and-run single to Knoblauch that barely cleared the glove of Bream at first base. Braves manager Bobby Cox walked to the mound to remove a disgusted Smoltz. "I felt like Jack did," Smoltz says. "I was going to go as long as it took— 10, 11 innings. I'm amazed Kelly was able to leave Morris in, but that's what I grew up watching."

Reliever Mike Stanton intentionally walked Puckett to load the bases. Then Knoblauch made an even worse baserunning gaffe than Smith's. He took off from second on Hrbck's soft liner to second baseman Mark Lemke and was doubled off. Inning over.

MORRIS HAD reached the big leagues in 1977, a time when no one paid much attention to pitch counts or rotator cuffs or knew what a closer was. He was 22 years old when he made his first major league start. He walked the first four batters he faced. Manager Ralph Houk left him in for nine innings. He struck out 12; heaven knows how many pitches he threw. His arm hurt like hell for the next year and a half. Houk's successor, Anderson, reinforced the tenet that Morris should not look to the bullpen for help.

"During the '82 season Sparky left me out there to rot because he was teaching me something," Morris says. "He believed in me, believed I had the best stuff on the team. He knew I was strong, knew I was durable and knew I could handle it mentally. Once I got what he was doing, I wasn't going to let him take the ball from me ever again. I always looked at it this way: If the relievers came into the game, I screwed up. It wasn't, Jack, you did a good job for seven. Bull crap."

One day Morris was losing 5–4 in the fifth inning when he noticed "our 20th pitcher warming up." He saw Anderson leave the dugout for the mound, his second visit of the inning, which required Morris's removal once Anderson had crossed the third base line. Morris walked toward Anderson and grabbed him before he reached that line. "Get the hell out of here," he yelled, "because what you've got warming up is no better than what I've got right now."

Says Morris, "He looked at me like, You're nuts, but he turned around. I got out of the jam, and we won the game."

"We had more fights and arguments than the world would allow," Anderson says. "But I don't have more respect for anybody. This man was quality, the best pitcher I ever had in 26 years."

MORRIS BREEZED through the ninth inning, getting three outs on eight pitches. He had thrown 118 pitches in the game. His innings odometer for the year read 282. Kelly thanked him in the dugout, told him, "Great job, that's all we can expect from you," and walked away . . . even though no one was throwing in the bullpen.

"I'm fine," Morris said. "I'm fine."

Morris and Kelly had not always seen eye to eye. "I think when I came to Minnesota he didn't know how to handle me," Morris says. "It was all kind of trial and error for the first few months. One time I remember I got so pissed off at him that I wanted to kill him."

The Twins were holding one of their usual pregame meetings to review the opposing lineup when Kelly asked Morris how he would pitch to a particular hitter. Morris gave his answer.

"All right," Kelly said, "we're not going to do it that way." He then gave orders that contradicted Morris.

"Now," Kelly said, "anybody have a problem with that?"

"Yeah," Morris snapped. "Why the f--- did you ask me?"

"That's not important," he said. "We're going to do it this way."

Morris says, "T.K. wanted to show everybody—and I loved him for this—that he was in control."

Now, with the World Series on the line, Kelly was testing Morris again. He seemed to be saying somebody else would pitch the 10th inning. The pitching coach grabbed Kelly by the arm and said, "T.K., he said he's fine."

Kelly turned. He looked Morris in the eye.

"I can pitch," Morris said.

Kelly paused, then said, "Oh, hell. It's only a game."

"He was giving me the chance to take myself out," says Morris. "But

I think he wanted me to look him in the eye and say, 'I'm not going nowhere. This is my game.' "

So Morris pitched the 10th inning, the only starting pitcher to do so in the World Series since Tom Seaver, one of his heroes, did it in 1969. He pitched as if it were a balmy Florida afternoon in spring training, and he was fresh and full of vigor. Again he zipped through the inning with only eight pitches. He had pitched to eight batters since Pendleton hit that double, and none of them got the ball out of the infield. It made no sense. A 36-year-old pitcher, 283 innings into his season, working his second straight game on short rest, throwing 10 shutout innings . . . and he was getting *stronger*.

"Without question," MacPhail says, "it is the most impressive pitching performance I have ever witnessed, and, remember, I watched Kerry Wood's 20-strikeout game."

The bullpen phone remained still. Morris was prepared to go back out for the 11th, but Minnesota loaded the bases with one out against Alejandro Pena in the last of the 10th. Kelly sent Gene Larkin to pinchhit.

"They're pulling their outfield in," home plate umpire Denkinger said to Larkin. "I believe you could hit one over their heads." Larkin said nothing.

Weeks later, at a White House reception, Denkinger asked Larkin, "Didn't you hear what I said?"

Replied Larkin, "Yep. But you know what? My mouth was so dry I couldn't talk."

Larkin hit the first pitch over the leftfielder's head, and Gladden danced home with the game's only run. Never before or since had a run been so difficult to come by in a World Series game. Morris—his warmup jacket on, ready to pitch all night if he had to—was the first player to get to home plate, waving Gladden in.

There is a scene on the videotape in which Kelly first spots Morris in the clubhouse after the game. Kelly seems to be fighting back tears as he rushes toward his pitcher, then embraces him with a long, tight hug.

"Now, *that* ... " Morris says, choking up as he watches the tape. He lowers his head, gathers himself and continues, " ... that is worth more than any trophy or ring. To have the respect of your manager, your teammates .... What is greater than that?"

THE GAME has changed. Complete games, Morris's badge of honor, are more than twice as rare now as they were in 1991. Only twice in the 116 World Series starts since Morris's Game 7 has a pitcher thrown a shutout (Curt Schilling in 1993 and Randy Johnson in 2001). The next Jack Morris, Smoltz, isn't even a starting pitcher anymore. He's a closer. Smith is retired, raising a family in an Atlanta suburb. The Braves asked him last year to attend one of their promotions at Turner Field in which former team members sign autographs for fans. Smith was heckled there by some fans about 1991 and the Knoblauch decoy. He vowed he would not return. "I feel like an outcast," Smith says. "I'm the one they identify with losing that Series."

Says Smoltz, "Many times in sports guys are falsely accused of being the reason a team lost. This is one. We had men on second and third, nobody out, and we did not score .... "

Morris was 39 years old—with 10 wins by August—when Cleveland released him in '94. He squeezed in his starts that year between visits to a wheat and barley farm he had purchased in Montana after the '91 World Series. He lost $1 million that year. He made money with a bumper crop the next year, the only year of sufficient rain. He lost money for several more years until he sold the farm. "No matter how well you fertilized, how well you prepped the fields, you had to rely on Mother Nature," Arvid says.

It is not in Morris's blood to rely on anyone or anything. He did not make many friends in the game. He received one job offer in baseball after retiring: $50,000 to be a coach in Saskatoon, Saskatchewan, in the Toronto minor league system. He passed on it. Last season Detroit invited him to spring training as a special instructor to work with its pitchers. He saw firsthand how much the game has changed. "I expected them to care like I care," he says, "and they didn't."

Though he still lives in the Minneapolis area, Morris is mostly associated with Detroit—this season he will work 40 Tigers games as a broadcaster. He never pitched again for the Twins after that Game 7. He exercised his option for free agency and signed with Toronto, becoming baseball's highest-paid pitcher. Then he again pitched his team into the World Series, in 1992, and pitched against the Braves again, though poorly in Game 5. He gave up a grand slam—to Lonnie Smith. Smoltz was the winning pitcher. Morris knew that a night like Oct. 27, 1991, would not happen again.

"Other than my kids being born, I can't remember anything that meant more to me," Morris says. "It was the epitome of everything I'd ever tried to achieve in my life. And yet within 24 hours this sadness came over me, knowing I might not be back in Minnesota and I might not ever pitch a game like that for the rest of my life. . . . I wish everybody could experience what I experienced that day. The joy. Total joy. The world would be a better place if everybody could feel that at least once."

On that Sunday morning when Morris woke up and knew he would win Game 7, an old baseball wizard with gleaming white hair and a twinkle in his eye awoke with a similar premonition. Anderson, Morris's old skipper, met his friends for his daily game of golf that day in Sunset, Calif. The boys were talking about how the Braves would win the Series. The man with the white hair laughed. "Tell you what to do," Anderson told them. "Go home and get your bankbook. Clear it out and send it to Vegas. Morris is pitching. He will beat Smoltz. I promise you that."

"How do you know?" they said.

"Boys, I know that guy," Anderson said. "He's an animal. If he doesn't have a real challenge, he's liable to give up six runs. But don't get him in a position where you challenge him."

Anderson laughs when he tells the story. "[Jack] was the last of them," he says. It was 12 years ago. Another era. "When you talk to Cactus Jack, tell him he's still the meanest man I ever met."

Postscript: I met Morris for this story once over beers and then another time in a hotel suite, where we watched a tape of the game as he took me through it pitch by pitch. Cactus Jack wasn't mean at all. He was friendly, honest and, above all, proud. It still is the greatest baseball game I've ever seen, and deconstructing it through the eyes of Morris was as much fun as watching it unfold in real time.

What Is Rickey Henderson Doing in Newark?

The greatest leadoff hitter of all time beat the bushes, trying to get back to the majors—and still left 'em laughing at every stop

RICKEY HENDERSON WAS BORN ON CHRISTMAS DAY, 1958, in the backseat of a '57 Olds on the way to a hospital in Chicago. ❡ He was fast from the very beginning. ❡ There are certain figures in American history who have passed into the realm of cultural mythology, as if reality could no longer contain their stories: Johnny Appleseed. Wild Bill Hickok. Davy Crockett. Rickey Henderson. They exist on the sometimes narrow margin between Fact and Fiction.

"A lot of stuff [people] had me doing or something they said I had created, it's comedy," Henderson says. "I guess that's how they want to judge me, as a character."

Nobody in baseball history has scored more runs, stolen more bases, drawn more walks or provided more entertainment (some of it unintended) for so many teams than Rickey Henley Henderson, the greatest leadoff hitter ever, a superstar so big that his middle and last names became superfluous. Rickey is the modern-day Yogi Berra, only faster.

Whereas Berra contributed a new noun to the English language *(Yogiism)*, Henderson inspired that classic rejoinder muttered by many a manager, teammate, sportswriter or, especially, general manager come contract time: "Rickey is Rickey."

"I don't know how to put into words how fortunate I was to spend time around one of the icons of the game," says Padres All-Star closer Trevor Hoffman, a teammate of Henderson's in 1996, '97 and 2001. "I can't comprehend that yet. Years from now, though, I'll be able to say I played with Rickey Henderson, and I imagine it will be like saying I played with Babe Ruth."

The legend of Henderson is real, all right, as real as the check-cashing service with the metal security gates on Broad Street in downtown Newark, which is about all the local color there is in the neighborhood of the mostly empty Bears & Eagles Riverfront Stadium, home to the Newark Bears of the independent Atlantic League—and, at the moment, to Henderson.

"We need to shift the ballpark to another location or something," he says.

At age 44 the future first-ballot Hall of Famer is here on the wrong side of baseball's tracks, not to mention those of New Jersey Transit, whose cars clackity-clack a pop fly away from his leftfield post. He signed with the Bears and came to downtown Newark for one last shot at the major leagues, which makes him, in every sense, an urban legend.

Speaking of cashing checks. . . .

Once in the late 1980s, the Yankees sent Henderson a six-figure signing-bonus check. After a few months passed, an internal audit revealed that the check had not been cashed. Brian Cashman, then a low-level executive with the club, called Henderson to ask if there was a problem with the check.

"No problem," Henderson said. "I'm just waiting for the money market rates to go up."

And speaking of money. . . .

Over 24 seasons in the major leagues, Henderson never spent his meal money. Before each trip players get an envelope filled with cash equal to the daily rate as negotiated by the Players Association ($73 this year), multiplied by the number of days on the road. Henderson would take the envelopes home and put them in shoe boxes. Whenever his daughters, Angela, now 18, Alexis, 11, and Adriann, 9, did well in school, Henderson would allow them to choose an envelope from a shoe box, a little game he called Pick It. The jackpot was getting an envelope from one of those 13-day, four-city trips. The girls would keep the money.

"They do what they want with it," he said. "It gives them motivation for their school and something to do, like a job."

Rickey's Best Lines about Money

1. "If they're going to pay me like [Mike] Gallego, I'm going to play like Gallego."

2. "All I'm asking for is what I want."

ON THE SUBJECT of contracts. . . .

Henderson signed a minor league deal last year with the Red Sox that included an invitation to spring training and a $350,000 salary if he made the team. After he played his way onto the Boston roster with an impressive spring, Henderson groused that the Red Sox were underpaying him. Interim general manager Mike Port reminded Henderson of the conditions he had agreed to.

"Oh, that?" Henderson replied. "I canceled that contract."

Says Port, "It was the first and only time I've ever had a player tell me he canceled his contract."

Red Sox president Larry Lucchino telephoned San Diego G.M. Kevin Towers, asking how Towers had appeased Henderson during their contract squabbles in the past. "I was on the golf course late in spring training one year when Rickey called to close a deal," Towers says. "I was putting, and my wife took the call. I said to her, 'Ask him what he wants.' She said, 'He wants a living allowance.' And I did it. That's how we closed the deal."

Lucchino liked that idea. The Red Sox agreed to pick up the tab on the suite Henderson was renting at the Boston Ritz-Carlton, which ran $10,000 a month.

Then there was the time. . . .

Henderson was ready to sign a $1.1 million contract with Oakland in 1998 when he demanded a suite on the road. Athletics general manager Billy Beane told him it was club policy not to give such clauses. Henderson insisted.

"Tell you what," Beane said. "As general manager I get a suite on the road. I don't make a lot of trips. I'll give you my suite whenever I don't go."

Henderson signed.

And while we're on the subject of contracts. . . .

After he signed a four-year, $12 million deal with Oakland in 1989, Henderson complained every spring about being underpaid. To underscore his unhappiness, he made a habit of reporting to spring training after the team's reporting date, though before the mandatory date established by the Basic Agreement. Trouble was, one spring teammate and star rightfielder Jose Canseco adopted the same tactic.

"Rickey was in town," traveling secretary Mickey Morabito says.

"But he didn't want to report before Jose did. So Rickey would drive into camp, and if he didn't see Jose's car parked there, he'd drive back out. Rickey made sure he was the last one to report."

Rickey's Favorite Pregame Routines

1. Flexing and swinging a bat naked or in his underwear in front of a full-length mirror, saying, "Rickey's the best."
2. Playing cards.
3. Playing dominos.
4. Ignoring meetings held to review opposing pitchers. Henderson prefers knowing nothing about what they throw.

HENDERSON HAS played for eight major league teams, including the Athletics, with whom he has had four stints. It's easy for him to lose track of his teammates. "There're countless guys that he's been teammates with, he has no idea of their names—countless," says Colorado Rockies bench coach Jamie Quirk, who played with Henderson for three years in Oakland. "It's not like if you got brought up from Triple A and walked in the locker room, Rickey's going to stick out his hand [to greet you]."

Henderson lockered next to Beane, then an outfielder for the Athletics, in 1989. Oakland sent Beane to the minor leagues. Six weeks later, Beane was called back to the Athletics.

"Hey, man, where have you been?" Henderson said. "Haven't seen you for a while."

There was another time. . . .

Art Kusnyer was a coach on the Athletics staff. One day during the season, after Kusnyer threw batting practice, Henderson told him, "You throw good BP. Are you comin' on the road with us?"

A similar thing happened with the Mets. . . .

In June 1999, when Henderson was playing for the Mets, the club fired hitting coach Tom Robson. Henderson saw reporters scurrying around the clubhouse and asked a teammate, "What happened?"

"They fired Robson," was the reply.

"Robson?" Henderson said. "Who's he?"

Which calls to mind another story about how, when Henderson joined the Mariners in 2000, he saw first baseman John Olerud, his former Mets teammate, fielding grounders while wearing a batting helmet and remarked, "That's strange. I played with a guy in New York who did the same thing." Alas, the story, though it appeared in many publications, is one of the rare Rickey tales that falls entirely on the side of Fiction, having been fabricated by members of the Mets' training staff.

Then again, in San Diego. . . .

Padres G.M. Towers is often called KT. Fred Uhlman Jr. is his assistant. The two of them would often walk into the clubhouse together to meet with manager Bruce Bochy. Whenever Henderson saw Towers and Uhlmann he would say to his two bosses, "Hi, Kevin. Hi, KT."

There was another time in San Diego. . . .

Henderson was boarding the team bus, walking toward the back to sit near Hoffman and catcher Brian Johnson. Tony Gwynn, seated near the front, stopped Henderson and said, "Rickey, you sit up here. You've got tenure."

"Ten?" Henderson said defiantly. "Rickey got *20* years in the big leagues."

Ah, yes. If Henderson is not best known for his speed or his strike zone ("Smaller than Hitler's heart," the late Jim Murray wrote), it must be his penchant for referring to himself as Rickey. Or as Rickey says, "A lot of times people talk about [how I use the] third party."

One off-season, in search of a team, he left a message on Towers's voice mail that went like this: "Kevin, this is Rickey. Calling on behalf of Rickey. Rickey wants to play baseball."

"One time," says Mariners catcher Ben Davis, who played with Henderson on the Padres, "Rickey came walking into the clubhouse with this denim outfit and big suede hat. And he says, 'Rickey got a big ranch [in California]. Rickey got a big bull. Rickey got horses. Rickey got chickens and everything. And Rickey got a 20-gallon hat.' "

"In 2000," says Texas shortstop Alex Rodriguez, who played with Henderson that season in Seattle, "Rickey was scuffling down the stretch, and there was some speculation that he wouldn't even be on the postseason roster. Rickey would say, 'Don't worry about Rickey. Rickey's an October player. Rickey's a postseason player.' And he was. He helped us beat Chicago.

"Sometimes he'd come back to the dugout after an umpire called him out, and I'd say, 'Rickey, was that a strike?' And he'd say, 'Maybe, but not to Rickey.' "

Rickey's Rules for a Long Career

1. Run three to five miles every other day. "Some guys, once the season starts, they relax, eat, do nothing. I feel sluggish that way. I got to get up and do something, get the blood back circulating and get the oxygen back in my body."

2. Do 200 sit-ups and 100 push-ups a day. "I don't do a lot of weights. Some guys, they want to be Hulk Hogan. Not me."

3. Stretch before bedtime. "Do your stretching before you sleep. That way you wake up loose."

4. Eat plenty of ice cream. "I like to eat ice cream at night. I got to have something sweet before I go to sleep."

Late one night, after a game in New York, Henderson ordered room service, but the order wound up going to Bochy's room. "I couldn't believe it," the manager says. "A huge bowl of ice cream and a big slab of cheesecake with sauce on it. I'm thinking, Where does it go?"

HENDERSON LED the league in stolen bases at age 39, the oldest player to do so, with 66. (The Marlins' two-time stolen base champ Luis Castillo, 27, has never had that many in a season.) When Rickey was 40, his on-base percentage was .423. He has played 24 big league seasons; no outfielder has played more. At 44, according to Bears teammate Mike Piercy, 26, "His flexibility is amazing. I'd get hurt if I tried to stretch like him. He's like Bruce Lee. I grew up idolizing him. And he doesn't look any different now."

Henderson's durability is remarkable considering the pounding his body has taken from his baserunning and hundreds of headfirst slides using a technique borrowed from . . . commercial airliners.

"It was really like a dream," he says. "I learned that the more closer to the ground [you are], the less pounding you take. We were going to Kansas City in an airplane, and we came in and bounced. Boom, boom, boom. Then we left there, came in I don't know where, and the plane came in smooth. I thought [the pilot] got lower to the ground, and that's how I developed my slide. I started to see how low I could get to the ground."

Tony La Russa managed Henderson for parts of seven seasons in Oakland. He reached an agreement with Rickey: Henderson would tell him directly, rather than through the trainers, when he needed a day off.

"He rises to the occasion—the big moment—better than anybody I've ever seen," La Russa says. "But when he was tapped, he'd take a couple of days off. One day [in 1993] he came in and said, 'My head's not right.' It turns out he was mad about the rumors he was getting traded. I wasn't going to push him. If you pushed him and he didn't want to play, he played like a cigar-store Indian. He'd take an 0 for 4, and you were better off playing *me*."

HENDERSON IS an avowed card shark and competition junkie. He will play almost anything with scoring, especially if it involves a friendly wager. Two years ago Shooty Babitt, a former Oakland teammate and current Diamondbacks scout, chided him for not playing well in spring training.

"Next thing you know we're playing Strikeout [a simple pitcher-versus-batter game] on the tennis court next to where he was staying," Babitt says. "He challenged me. We played for an hour—with a tennis ball. And he still owes me 50 bucks for a game of H-O-R-S-E we played."

"Every day," says Yankees third baseman Robin Ventura, who played with Henderson on the Mets, "there would be a big argument in the clubhouse, with guys accusing Rickey of cheating at cards. He'd get up and say, 'I don't know what you're talking about. I'm always winning.'"

That Christmas morning when Rickey was born in the backseat? His mother, Bobbie, had gone into labor late on Christmas Eve. It was snowing in Chicago. She telephoned her husband, John Henley, to come home and drive her to the hospital. John said no, he didn't want to rush home right away.

Rickey's father was playing poker—and he was winning big.

Rickey's Rankings on Alltime Lists
1. Runs: First (2,288)
2. Walks: First (2,179)
3. Stolen Bases: First (1,403)
4. Leadoff home runs: First (80)
5. Times on base: Third (5,316)
6. Games: Fourth (3,051)

BASEBALL IS designed to be an egalitarian sort of game in which one player among the 18 is not supposed to dominate. Basketball and football can stop the proceedings and design a play to put the ball in the hands of a chosen player. A starting pitcher, who begins the action in a game, takes four days off for every one he works. Yet in the past quarter century Henderson and Barry Bonds have come closest to dominating a baseball game the way Michael Jordan could a basketball game.

"If you're one run down, there's nobody you'd ever rather have up at the plate than Rickey," says Mariners coach Rene Lachemann, a former Oakland coach. "You didn't want to walk him, because that was a double—he'd steal second—but if you didn't throw it over the plate, he wouldn't swing. And if you *did* throw it over the plate, he could knock it out of the park."

There was one time. . . .

Henderson was taking a lead off first base when he held up two fingers toward Orioles third baseman Floyd Rayford. Rayford was perplexed . . . that is, until Rickey was standing next to him two stolen bases later.

And another time. . . .

In the 1989 World Series, during which the A's swept the Giants, Henderson reached base 11 times in the four games and stole three bases. Giants catcher Terry Kennedy grew so weary of seeing Rickey at first base that he grumbled, "Just go ahead and steal the base!"

With his showman's style—he invented the snatch catch and the slo-mo home run trot—Henderson was hated as an opponent, beloved as a teammate.

"One of my favorite teammates of all time," Brian Johnson says. "I grew up in Oakland, and he was an icon to me. When I was in San Diego I lockered next to him, and my biggest fear was that he was a bad guy. It was a breath of fresh air to find out he was the nicest guy, a genuine good guy and a great teammate."

"One of the best teammates I've ever had," Rodriguez says. "He made the game fun every day,"

Says La Russa, "In the clubhouse, on the plane, on the buses, Rickey was anything but the egotistical superstar who kept to himself. He was right in the middle of all the conversations, the cutting up. If you asked anybody on those Oakland teams, I would bet you'd find that everybody liked Rickey."

"Let me tell you something," Towers says. "I get e-mails daily from fans saying, 'Sign Rickey.' I get up to 100 a day. I get more calls and e-mails about him than anybody. I understand. We've had some special players come through San Diego. But there's an aura about him nobody else has."

Rickey's Top Forrest Gump–like World Series Whereabouts

1. Joe Carter's series-ending home run in 1993: on second base (which caused pitcher Mitch Williams to use a slide-step and hurry his delivery).

2. The 1989 earthquake: on a clubhouse toilet.

IT SHOULDN'T end like this for the Greatest Leadoff Hitter Ever, not here on Broad Street, not here with only about 1,000 people in the stands and kids in hot-dog costumes racing around the bases; not here, where players have to slip 75 cents into a vending machine if they want a soft drink in the clubhouse and the meal money is $18, which doesn't make for a very exciting game of Pick It.

"I wish he wouldn't have done it," Quirk, Henderson's former teammate, says of his signing with Newark. "I played with him three years. I wish he would retire, wait his five years and go to the Hall of Fame and live happily ever after. I don't know why he needs to do what he's doing. But who are we to say?"

Rickey played sparingly for Boston last year, getting 179 at bats. He hit .223 with five homers, 16 RBIs, eight stolen bases and a .369 on-base percentage. (The league average was .331.) John Vander Wal, Ron Coomer, Carlos Baerga and Lou Merloni all had similar seasons or worse. All of those veterans were invited to big league camps this spring and are still playing. No one offered Henderson that chance. His main team, the Athletics, invited Ron Gant (.338 OBP last year) to camp as a righthanded-hitting backup outfielder.

The word among G.M.'s was that Henderson's bat had slowed and that he appeared to have trouble accepting a limited role after years of stardom. "His bat had slowed two years ago," Towers says. "I think he's a decent platoon player. But if he's a part-time player playing once a week, people think he would have a hard time handling that. Rickey's game has always been about being out there every day and putting on a show. It's tough for him to sit and watch. We're going with young players right now, but I can tell you I'd hate to see him go out the way he's going out. If he's still there in September, I'd like to think we could work something out to see him back in the big leagues."

Rickey has interpreted the silence of the general managers differently. Instead of hearing a no-confidence vote on his skills, he heard them challenging him to a game of Strikeout. *Oh, yeah? Bring it on. I'll show you.*

Rickey knows that he can still play baseball. He can still lay off pitches dangerously close to the strike zone, he can still make a pitcher perspire just by taking that cocksure lead off first base, he can still fly close to the ground, jetlike, into second base, and he can still give value to a paying customer.

Newark isn't Utopia. But it is baseball. And, on balance, he is paying to play it. He took the job for $3,000 a month and rented an apartment in Manhattan for $4,000 a month. He travels with a longtime friend to every home and away game (except those in Nashua, N.H., where he stays at the team hotel) by commuting, like some Pony League player, from Manhattan. Sometimes his ride home takes two hours. At week's end the Bears' leadoff man was hitting .352 with a .477 on-base percentage.

"If I feel I don't have the skills, I'd be happy to hang up my shoes and go be with my kids," he says. "But I know I have the skill. The speed guys who can score runs? I think I'm better than the guys in the major leagues. Will I get the chance?"

Henderson sits on a gray folding metal chair in front of his locker in the Bears' clubhouse. These are gym lockers—red metal lockers with doors and vents—not the cherrywood stalls you find in plush big league clubhouses. Strips of adhesive tape serve as name tags for the has-beens, never-weres and hardball lifers of the independent team, including one for the impossibly named Damon Ponce DeLeon, a pitcher.

One of the two overhead television sets carries the news that David Cone, four years younger than Henderson, has retired, this time for good. It was Jim Bouton who wrote that a ballplayer dies twice—once like everybody else, but first, when his career ends. Cone has found his baseball mortality. Then Henderson is told that the Athletics have cut Gant. His eyes moisten on that news. He cannot help but think that was his roster spot, his shot.

"I'm trying to figure what's the problem," he says. "Why I can't get a chance. Who did I step on? Who did I do something bad to? If [that's it], I apologize, because I'm not that kind of person."

Rickey needs a Day. He needs the microphone, the gifts, the good-byes, the proper eulogy for a Hall of Fame career. "If I was still playing baseball and went off that way, it would be fine," he says. "If I'm not playing baseball, I don't feel that is the way I'd want to go. Why bring me back [only] for a Day when I can play the game?"

Boston gave him a Day last year, though it was more an appreciation than a send-off.

And that was the time. . . .

One of the team's owners, Tom Werner, asked Rickey what might be a good idea for a gift from the team.

"I always wanted a mobile home," Rickey said.

Werner, staggered, said, "A mobile phone?"

"No," Rickey said, "a mobile *home*."

Werner asked Rickey for another suggestion. He asked for "John Henry's Mercedes," referring to the vehicle of another of the team's owners. Werner explained the club might have difficulty finding and taking delivery of the same make and model on short notice.

"No, I mean *John Henry*'s Mercedes," Rickey said.

Henry wasn't about to hand over his car. On Rickey's Day, a new car was being delivered to Fenway Park just as Henderson arrived. It was a shiny red Thunderbird.

"Whose ugly car is that?" Henderson said.

That was the car the Red Sox purchased for him as a gift. "It's an old man's car, and I'm not an old man," Henderson said. He told the club it would have to pay to have the car shipped to his home in Arizona. He gave the car to Angela.

Yes, he needs one last Day in a big league park if only to give him an ending that isn't so messy. And so people can get together and tell their favorite Rickey stories.

Like the time. . . .

Rickey was pulled over by a police officer after a night game in San Diego for speeding with his lights off. As the officer approached the car, Rickey, without saying a word, lowered his window only about an inch, just far enough to stick out two fingers holding a $100 bill. (The officer let him and his money go.)

Or the time. . . .

Rickey was asked if he owned the Garth Brooks album that has the song *Friends in Low Places*. "Rickey doesn't have albums," he answered. "Rickey has CDs."

Or the time someone asked him what he thought about speculation that as many as 50% of big leaguers used steroids. "Well, I'm not," he said. "So that's 49 [percent] right there."

Or the time he developed frostbite in August. The Blue Jays used a newfangled ice treatment on his ankle. "What is Rickey, a guinea pig?" he asked.

Or the time he bragged that his Manhattan apartment had such a great view he could see "the Entire State Building."

Or the time he settled a feud with Yankees manager Lou Piniella, saying, "Let bye-byes be bye-byes."

Until that Day he waits and wonders. He thinks about winter ball after this and maybe Japan if the majors still haven't called. He is one of the treasures of the game, and he is left behind in its basement—

Sinatra playing the Catskills, Olivier doing summer stock, Toscanini at the Elks band shell.

"If they say your skill's gone and you can't do nothing, then I can see it's time, but I ain't had a club yet that says that," Henderson says. "And that's the shame. As long as I've been playing the game, what I accomplished . . . for me to be in this situation, really, it's a shame to major league baseball.

"But that's life. And I digest it. Because I believe the Good Lord has put me here for something. And He never tells me that road I'm going to put you on is always going to be gravy."

A road without gravy is no sort of place for this kind of story to end. And so, at 44, ever independent, the legend goes on.

Postscript: Rickey was still playing independent ball, in San Diego, in 2005. It is hard to find anyone who loves playing the game and loves life more than he does. When we were done talking in that spartan Newark Bears clubhouse, Rickey surprised me with something no player ever did before or since: He gave me a big hug.

Hitting Bottom

*Even great hitters aren't immune to horrific slumps. How does
a player like Derek Jeter suddenly lose his way at the plate—
and how does he find his way back?*

A BATTING SLUMP IS BASEBALL'S VERSION OF THE
common cold. Sooner or later every hitter gets one, it
can keep him up at night, and there is no known cure,
though that does not prevent everyone and his doorman from passing on homemade remedies and get-well wishes. Derek
Jeter of the Yankees came down with a whopper of a case in April—he
was 0 for 32 at its head-throbbing worst—that was so bad that he
couldn't leave his Manhattan apartment without being reminded of it.

"The doorman would tell me, 'Tonight's the night! I've got a feeling
this is it!' " Jeter says. "You're trying not to think about it, yet everywhere you go, you're constantly reminded of it. It wasn't so much people giving me advice as it was people saying, 'We're pulling for you.'
It's everywhere you turn—people on the street, the questions from the
media every day."

This season has produced even more proof that no one is immune.
Career .300 hitters Jeter, Chipper Jones of the Braves and Jose Vidro

of the Expos—who ranked seventh, 12th and 18th, respectively, in career batting average among active players entering this season—all were hitting worse than .250 at week's end. Fellow perennial All-Stars Carlos Delgado of the Blue Jays (.227), Bret Boone of the Mariners (.231) and Shawn Green of the Dodgers (.229) were similarly stricken. Welcome to the cold-and-flew-out-weakly-to-leftfield season.

"These guys are all proven hitters, and they're not old, either," Brewers general manager Doug Melvin says. "I think [at the end of the season] the numbers will be there. But some are digging such a big hole that they won't be able to put up the big numbers they have in the past."

Jones, for instance, had only two doubles and 13 RBIs at week's end, jeopardizing his streaks of five years with 30 doubles and eight years with 100 RBIs. Delgado had eight homers and 32 RBIs, and was facing an uphill climb to continue his streak of six consecutive seasons with at least 33 homers and 102 RBIs.

For young hitters, a slump can infect an entire year, which is what happened last season to the Phillies' Pat Burrell (.209), the Reds' Adam Dunn (.215) and the White Sox' Paul Konerko (.234). Jeter, however, showed last week how stars with long track records of success can get well soon. Entering the Yankees' May 26 game against the Orioles, Jeter, who hit .324 in 2003, was batting .189 after 190 at bats. Suddenly, facing the Orioles and the Devil Rays, he pounded out 11 hits in his next 24 at bats, raising his average 31 points in five days, to .220. To hit .300 for the season—assuming he maintained his rate of at bats—Jeter would need to hit .335 the rest of the way, not an unreasonable task for a career .317 hitter.

"I didn't see how people could be writing my obituary after one month," Jeter said last Saturday before hitting safely in his sixth straight game. "I knew all along there was a lot of the season left to play, so I wasn't concerned. It's frustrating when you're not getting your hits. I'm not going to lie to you about that. But you don't spend time thinking about what's already happened. You can't change it. You just look forward to the next game, especially when you know there are about 120 left."

Not coincidentally, the Yankees also began to look more like themselves last week, putting together their highest-scoring (61 runs) six-game winning streak in 46 years. "We feed off his energy, without a doubt," Yankees third baseman Alex Rodriguez says of Jeter. "He's a hitting machine. A lot of good things happen when he gets going. He's the heartbeat of this team."

The slump—or at least its derivation in the English language— traces from the appropriately cold climes of Scandinavia and the Norwegian verb *slumpa* ("to fall"). In America a *slumpa* can take on many forms, though none as vivid as the one that falls at the beginning or end of a season and strikes a star player. Combine those elements, and you get historic droughts at the plate, such as the 0 for 21 suffered in the 1952 World Series by the Dodgers' Gil Hodges, whose slump the following season prompted Brooklyn priests to entreat their parishioners to pray for him; the 5-for-25 performance by the Red Sox' Ted Williams in the 1946 World Series, which turned out to be his only postseason appearance; and Jeter's 0-for-32 run, which drew much more attention than the virtually simultaneous 0-for-37 skid by the Devil Rays' José Cruz Jr., a lifetime .251 hitter.

Bob Uecker, the former backup catcher, once said, "I had slumps that lasted into the winter." But with players such as Uecker, a career .200 hitter, it's hard to tell when a slump begins and ends. Likewise, pitcher Bob Buhl owns the worst 0-fer in major league history—0 for 88 over two seasons—but he was a career .089 hitter.

Dodgers infielder Robin Ventura went 0 for 41 as a rookie with the White Sox in 1990. Hall of Fame shortstop Luis Aparicio once endured an 0-for-44 slump. For position players, however, the sultan of slump is Bill Bergen, a Brooklyn catcher who went 0 for 46 in 1909 on his way to becoming the worst hitter of all time (minimum 1,000 at bats), with a .170 batting average over 11 seasons. That an accomplished hitter such as Jeter could look like Bergen is testament to the humbling nature of baseball.

"Slumps are powerful things," says Rodriguez, who endured an 0-for-21 stretch with the Rangers in 2002. "Sometimes players are going so badly that, if they hit a pop-up near the third base stands, they root for the ball to stay in play so the third baseman can catch it, just so they don't strike out again. I've heard of guys telling the catcher, 'Just tell me what pitch is coming because there's no way I'm getting a hit right now and I don't want to punch out again. Just let me put one ball in play.' "

Says Yankees DH Jason Giambi, "There are times you're going so bad you swing at the first pitch just so you don't get to another two-strike count, because you know you'll strike out. So you'll take your ground ball to second base and get out of there thinking, O.K., at least I made contact. That's *something*."

Slumps can be all-consuming, affecting a hitter's mood, appetite and behavior. Former Yankees outfielder Paul O'Neill says that when he was in a slump, it "never really left me. It was what I thought about as I went to bed and the first thing when I got up in the morning."

Says Devil Rays manager Lou Piniella, a former player notorious for his intensity, "When you're in a slump, thank God for the invention of the watercooler."

Slumps would awaken Piniella, a lifetime .291 hitter, in the middle of the night and, eventually, would rouse his wife too. Anita Piniella would hear yelling coming from downstairs and fear a burglar had entered the house. Instead she would find her frustrated husband swinging a bat in front of a mirror, talking to himself.

Hitting is an art with karmic overtones. Cold streaks are charged by the static of many disjointed thoughts. Hot streaks are marked by the absence of thought, or as the great philosopher Yogi Berra once said, "How the hell are you going to think and hit at the same time?"

Like an artist visited by a muse, the hitter has an elusive relationship with the baseball goddess known as *Feel*. Explains Yankees centerfielder Bernie Williams, "You get the feeling that they can't get you out. It's something that seems to come from your inner being. You can't wait for your next at bat. It's like riding a wave, being right in the middle of a 50-foot swell and riding it all the way in to shore, and then you paddle back out and do it as long as you can. And then [the feeling's] gone."

The loss of that feeling, however, can have practical explanations. As Jones says, "When I'm not hitting, 95 percent of the time it's something mechanical. So the key is to figure out what the mechanical flaw is. You get in the cage and try to work yourself out of it. The other five percent of the time, it's mental. Every time you go to the plate, you feel like they've got 12 people out on the field, there are no holes, and you're not going to get any hits."

Jeter's slump had mental *and* physical origins. As he pressed to get off to a good start, Jeter admits, his anxiety had him "jumping at the ball." Rather than waiting for a pitch to get to him, especially an outside pitch, Jeter would lean forward in his haste to hit it, jerking his head instead of keeping it steady. He was particularly hard-pressed to hit fastballs, which he previously had feasted on. Last year, for instance, he batted .330 against fastballs from righthanders on the outer third of the plate, according to the scouting service Inside Edge. In his first 43 games this year, however, Jeter was hitless in 16 at bats decided by those same pitches. He struggled when hitting with two strikes (.127, versus .235 in 2003) even when he was ahead in the count (.250, versus .459). Furthermore, his "well-hit average"—Inside Edge's category for hard-hit balls, regardless of whether they end up as base hits—dropped from .316 to .245.

"You're trying so hard to get hits instead of just hitting the ball," Jeter says. "But you can't guide the ball. Your eyes are the key. When your head moves, your eyes move, and you don't see the pitch as long. That's why when you're going good, the ball looks slower. You see it longer. Now I'm staying back, letting the ball get to me instead of trying to go out and get the ball."

Moreover, Jeter sometimes caught himself guessing the type and location of the next pitch. "I'm no good when I look for pitches," he says, "because if I look for something [and it comes close to that location], I'll swing no matter what. Like if I'm looking inside, the pitch could be about to hit me and I'll still swing at it."

Before his 0-for-32 slide, Jeter had never gone more than 18 at bats without a hit. When he finally ended the drought with a leadoff home run against Barry Zito of the A's on April 29, he said after the game, "It's like a bad dream is over." He added, "I wouldn't wish it on anybody." Not long thereafter, he fell into a 1-for-26 funk.

"[It] never really changed much," Giambi said about Jeter's demeanor, "and that's hard to do when it seems like nothing is going right. I remember in Boston he hit a couple of line drives to right-field that would have been hits except Kevin Millar was playing a Little League rightfield. When you're going bad, guys make plays on you that they're not supposed to make."

Says Jeter, "I never lose my confidence. It doesn't mean I'm going to get hits, but I have my confidence all the time."

According to New York manager Joe Torre, two of Jeter's three hits—flared doubles—in his breakout game against Baltimore were typical slump breakers. "All of a sudden you realize you don't have to hit it on the screws to get a hit," says Torre, a lifetime .297 hitter. Jeter added three hits in each of the next two games, after which Torre observed, "He looks very confident up there now, and he's got an edge to him. His body language says, 'I know you're going to challenge me,' and he's up for it."

Says Piniella, who watched the Yankees shortstop go 5 for 15 last weekend against his Devil Rays, "Jeter can run, he hits the ball to all fields, and he can even bunt, so for a player like him to be in a prolonged slump is hard to imagine. But [it happens, and] it's humbling because you can't get away from it. It's on the talk shows, it's in the newspapers, it's on TV, and pretty soon it's larger than life. That's when I tell my guys, 'Look, your wife is still going to be there when you get home, your dog will still like you, and you'll still drive the same car. Just relax and hit the ball.' "

One AL scout says, "Slumps become worse when guys try to do too much. Boone is an example. He's trying to carry the club, and he's expanding his strike zone. He's swinging harder than I've ever seen him. He's not recognizing sliders away—he's just hacking up there. He's lost at the plate right now."

Stars such as Jeter, Delgado, Jones, Vidro, Boone and Green still have more than two thirds of the season left to approach their typical numbers. In 1941, for instance, Joe DiMaggio had been mired in one of the worst slumps of his career—a 20-game stretch over April and May in which he hit .184—when on May 15 he singled off White Sox lefthander Eddie Smith in the first inning. It was the start of his 56-game hitting streak, and he finished the year batting .357.

"People kept asking me if I was worried about Derek," Yankees G.M. Brian Cashman says. "My answer was always the same: No. Because if you look at late May every year, there are a couple of stars struggling to get out of the gate. And by the end of the year their numbers are there regardless. They've proven themselves over time, so you don't worry. It just happened to be Derek's turn this year. Next year? It'll be somebody else's turn."

Postscript: Jeter started crushing the baseball as soon as I began reporting this story. Most players suffer through painful stretches during which their confidence is shaken, but Jeter is one of the rare players I've met— Roger Clemens is another—who never succumbs to such doubts. Jeter finished that 2004 season with a .292 batting average.

Heady Stuff

*As remarkable as it is to win 300 games, Greg Maddux's real feat
has been to thrive as a finesse pitcher in a power era*

T HE MASTER LEARNED TO PITCH WITH A VOICE IN HIS EAR.
It was the voice of a man who would be dead inside of
two years. That would be enough time though—this
brief convergence of skinny kid and wise old muse—to
engender what may be the most sophisticated evolution of the art of
pitching ever witnessed.

"First pitch, fastball in," the voice said.

Greg Maddux was 15 years old when he heard that. The batter was
Marty Barrett, a 23-year-old minor leaguer headed for a 10-year career
in the bigs. The voice belonged to Ralph Medar, a former scout who assembled pickup baseball games every Sunday at nine in the morning
in Maddux's hometown of Las Vegas. The good ballplayers somehow
always knew about the games, the same way basketball players know
when and on which court to find the best neighborhood run. See you at
Medar's, they'd say. Medar would stand behind the pitchers and give
instruction. Maddux listened to the voice. The kid threw a fastball in.

Barrett pounced on it, sending a double screaming out to leftfield.

The next inning Barrett stepped in again. (The games almost never drew enough players for nine to a side.)

"First pitch, breaking ball," came the voice.

The kid broke a decent curve over the plate. The pro took it for a strike.

"O.K. Now, fastball in."

Maddux threw it. This time the barrel of Barrett's bat was not so quick. He connected, only not as solidly. The same pitch, but this time cleverly set up by slow stuff, produced a lazy fly ball to centerfield.

Oh, O.K., the kid said to himself. Now I get it.

VAN GOGH had the south of France, Hemingway the battlefields and bullrings of Europe. Maddux had Medar's. The genius of the 22nd, and perhaps last, 300-game winner in the major leagues was inspired by the old man's voice. "Kid," the sage said, "you throw hard enough to get drafted. But movement is more important than velocity."

"I believed it," says Maddux, now 38 years old and in his 19th big league season. "I don't know why. I just did."

How do you explain it? The kid heard it, and he believed it, the way a seminarian hears with clarity the call of God in a noisy, profane world. He was born to this calling. The other kids, muscles growing and hormones flowing, wanted to throw baseballs through brick walls, and the other coaches kept imploring them, "Throw strikes!" But the old man would say, "Bounce a curveball in the dirt here," and the kid would understand the intended subterfuge. It didn't hurt, either, that when the kid threw a baseball with his right index and middle fingers atop the seams, the ball darted and sank with preternatural movement.

"God gave it to him, I guess," says Cubs bench coach Dick Pole, who worked with Maddux as far back as 1987, when the Cubs righthander was in his first stint with the team. "It's always moved like that."

Maddux is sitting in the visitors' dugout at Miller Park in Milwaukee the day after career victory 299, a 7–1 win over the Brewers in which he'd given up four hits and one run in six innings. Only three 300-game winners have ever had better control, as measured by walks per nine innings, than Maddux (1.90): Cy Young (1.49), Christy Mathewson (1.59) and Grover Cleveland Alexander (1.65). All of them were done by 1930. Only two pitchers, Lefty Grove and Walter Johnson, ever won this many games with a relative ERA (that is, ERA measured against his contemporaries') better than Maddux's 28.2% differential. Grove's ERA was 33.2% better than his peers', and Johnson's was 30.8% better. Both of those pitchers were finished by 1941. Maddux is, to most of us, unlike anyone else we've ever seen.

Once Maddux nails down number 300, only he and Roger Clemens will have survived maple bats, billiard-hard baseballs, steroid-juiced lineups, a construction boom of hitter-friendly ballparks and a laser-guided tightening of the strike zone—in short, the greatest extended run of slugging the game has known—to reach that milestone. Clemens did so with the sledgehammer of a mid-to upper-90s fastball. Maddux has needed stealth and intellect. A beautiful mind, but with a killer changeup.

So expertly has Maddux mastered the subtleties of pitching that he has become an iconic presence. What Ripken is to durability and Ruth is to power, Maddux is to finesse, forever the measuring stick for the few who might follow in his path. "It's amazing," Pole says of the Maddux-Medar relationship, "to think what came about when those two people collided. Right time, right place."

Maddux still hears the voice of the old man when he pitches, only the voice long ago became so familiar that it now sounds the same as his own. These are the commandments of pitching that he hears:

1) Make the balls look like strikes and the strikes look like balls.

2) Movement and location trump velocity every time.

3) When you're in trouble, think softer. Don't throw harder; locate better.

4) Have fun.

His physical gifts fading, Maddux must work harder than ever to obey those commandments. All except the last one, anyway.

MADDUX'S OLDER brother Mike, now the pitching coach for the Brewers, pitched with modest success for 15 seasons, the last in 2000. "I remember my brother telling me in his last year or two, 'You don't know how good I have to pitch just to get out of an inning,' " Greg says. "I'm thinking, What's he talking about? I'm starting to understand more and more what he meant by that."

At his very best, Maddux won four consecutive Cy Young Awards (1992 to '95) and had the lowest ERA (2.14) in any six-year span since World War II (1992 to '97), lower than the sublime six-year prime of Sandy Koufax (2.19) in a pitcher's era. Such was Maddux's sleight of hand with a baseball that future Hall of Fame third baseman Wade Boggs called him "the David Copperfield of pitchers" after he shut out the Yankees over eight innings in Game 2 of the 1996 World Series.

Maddux, however, never did get enough credit for just how nasty his stuff was. He threw his fastball 90 or 91 mph with the sudden movement of a jackrabbit flushed from the brush. The ball naturally sank and ran away from lefthanders. A slight twist of the wrist, and it cut toward their hands. "I pulled out tapes from 10 years ago, back when I was throwing up those really good years," Maddux says. "I made more mistakes then than I do now! It's just that I got away with them. My movement was better because my velocity was better."

Maddux typically throws at about 85 mph now. "I may not have the same success as I did earlier when I was doing it at faster speeds, but I can still have success," he says. "My bad games may be worse, though. I think I have to pitch better now than 10 years ago. I have to locate better because my stuff is not as good. It's still good enough to win, but not good enough to make mistakes. I don't throw hard enough for the ball to break as much as it used to."

Brewers outfielder Geoff Jenkins says of Maddux, "He still keeps the ball down in the zone. I try to be aggressive against him and attack early in the count because the deeper you get in the count against him the more he seems to mess with you and outthink you. It just seems like he hits his spots and all of a sudden it's the end of the night and you have a comfortable 0-fer."

The more Maddux's physical skills decline, the deeper he must tap his mental well to stay sharp—and at that he is unrivaled. He is, for instance, a voracious observer. He often can tell what a hitter is thinking by where he stands in the batter's box, how he takes practice swings, how he fouls off a pitch or takes a pitch. "It's like kids at school—some pay more attention than others," Pole says. "He's on a different level from everybody else when it comes to attention."

Says Mets lefthander Tom Glavine, Maddux's rotation mate with the Braves for 10 years, "That's the biggest part of what sets him apart. It helped me. I never really paid attention to any of that stuff until Greg came to Atlanta [in 1993]. It opened up a whole new world I had never seen before. He was way ahead of everybody else in that regard."

Once while seated in the Braves' dugout as third baseman Jose Hernandez batted for the Dodgers, Maddux blurted out, "Watch this. The first base coach may be going to the hospital." On the next pitch Hernandez drilled a line drive off the chest of the first base coach.

Another time Atlanta manager Bobby Cox visited Maddux on the mound with runners on second and third and two outs. Cox suggested an intentional walk.

"Don't worry," said Maddux, who then spelled out to Cox the sequence of his next three pitches: "And on the last pitch I'm going to get him to pop up foul to third base." Maddux proceeded to escape the jam on his third pitch—getting a pop-up to third base that was a foot or two from being foul.

Cubs ace Mark Prior, a 23-year-old power pitcher, says he likes to sit next to Maddux in the dugout on days when neither is pitching. "He's helped me tremendously," Prior says. "I've always gone harder whenever I've been in trouble. He's got me thinking, Go softer when I'm in trouble. I never thought that way before, and it's helped me develop confidence in my changeup. As we watch games, he'll talk about what I might throw in certain situations."

Maddux prefers to downplay his reputation as a mound savant. He has told teammates, "People think I'm smart? You know what makes you smart? Locate that fastball down and away. That makes you smart.

"I don't surprise anybody with what I throw anymore," Maddux says. "You just have to mix your pitches up. And even if the hitter is guessing right, if you locate it, you won't get hurt. You might give up a single or a double, but it's not the end of the world. Yeah, the hitters are stronger, the balls are harder, some parks are smaller and the strike zone's smaller. Still, for me, it's all about movement and location. If you have those, you're going to have success."

Episodes of Maddux's clairvoyance, however, still abound. Last week before his start in Milwaukee, he shouted to Pole in the clubhouse, "Hey, what's Brady Clark hitting with runners in scoring position?"

"How the hell do I know?" Pole replied.

"Well, find out for me, will you?" Maddux said.

Pole tracked down and passed along the information: The outfielder was hitting .226 with runners in scoring position. That night Maddux pitched around slugging first baseman Lyle Overbay with a runner on second and Clark on deck, then whiffed Clark on a change-up. "He knew which hitter he wanted to face if that very situation came up," Cubs lefthander Kent Mercker said afterward. "He doesn't miss anything."

Maddux lives for such moments, like a chess grandmaster who has specific killer moves cataloged in his head and finds utter joy when the board suddenly presents the perfect opening to employ one. Three hundred wins? It is just a number to him right now. That is not why he pitches. He pitches for the intellectual and physical challenges, the small moments that go unseen by most.

Asked to explain the best part of pitching, Maddux says, "I enjoy watching the other guys, talking on Monday [about a game plan] and trying to do it on Tuesday. Guys who just show up on Tuesday and pitch, I don't understand that.

"The best part? The best part is knowing on Monday you're going to do something and then actually doing it on Tuesday. You know what? It might be just a strike. It might be a foul ball, [telling yourself,] If I throw this guy this pitch, he's going to hit it foul right over there. And then to go out there and do it, that's pretty cool. To me, that's fun.

"You're only talking about 10 pitches a game where that may happen. The other 80 or 90 pitches you're trusting what you see and what you feel. It's still just fun playing the game."

It's still so much fun that he cannot yet imagine it ending. "Who knows?" he says, when asked how long he will pitch. "As long as I can do it. I don't want to embarrass myself, by any means. But I'd rather pitch bad than not pitch at all."

"THERE'S ONE thing I've learned about Greg Maddux," Cubs manager Dusty Baker says. "He shags better than anybody I've ever seen. I don't see him out there running foul poles, but I see him out there getting his running in shagging."

It's not uncommon for a pitcher, especially a veteran, to loathe workouts, but two or three times on his off days between starts Maddux chases fly balls during batting practice like an eager teenager hauled out of the stands. "I like to stay in shape, baseball shape, by playing baseball," Maddux says. "And it's fun. It's a lot more fun running around the outfield pretending you're Andruw Jones than running on a treadmill watching *Jerry Springer* reruns. To me, even the four days in between starts are fun."

Maddux makes certain that every throw he makes, even when shagging flies, is delivered from the same arm angle as one of his pitches, and never off-balance. He lifts light weights for his arm and shoulders from December through April, then, he says simply, "I trust my arm." At week's end he had thrown 4,110⅓ innings in his career and had never been placed on the disabled list with an arm injury of any sort.

There are model Rockets all around baseball, tall power pitchers in the mold of Clemens with here-it-comes fastballs. The next Maddux, however, may be a long time coming. "Now," says Maddux, who stands six feet tall and weighs 185 pounds, "if you don't throw 95, you're a wimp. If you're not 6' 4" with a 90-plus fastball, you'll never get drafted."

Says Glavine, "It's such a game of power pitching and power hitting now. Every pitcher throws flat-out gas with maximum effort. I don't know if we'll ever see anyone like Greg."

Here is the next Maddux. He is throwing a baseball against a dugout fence at Miller Park. Chase Maddux, Greg's son, is seven years old. He throws a pitch submarine-style. "Like the guy from Oakland," he says, referring to reliever Chad Bradford.

"Stay on top, kid. Stay on top," Greg says.

The father raises his right arm in a classic L shape, his elbow slightly above the height of his shoulder. "Look," he says. "Like this."

That voice is a familiar one. Medar, who died in 1983 at age 69, never lived to see one of Maddux's 300 wins, never lived even to see him selected by the Cubs in the second round of the 1984 draft.

Chase winds up and, with a still head and properly raised elbow, lets fly a perfect strike.

"That's better," the sage says. "That's much better."

Postscript: I've never known a smarter ballplayer than Maddux—I learn something about baseball during every conversation with him. His humility, however, is just as impressive as his genius. His achievements have exceeded his own expectations—and just about everyone else's. And even as he was racking up Cy Young awards, he would marvel at that recognition, as if he were a schoolkid who'd just received extra credit.

Five Outs
Away

In the 2003 playoffs the Cubs and Red Sox each came that close *to the World Series, only to see it all blow up in eerily similar—and all-too-familiar—fashion*

I N THE CAVITY OF THE CATHEDRAL, HISTORY SOUNDS LIKE A freight train rumbling through a concrete tunnel. Roger Clemens recognized the rumble. Clemens, his retirement plans not yet amended, had spent the last seven innings of Game 7 of the 2003 American League Championship Series in the home clubhouse at Yankee Stadium, nervously wondering if his career and the Yankees' season were about to be extinguished by the Red Sox. It was 12:16 a.m. on Oct. 17 when he heard the answer from above.

The Yankees clubhouse is carved out among the catacombs and narrow hallways beneath the first base stands. When a moment of excitement— such as the solid thwack of a Louisville Slugger upon a benign knuckleball— brings the fans to their feet, the clatter of thousands of blue plastic seat bottoms snapping upright reverberates through the clubhouse below.

The noise sent Clemens to his feet and then to the door and finally toward the ramp to the field as the pennant-winning home run by Aaron Boone was floating into the leftfield seats.

"I knew that sound," Clemens would later say.

This kind of history sounded familiar. The home run ensured that Boston's 1918 World Series championship would remain its most recent, a streak of futility so long and chock-full of so many absurd near misses that it feels organic and as immutable as a law of nature. Boston is 0 for 85 since Babe Ruth pitched them to the '18 title, including four seasons that ended with defeats in Game 7 of the World Series.

Red Sox seasons die the deaths of spaghetti western cowboys: never graceful, but rather writhing, painful and melodramatic. This ending, at the hands of Boone and the Yankees, was true to form. Five outs from the World Series with a three-run lead, no one on base and their best starting pitcher on the mound, the Red Sox lost the lead without ever using their bullpen. Nobody but the Sox could lose a game so spectacularly.

Nobody, that is, except the Chicago Cubs, Boston's fraternal twin in despair.

The Cubs' institutional losing dates to 1908, when they last won the World Series. After that they are 0 for 96. Since 1945 they have played six games in which a victory would have sent them to the Series—and lost all of them. That agony includes the preposterous Game 6 of the 2003 National League Championship Series against the Marlins. Like the Red Sox, the Cubs were five outs away from the World Series with a three-run lead, no one on base and their best starting pitcher on the mound.

There have been 1,077 postseason games in the history of baseball. In only 13 of them did a team lose after it led by at least three runs with no more than five outs to go. But only twice did the losing team blow a lead that big and that late while leaving its starting pitcher in the game: the Cubs in Game 6 with Mark Prior and, two nights later, the Red Sox in Game 7 with Pedro Martinez. Two losses with matching DNA. Two out of 1,077. A .2% match. Crazy.

How the Cubs and the Red Sox invented a new way to lose within 48 hours last October is, prosaically, the story of how fatigue rendered each team's ace incapable of holding a lead. Revisiting the two games with the principal figures involved also reveals that this is a story of how baseball can take on religious properties, when belief in the unseen is as good an explanation as any.

MARK PRIOR threw a 94-mph fastball with his 99th pitch, and Marlins pinch hitter Mike Mordecai lifted it into leftfield, where it settled into Moises Alou's glove. Five outs to go.

Cubs president and CEO Andy MacPhail, sitting in a mezzanine box, began rehearsing in his head what he would say to the national television audience upon being presented with the NL championship trophy. He reminded himself that he would need to find his tie in order to look proper for such a moment.

Prior, the Cubs' ace righthander, had retired eight straight hitters while working on a three-hit shutout. Chicago led 3–0.

Waveland Avenue felt like Times Square on New Year's Eve, though a crowd waiting for a ball to drop would prove to be a cruelly prophetic image. About 3,000 people packed shoulder to shoulder in the autumnal chill on the famous street that runs parallel to the leftfield wall at Wrigley Field, the little jewel box of a ballpark that was quaking with excitement. The Cubs were going to the World Series, something no one under the age of 58 had ever witnessed, including Hillary Clinton, who once said, "Being a Cubs fan prepares you for life—and Washington."

Chicago police had decided before the game that the Wrigleyville streets would be given over to 90 minutes of celebration immediately after the game, as long as there were—hey, hey—no open containers. The crowd was ready. Everyone thought Prior looked great. Everyone thought Prior looked strong.

Everyone, that is, except Prior.

"Most times when I pitch," he says, "I feel like in the second, third, fourth innings I'm just getting warmed up. If things go according to plan, I get a little boost after that in the middle innings, and I feel stronger at the end of the game.

"This time I didn't feel that. I felt like I had the same energy level the whole time. I never got that second wind."

Prior, 23, was drafted by the Cubs out of USC in 2001 and won 18 games for Chicago last season. This night, however, would be his official Cubs baptism.

The Cubs are a Franciscan franchise. For core virtues they embrace humility (they welcome opponents to "the friendly confines" of Wrigley), poverty (as it relates to winning) and love of nature (especially sunshine, grass, ivy and choice hops and barley). The Cubs may not have invented the concept of lovable losers, but they certainly have perfected it.

"I was excited to be drafted by the Cubs," Prior says. "But I got called up in a year we lost 95 games, and you start hearing all the time about the negatives. It gets drilled into you. Even while we were winning last year, people were bringing up 1908 or 1984 or 1969 over and over again. It wears on you."

The Cubs' first-year manager, Dusty Baker, had left a successful 10-year run in San Francisco to change the culture in Chicago. He was the embodiment of cool, grooving to Coltrane or Miles Davis in his tiny office while munching on a toothpick and speaking a language of optimism that sounded Greek to the Windy City. Winning baseball seasons in Chicago were treated like mild winters, totally unexpected flukes that surely meant hell to pay the next year. "It was probably my most difficult year managing," Baker says. "Toward the end of the year I was psychologically worn out. I thought at the end of the year we were pretty close to getting the mind-set turned around."

Pretty close. Five outs from the World Series, and one strike away from whiffing centerfielder Juan Pierre, Prior fired a 96 mph fastball. Pierre swatted the pitch hard, just inside the leftfield line, for a double. Alou fielded the ball in foul ground, near the brick wall of the stands. A few feet away, in the front row of those stands, a 26-year-old man raised in the religion of the Cubs—in his lifetime the team had accrued only seven winning seasons, none consecutively—wished hard for those five outs.

The man looked like a *Sibley Guide* version of a Cubs fan, if the bird experts had ever expanded their artistry into the domain of sports spectators. Bespectacled, he wore a Cubs cap with earphones atop it, listening to the broadcast of the game. Over a green turtleneck he wore a black sweatshirt emblazoned with RENEGADES, the name of the youth baseball team he helped coach. He was unaware that the quiet life he knew was about to end.

MARTINEZ THREW a 93 mph fastball with his 107th pitch, and Yankees first baseman Nick Johnson lifted it to shortstop, where it settled into Nomar Garciaparra's glove. Five outs to go.

The Red Sox held a 5–2 lead. Martinez was still throwing hard. He knew, however, that the radar gun was an inadequate indicator of how he was feeling. "Even when I'm fatigued, I can still throw hard," he says. "My arm speed may be there, but location is where I suffer, and that's because my arm angle drops. I throw three quarters, yes, but it's three-quarters steady. If I start to get tired, my arm drops a little more, and that causes the ball to stay flat over the plate. My velocity doesn't change, but I can't spot the ball as well when I'm tired. That's what happened."

Martinez had not slept well on the eve of Game 7. He was anxious, sure, but his body clock was off: He'd flown from Boston to Tampa (where the Red Sox had ended the regular season) to Oakland (where they had opened the playoffs) to Boston to Oakland to New York to Boston to New York in the previous 20 days.

The fallout from Game 3 had also taken its toll on Martinez. That epic, six days earlier at Fenway Park, had been the sizzling prelude to Game 7. New York had knocked Martinez around for four runs on six hits before the righthander was even out of the fourth inning. So emboldened were the Yankees by the hard swings they took at Martinez that they yelled at him from the dugout, "You've got nothing!"

The fourth inning of Game 3 began with a walk to Jorge Posada, followed by a single by Johnson and a double by Hideki Matsui. Martinez, working with a base open, had seen enough. With his next pitch he whistled a fastball behind the head of Karim Garcia. The pitch hit a stunned Garcia in the back.

"I don't think Pedro was trying to hurt him," says John Burkett, a Red Sox righthander since retired. "He was trying to send a message. It was, F--- this, I've got to put a scare into somebody. And he did." (Martinez claimed the pitch simply got away.)

In the bottom of the fourth inning that day, Red Sox leftfielder Manny Ramirez caused both benches to empty when, bat in hand, he glowered at Clemens after a pitch that was nowhere close to hitting him. Don Zimmer, the portly 72-year-old Yankees bench coach, charged across the field at Martinez. "He reached for my right arm," Martinez says. "I thought, Is he going to pull it? Is he trying to hurt me? I tossed him down."

Zimmer fell awkwardly to the ground in front of the Red Sox dugout. He would apologize through tears the next day for his actions, but that did not stop New York City mayor Michael Bloomberg from suggesting that Martinez would be arrested if he had acted that way in New York.

So it should have come as no surprise when, ahead 4–1 after a rather easy sixth inning in Game 7, Martinez sat next to assistant trainer Chris Correnti and said, "Chris, I'm a little fatigued."

The Red Sox are a Calvinistic franchise. Fathers have passed to their sons, who have passed to their sons, a doctrine of predestination. Only by the grace of God, and not by a wicked starting rotation, can the Red Sox ever win a World Series again. The Calvinists' God, however, also marks certain souls for damnation. So it is that Fenway Park in the late innings of a close game can be churchlike in its silence. The faithful can only wait for God to do His work, knowing that it includes more damnation.

"I want to win a World Series with Boston more than anything else," Martinez says. "I'd rather win one with Boston than three or four with any other team. I've had so many people say to me they pray to God they don't die before the Red Sox win the World Series. But after that, they're satisfied, they can die."

The Yankees made Martinez exert himself in the seventh. Jason Giambi hit his second homer of the night to cut the lead to 4–2. Enrique Wilson and Garcia followed with singles. Martinez gamely fanned Alfonso Soriano, though it took a grueling six-pitch at bat to do so. He had thrown 100 pitches. As he walked off the mound, Martinez gave thanks to God by pointing to the sky, his usual coda to a full night's work.

In the far end of the dugout Garciaparra threw his arms around Martinez, a gesture of appreciation for his effort. At the other end of the dugout pitching coach Dave Wallace pulled his pitching log notebook from his pocket, scratched out Martinez's name and, with the lefthanded Johnson due up next inning, wrote in the name of lefthanded reliever Alan Embree.

"After the seventh," Martinez says, "Chris and Wallace told me that was pretty much it. They were going to talk to Grady [Little, the Boston manager]."

For a moment, Martinez figured he was done. And such a moment is all it takes to trigger the shutdown of a pitcher's competitive systems. Rebooting is never easy. "Your energy level drops," Martinez says. "As soon as you think you're out, even for 30 seconds, you get tired and out of focus."

Martinez was getting ready to leave for the clubhouse with Correnti when Little approached him. According to Martinez, Little told him, "I need you for one more [inning]. Can you give me one more?"

"I didn't know what to say," Martinez says. "If anything happens, everyone will say, 'Pedro wanted to come out.'

"I wasn't hurt. I was tired, yes. I never expressed anything about coming out. The only way I would say that is if I was physically hurt. The only way."

So Martinez told Little he would try to give him another inning. Little, sensing Martinez's fatigue, decided on a backup plan. "I'll tell you what, Petey," Martinez says Little told him. "Why don't you try to start the eighth. I might even send you out there just to warm up."

The implication was that Embree would be summoned at any sign of distress, even if it occurred as Martinez threw his warmup pitches.

"Help is on the way," Little told Martinez.

Says Martinez, "At that point, I thought I was batter by batter"— that he would be removed if a runner reached base.

David Ortiz gave Boston another run to spare with a homer off David Wells in the top of the eighth. Martinez, the game more secure, marched back to the mound with a 5–2 lead. "I was a little fatigued," he says. "But I did not believe I was giving up that lead. That had never happened to me. You might as well be up 10 runs instead of three—that's what it seemed like to me. We had enough to win."

Little, then 53, slightly plump, twinkle-eyed and gray-haired, speaks slowly in a soft voice with a lilting Southern accent. He was Central Casting's version of a big league manager, popular with his players. Indeed, when Red Sox CEO Larry Lucchino had introduced Little, a former Boston coach, as manager during a hastily called team meeting in spring training 19 months before, a happy Martinez had celebrated in front of Little with a raunchy jig in the nude.

As Martinez tossed his eighth-inning warmup pitches, Embree threw in the bullpen. Mike Timlin and Scott Williamson were available too. The three relievers had dominated New York throughout the series, allowing only one run in 11⅓ innings and just five hits in 36 at bats. Little would later tell club officials that, as well as the trio had pitched, he did not trust them to keep their nerves under control in such a pressurized spot. He trusted no one more than Martinez.

Little preferred a fatigued Martinez to any of the fresh relievers, and not just to start the inning. The manager would make the same decision a second, third and fourth time when trouble arose in the eighth. "It's the way we've always done it," Little says. "Ninety percent of the time when we send Pedro back out there he completes the inning. He gets out of his own jams. I'd rather have a tired Pedro Martinez out there than anybody else. He's my best."

Until Game 5 of the AL Division Series against Oakland, Martinez had been removed eight times mid-inning in his 60 starts for Little—four of them against the Yankees—and only once after the seventh. But in a subtle bit of foreshadowing, Martinez had not been able to get through the eighth inning of that game in Oakland. Little had pulled him after two hits and used four relievers to secure the final six outs to make possible the New York–Boston steel cage match.

Ten days later, with a World Series berth on the line, the manager had more confidence in Martinez. Little was unaware that the quiet life he knew was about to end.

LIKE JUAN Pierre, who had doubled on 2 and 2, Luis Castillo made Prior exert himself. He worked the count to 3 and 2. No one was throwing in the Cubs bullpen. Mets lefthander Al Leiter, working as an analyst for Fox, remarked, "[Prior] hasn't shown any reason to have any [bullpen] activity. His stuff's the same."

When Castillo fouled off the sixth pitch of the at bat, however, Cubs pitching coach Larry Rothschild stood up in the dugout, picked up the phone and ordered reliever Kyle Farnsworth to start getting loose.

Prior had averaged 113 pitches per start during the regular season, the most in baseball. Baker pushed him beyond that in the postseason. Prior had thrown 133 and 116 pitches in his two previous starts, the most recent one a 12–3 win in Game 2 in which Baker sent him back out for the eighth inning with his team leading by 10 runs. Baker explained that nothing can be taken for granted in a playoff game. Now Prior's odometer had hit 234⅔ innings for the year—a leap of

167⅔ from his combined minor and major league total as a rookie.

"My bullpen was tired," Baker says. "[Mike] Remlinger's arm was barking like a dog. [Antonio] Alfonseca wasn't throwing the way he's capable. [Mark] Guthrie wasn't throwing like he usually does. [Dave] Veres wasn't ready. And then there wasn't a spot to take Prior out. It happened real quick."

Prior could no longer finish hitters. He would throw 24 pitches in the inning and get the Marlins to swing and miss only once. He would get two strikes on three batters and retire none of them.

"That's where the second wind comes in," Prior says. "I didn't have it."

Castillo fouled off another pitch. And now it was time. The Cubs, the fans and Fox had enjoyed scads of dreamy fun—the Charlie Brown appeal of the Cubs and the Sox had prompted the other networks to scrap original programming and offer up sacrificial reruns for the ratings slaughter—but now it was time to start restoring order to the baseball universe. It was time for humility and poverty. It was time for the Cubs to be Cubs.

In a span of 12 pitches (not including intentional balls), the Marlins scored eight runs, the Cubs used three pitchers, Waveland Avenue fell as silent as a tomb and Steve Bartman, the *Sibley* Cubs fan, unintentionally created such infamy for himself that he would have to go into hiding.

The beginning of the end was a foul pop-up by Castillo. Alou drifted across the leftfield line to the padded side wall and jumped to make a backhand catch, his glove just above the green railing atop the wall. He had no doubt that he was about to catch the ball. Three fans seated in the first row, their eyes fixed not on Alou but on the falling baseball, also reached for the pop-up. It was Bartman who touched it. The ball clanked off his left hand. Alou came away with nothing but anger.

By sunrise Bartman's life would become a nightmare. News helicopters hovered over his suburban home; his phone had to be disconnected; he could not go to the consulting firm where he worked; the domain names stevebartman.com, .net and .org all had been claimed; writers for Letterman and Leno were scribbling Bartman jokes as fast as they could; people were planning their Bartman Halloween costumes; and actor Kevin James was preparing a pitch for a movie titled *Fan Interference*. A Chicago alderman, Tom Allen, told the *Chicago Sun-Times*, "He better get a new address. He ought to move to Alaska." Florida governor Jeb Bush offered Bartman asylum.

In a statement read by his brother-in-law, Bartman apologized the next day "from the bottom of this Cubs fan's broken heart." He never made a public appearance thereafter. He spoke with MacPhail and briefly maintained private correspondence with baseball commissioner Bud Selig.

"That's not what lost it for us," Baker says. "We had our chances."

And then Baker utters what passes for the Nicene Creed of the Cubs' and the Red Sox' congregations: "Maybe it was just not meant to be."

All hell broke loose. Not only did Prior walk Castillo with the next pitch, but the ball got by catcher Paul Bako, allowing Pierre to advance to third.

Rothschild visited Prior. Wrigley security officers visited Bartman. Both meetings concerned plots for emergency escapes. Only one succeeded.

Now fatigue owned Prior. He tried a breaking ball with his next pitch, to Ivan Rodriguez, but it had none of the snap or tight spin of those from the early innings. The pitch rolled more than it broke, and Rodriguez hammered it, but foul. Prior muscled a fastball past the Marlins catcher on his next pitch. Then he returned to the breaking ball at 0 and 2. Again, he did not have the arm strength to finish off the pitch with the proper snap. It hung over the plate, and this time Rodriguez drilled it fair for a run-scoring single.

"That's what sticks with me," Prior says. "The pitch to Rodriguez. I felt that I hung it. That pitch has got to be down in the dirt. If I get that pitch down maybe he grounds out. I think that's the one pitch that bothers me. Late in the game it's not your velocity that goes. It's your location."

Miguel Cabrera pounded the next pitch into the hardpan in front of home plate. Shortstop Alex Gonzalez moved to his backhand while thinking about starting a double play. The baseball bounced again on the infield dirt, only this time, propelled by topspin, it seemed to accelerate, and it was quicker than Gonzalez's hands. The ball clunked off the heel of his glove.

"The ball just ate me up," Gonzalez says. "I don't think I hurried it as much as it was the ball got on me so fast."

Even though Prior had induced a playable foul pop-up and an infield grounder, the Cubs still needed five outs. Now the score was 3–1, the bases were filled with Marlins and the air was filled with dread. Florida first baseman Derrek Lee, 3 for 25 in the series, was the hitter. The Cubs' scouting report said to pound Lee on the hands with fastballs, and the pitchers had done so successfully almost without exception. Lee's bat had not been quick enough against Chicago's steady diet of power.

Lee told himself to look for something hard inside. Prior wasn't about to deviate from the report at a time like this. Bako called for an inside fastball, and Prior unleashed a 95 mph screamer. Again, however, Prior missed slightly with his location. It was a decent pitch, just not far enough inside, especially to a hitter looking in that area. Lee smoked a line drive into leftfield, good for a game-tying, two-run double. Baker was out of the dugout to pull Prior even before the baseball was returned to the pitcher.

The bullpen could not stem this mud slide of a rally. An intentional walk, a sacrifice fly to break the tie, another intentional walk, a three-run double, a run-scoring single . . . and it was 8–3 before you could say 1908. The next night, in Game 7, the Marlins would rake Kerry Wood for seven runs ("I choked," Wood would say) in a pennant-clinching 9–6 win, a score that seemed to mock the Cubs' congregation. Year 96 of the wait had officially begun.

BACK IN New York for the final leg of the ALCS, Martinez did not leave his hotel room. He finally got some sleep before Game 7, and not long after he woke up, he ate lunch in his room. A friend brought Dominican food to him. He watched some television to kill time, then made sure to take the team bus to the ballpark. He wasn't comfortable taking a taxi. "People said I should be in jail because of the Zimmer stuff," Martinez says. "The fans were saying they were going to bring rocks and batteries. Ramon [Martinez, his brother] wanted to come, but I said, 'Stay in Boston. Anything could happen.' "

Burkett, knowing this was likely to be his final season, had toted a video camera throughout the playoffs. The tape was rolling in the clubhouse before Game 7. One of his favorite images, taken unobtrusively, is of Martinez, sitting alone, facing into his locker, his face taut with concentration and anxious anticipation.

Clemens and Martinez had combined for 476 wins, second most ever for two Game 7 starters. Clemens would be gone in the fourth, down 4–0 and leaving a no-outs and first-and-third mess. Mike Mussina, having never pitched in relief in his 400-game pro career, escaped with a strikeout and a double-play grounder.

Out by out, Martinez drew Boston closer to the finish. The Red Sox paradox is that each out brings the club as close to infamy as it does to fulfillment. "As Game 7 was going on, the drama kept building," Burkett says. "You have people on our team thinking, I don't want to be the one to make the mistake. You know, the Bill Buckner thing. I'm sure it entered people's minds."

After Johnson popped up for the first out of the eighth, Martinez jumped ahead of Derek Jeter, 0 and 2, with fastballs. Catcher Jason Varitek called for another fastball, wanting it so far out of the strike zone that he was nearly standing when he gave the target. Martinez threw to the spot, up and away, but Jeter smacked the pitch to right-field on a line. Rightfielder Trot Nixon misjudged the ball, and it sailed over his head for a double.

In the immediate aftermath of the game, one of the Red Sox coaches would grab a reporter and ask, "Was Jeter's ball catchable?" Told that it was, he sighed, crestfallen, "I thought so."

Embree still was throwing in the bullpen, but with switch-hitting Bernie Williams at bat and the lefthanded Matsui on deck, no help came for Martinez. Fox analyst Tim McCarver noted, "You get the feeling [Embree] will be the pitcher against Matsui one way or the other."

Martinez worked to a two-strike count again, this time 2 and 2, and again could not finish off the hitter. Williams drove home Jeter with a hard single off a 95-mph fastball that caught too much of the plate. As expected, Little left the dugout and walked to the mound. Unexpectedly, he returned without Martinez. Writers in the press box above the field howled, "What is he doing?"

Little had left the decision to Martinez.

"He came out, and he asked me, 'Can you pitch to Matsui?' " Martinez says. "I said, 'Yeah, of course. Let me try to get him.' He didn't ask me about anybody else. Just Matsui."

Martinez seized control of the at bat with another 0-and-2 count, getting called strikes on a fastball and a curve. Varitek called for a fastball up and in. "We've probably thrown Matsui 80 pitches up and in," Martinez says, "and he's never hit that pitch."

Again, Martinez missed slightly with his location. The pitch wasn't far enough inside. Matsui blasted a line drive that bounced into the rightfield stands for a double. The Yankees had runners at second and third. Now Martinez thought for sure he was out of the game. He had thrown 118 pitches, a number that he had reached only five times that year. But Little didn't move.

"I was actually shocked I stayed out there that long," Martinez says. "But I'm paid to do that. I belong to Boston. If they want to blow my arm out, it's their responsibility. I'm not going to go to the manager and say, 'Take me out.' I'm not going to blame Grady for leaving me out there."

Yankees closer Mariano Rivera was throwing in the bullpen. The next batter was Posada. One more duel between the arch enemies.

Posada had loathed Martinez even before the Game 3 fracas. The two had exchanged heated words that afternoon, and according to Martinez, "Posada started screaming at me in Spanish. He made a comment about my mother. Posada is Latin. He should know, if you don't want to f--- with someone, you don't say anything about their mother." Martinez had turned to Posada, pointed to his head and, he claimed, yelled to him in Spanish, "I'll remember what you said." (Posada denies making any such comment.) The Yankees interpreted Martinez's actions as threatening to hit Posada in the head with a pitch.

Martinez is a renowned bench jockey who enjoys riding opposing

players when he is not pitching. He takes particular delight in rib-
bing Posada, calling him Dumbo, in reference to the catcher's prominent ears. Posada tries so hard to get back at Martinez in the batter's
box that he typically fails. He entered last year's postseason 9 for 48
(.188) against Martinez.

Once again Martinez forged a two-strike count: He missed with a cut
fastball before throwing three straight curveballs, getting a called strike
on the first, missing with the second and getting a swinging strike on the
third. Varitek called for a fastball. And for the fourth consecutive time the
Yankees jumped on a two-strike fastball for a hit. Posada did not hit it
well—the 95-mph pitch jammed him—but he did hit it fortuitously. As
if by parachute, his little pop fly drifted onto the grass in shallow center.

Williams and Matsui scored to tie the game at 5. No one covered
second base as Posada chugged into the bag easily for a double. A
tremendous wall of sound rose up, the kind of roar that comes not
just from the throat but from the soul. "That," Posada says, "was the
loudest I have ever heard Yankee Stadium."

Suddenly, Rivera ran off the bullpen mound. The Yankees' bullpen is
a two-tiered arrangement. The throwing area is at field level, behind
the left-centerfield wall, and up a short flight of stairs is a sort of staging
area, with a small dugout and bathroom. Without a word of explanation, Rivera climbed the steps, ran into the bathroom, closed the door
and, with the joyous music and noise shaking the walls of the stadium,
starting crying. "It was just too much," Rivera says. "I needed to be
pitching, yes, but that's how awesome the moment was. I didn't want
people to see me standing there with tears coming out of my eyes."

At that moment, Little was walking out to the mound. He sig-
naled for Embree to replace Martinez. In Boston, where more people were watching than would see the New England Patriots win

the Super Bowl four months later, those who did not weep cursed.

After a combined 324 games—a record 26 against each other—the Yanks and the Sox were tied. Each team had won three games in the ALCS and scored 29 runs. The next run would be the last.

Rivera, the sixth pitcher for the Yankees, threw three scoreless innings, a courageous marathon for a closer and his longest outing in seven years. "Every inning we thought that was it for him," Burkett says, "and every inning we were like, 'Oh, s---, he's still pitching.'"

Tim Wakefield of Boston threw the last pitch, a knuckleball that Boone walloped. Boone wasn't yet to second base on his home run trot when Rivera sprinted to the pitching mound and collapsed atop it in supplication, crying once more. This time he didn't care if the whole world saw the tears falling from his eyes.

The Red Sox slunk wordlessly back to their clubhouse. Several players were crying. Once inside, Little spoke briefly, telling the players they should hold their heads high with pride. Relievers Timlin and Todd Jones also spoke, making a similar point.

Sometime later, amid the profound sadness in the Boston clubhouse, Little and Martinez shared a hug in a brief, private moment. Then the manager, a different kind of twinkle in his eye, looked at the pitcher he trusted more than anyone. "Petey," Little said, "I might not be here anymore."

"Why?" Martinez said. "It's not your fault. It's up to the players. Any other situation I get the outs, and you're a hero."

And then Martinez spoke the creed. "It wasn't meant to be."

PRIOR PITCHED in September and October last year with pain in his right Achilles tendon. After a winter of rest, it was no better in spring training. His throwing elbow throbbed too. He missed the first two months of this season. He finished 6–4 with a 4.02 ERA. When he looks back on Game 6, he likes to think the Marlins won it as much as the Cubs lost it. "They had a good team," Prior says. "What happened out in leftfield, you wish it didn't happen. But they're not getting the respect they deserve as world champions. They played extremely hard. They kept coming at us with tough at bats.

"I remember feeling upset after the series. I was upset we lost. I wasn't upset with myself. I wasn't upset with Gonzo. He saved us runs all year. We just basically didn't execute."

After Game 7 of the ALCS, Martinez spent a few days sequestered in his Boston home, playing pool, watching television and reading. "Nothing to do with baseball," he says. He finally decided to go out. He went to the Prudential Center mall in downtown Boston to begin his Christmas shopping. "As soon as I got in the Prudential, I was surrounded by people," he says. "Everyone just came up to me and said, 'We're so proud of you. It doesn't matter if we're not going to the World Series. You did all you had to do.' It really made me feel better.

"I was hoping we would make it and Chicago would make it. It would have been great for the fans."

Little, as he predicted, was fired. In an odd bit of cross-pollination, the Cubs hired him as a scout and the Sox replaced him with a former Cub, Terry Francona. The Cubs also signed Sox second baseman Todd Walker and on July 31 traded for Garciaparra. The Cubs dealt Gonzalez to Montreal, by way of Boston. Bartman? Who knows? "Personally," Baker says, "I'd like to win it all and put him at the front of the parade, to exonerate him for the rest of his life."

In front of millions of slack-jawed, rubbernecking viewers, the Cubs and the Red Sox chose the same point in baseball time to reaffirm their raison d'être: five outs to go. But to those faithful to the Cubbies and the Sawx, what defines the ball clubs better than the catastrophes themselves is what follows. The franchises exist not to fail but to try and try again. They exist for that one time when it *is* meant to be.

In 1922, four years after the Sox had won the Series and 14 after his hometown Cubs had done so, Carl Sandburg wrote a poem entitled *For You* that included this inadvertent article of faith.

> *The peace of great changes be for you.*
> *Whisper, Oh beginners in the hills.*
> *Tumble, Oh cubs—tomorrow belongs to you.*

And still they faithfully wait, Cubs and Sox alike, for tomorrow. They believe, God willing, in the life of the world to come. Amen.

Postscript: Baseball games are often decided on the unseen margins, and examining the details that made fraternal twins of these historic ballgames was one of the joys of this job. I spoke extensively with Prior and Martinez in spring training, when the wounds were fresh. The story ran in advance of the 2004 playoffs. Three weeks later, the Red Sox won the World Series.

At the End of the Curse, a Blessing

The 2004 Boston Red Sox staged the most improbable comeback in baseball history and liberated their long-suffering fans

THE CANCER WOULD HAVE KILLED MOST MEN LONG AGO, but not George Sumner. The Waltham, Mass., native had served three years aboard the USS *Arkansas* in World War II, raised six kids with a hell of a lot more love than the money that came from fixing oil burners, and watched from his favorite leather chair in front of the television—except for the handful of times he could afford to buy bleacher seats at Fenway—his Boston Red Sox, who had found a way not to win the World Series in every one of the 79 years of his life. George Sumner knew something about persistence.

The doctors and his family thought they had lost George last Christmas Day, more than two years after the diagnosis. Somehow George pulled through. And soon, though still sick and racked by the chemo, the radiation and the trips in and out of hospitals for weeks at a time, George was saying, "You know what? With Pedro and Schilling we've got a pretty good staff this year. Please let this be the year."

On the night of Oct. 13, 2004, George Sumner knew he was running out of persistence. The TV in his room at Newton-Wellesley Hospital was showing Pedro Martinez and the Red Sox losing to the Yankees in Game 2 of the American League Championship Series— this after Boston had lost Game 1 behind Curt Schilling. During commercial breaks Sumner talked with his daughter Leah about what to do with his personal possessions. Only a few days earlier his wife, Jeanne, had told him, "If the pain is too much, George, it's O.K. if you want to go."

But Leah knew how much George loved the Red Sox, saw how closely he still watched their games and understood that her father, ever quick with a smile or a joke, was up to something.

"Dad, you're waiting around to see if they go to the World Series, aren't you?" she said. "You really want to see them win it, right?"

A sparkle flickered in the sick man's eyes and a smile creased his lips.

"Don't tell your mother," he whispered.

At that moment, 30 miles away in Weymouth, Mass., Jaime Andrews stewed about the Red Sox' losing again but found some relief in knowing that he might be spared the conflict he had feared for almost nine months. His wife, Alice, was due to give birth on Oct. 27. Game 4 of the World Series was scheduled for that night. Jaime was the kind of tortured fan who could not watch when the Red Sox were protecting a lead late in the game, because of a chronic, aching certainty that his team would blow it again.

Alice was not happy that Jaime worried at all about the possible conflict between the birth and the Sox. She threatened to bar him from the delivery room if Boston was playing that night. "Pathetic," she called his obsession with his team.

"It's not my fault," Jaime would plead and fall on the DNA defense. "It was passed through generations, from my grandfather to my mother to me."

Oh, well, Jaime thought as he watched the Red Sox lose Game 2, at least now I won't have to worry about my team in the World Series when my baby is born.

Dear Red Sox:
My boyfriend is a lifelong Red Sox fan. He told me we'll get married when the Red Sox win the World Series. . . . I watched every pitch of the playoffs.
                                    —SIGNED BY A BRIDE-TO-BE

THE MOST emotionally powerful words in the English language are monosyllabic: love, hate, born, live, die, sex, kill, laugh, cry, want, need, give, take, Sawx.

The Boston Red Sox are, of course, a civic religion in New England. As grounds crew workers tended to the Fenway Park field last summer after a night game, one of them found a white plastic bottle of holy water in the outfield grass. There was a handwritten message on the side: GO SOX. The team's 2003 highlight film, punctuated by the crescendo of the walk-off home run by the Yankees' Aaron Boone in ALCS Game 7, was christened, *Still, We Believe.*

"We took the wording straight out of the Catholic canon," club president Larry Lucchino says. "It's not *We Still Believe*. Our working slogan for next year is *It's More than Baseball. It's the Red Sox.*"

Rooting for the Red Sox is, as evident daily in the obituary pages, a life's definitive calling. Every day all over New England, and sometimes beyond, death notices include age, occupation, parish and allegiance to the Sox. Charles F. Brazeau, born in North Adams, Mass., and an Army vet who was awarded a Purple Heart in World War II, lived his entire 85 years without seeing the Red Sox win a world championship, though barely so. When he passed on in Amarillo, Texas, just two days before Boston won the 2004 World Series, the *Amarillo Globe News* eulogized him as a man who "loved the Red Sox and cheap beer."

Rest in peace.

What the Red Sox mean to their faithful—and larger still, what sport at its best means to American culture—never was more evident than at precisely 11:40 EDT on the night of Oct. 27. At that moment in St. Louis, Red Sox closer Keith Foulke, upon fielding a ground ball, threw to first baseman Doug Mientkiewicz for the final out of the World Series—and the first Red Sox world championship since 1918. And then all hell didn't just break loose. It pretty much froze over.

All over New England, church bells clanged. Grown men wept. Poets whooped. Convicts cheered. Children rushed into the streets. Horns honked. Champagne corks popped. Strangers hugged.

Virginia Muise, 111, and Fred Hale, 113, smiled. Both Virginia, who kept a Red Sox cap beside her nightstand in New Hampshire, and Fred, who lived in Maine until moving to Syracuse, N.Y., at 109, were Red Sox fans who, curse be damned, were *born before Babe Ruth himself.* Virginia was the oldest person in New England. Fred was the oldest man in the world. Within three weeks after they had watched the Sox win the Series, both of them passed away.

They died happy.

Dear Red Sox:
Can you get married on the mound in, say, November at Fenway?

ON ITS most basic level, sport satisfies man's urge to challenge his physical being. And sometimes, if performed well enough, it inspires others in their own pursuits. And then, very rarely, it changes the social and cultural history of America; it changes *lives*. The 2004 Boston Red Sox are such a perfect storm.

The Red Sox are SI's Sportsmen of the Year, an honor they may have won even if the magnitude of their unprecedented athletic achievement was all that had been considered. Three outs from being swept in the ALCS, they won eight consecutive games, the last six without ever trailing. Their place in the sporting pantheon is fixed; the St. Jude of sports, patron saint of lost athletic causes, their spirit will be summoned at the bleakest of moments.

"It is the story of hope and faith rewarded," says Red Sox executive vice president Charles Steinberg. "You really believe that this is the story they're going to teach seven-year-olds 50 years from now. When they say, 'Naw, I can't do this,' you can say, 'Ah, yes you can. The obstacle was much greater for these 25 men, and they overcame. So can you.' "

What makes them undeniably, unforgettably Sportsmen, however, is that their achievement transcended the ballpark like that of no other professional sports team. The 1955 Brooklyn Dodgers were the coda to a sweet, special time and place in Americana. The 1968 Detroit Tigers gave needed joy to a city teeming with anger and strife. The 2001 Yankees provided a gathering place, even as a diversion, for a grieving, wounded city. The 2004 Red Sox made an even deeper impact because this championship was lifetimes in the making.

This Boston team connected generations, for the first time, with joy instead of disappointment as the emotional mortar. This team changed the way a people, raised to expect the worst, would think of themselves and the future. And the impact, like all things in that great, wide community called Red Sox Nation, resounded from cradle to grave.

On the morning after the Red Sox won the World Series, Sgt. Paul Barnicle, a detective with the Boston police and brother of *Boston Her-*

ald columnist Mike Barnicle, left his shift at six, purchased a single red rose at the city's flower market, drove 42 miles to a cemetery in Fitchburg, Mass., and placed the rose on the headstone of his mother and father, among the many who had not lived long enough to see it.

Five days later, Roger Altman, former deputy treasury secretary in the Clinton Administration, who was born and raised in Brookline, Mass., flew from New York City to Boston carrying a laminated front page of the Oct. 28 *New York Times* (headline: RED SOX ERASE 86 YEARS OF FUTILITY IN FOUR GAMES). He drove to the gravesite of his mother, who had died in November 2003 at age 95, dug a shallow trench and buried the front page there.

Such pilgrimages to the deceased, common after the Red Sox conquered the Yankees in the ALCS, were repeated throughout the graveyards of New England. The totems changed, but the sentiments remained the same. At Mount Auburn Cemetery in Cambridge, for instance, gravestones were decorated with Red Sox pennants, hats, jerseys, baseballs, license plates and a hand-painted pumpkin.

So widespread was the remembrance of the deceased that several people, including Neil Van Zile Jr. of Westmoreland, N.H., beseeched the ball club to issue a permanent, weatherproof official Red Sox grave marker for dearly departed fans, similar to the metal markers the federal government provides for veterans. (Team president Lucchino says he's going to look into it.) Van Zile's mother, Helen, a Sox fan who kept score during games and took her son to Game 2 of the 1967 World Series, died in 1995 at 72.

"There are thousands of people who would want it," Van Zile says. "My mom didn't get to see it. There isn't anything else I can do for her."

One day last year Van Zile was walking through a cemetery in Chesterfield, N.H., when the inscription on a grave stopped him. BLOUIN was the family name chiseled into the marble. Beneath that it said NAPOLEON A. 1926–1986. At the bottom, nearest to the ground, was the kicker of a lifetime.

DARN THOSE RED SOX.

Dear Red Sox:
Thanks for the motivation.
—JOSUE RODAS, MARINE, 6TH MOTOR TRANSPORT COMPANY, IRAQ

LIKE SNOWFLAKES in a blizzard came the e-mails. More than 10,000 of them flew into the Red Sox' server in the first 10 days after Boston won the World Series. No two exactly alike. They came from New England, but they also came from Japan, Italy, Pakistan and at least 11 other countries. The New England town hall of the 21st century was electronic.

There were thank-you letters. There were love letters. The letters were worded as if they were written to family members, and indeed the Red Sox were, in their own unkempt, scruffy, irreverent way, a likable, familial bunch. How could the faithful not love a band of characters self-deprecatingly self-dubbed the "idiots"?

DH David Ortiz, who slammed three walk-off postseason hits, was the Big Papi of the lineup and the clubhouse, with his outsized grin as much a signature of this team as his bat. Leftfielder Manny Ramirez hit like a machine but played the game with a sandlot smile plastered on his mug, even when taking pratfalls in the outfield. Long-locked centerfielder Johnny Damon made women swoon and men cheer and, with his Nazarene look, prompted a T-shirt and bumper sticker bonanza (WWJDD: WHAT WOULD JOHNNY DAMON DO? and HONK IF YOU LOVE JOHNNY).

First baseman Kevin Millar, with his Honest Abe beard and goofball personality, had the discipline to draw the walk off Yankees closer Mariano Rivera that began Boston's comeback in the ninth inning of ALCS Game 4. Righthander Derek Lowe, another shaggy eccentric, became the first pitcher to win the clinching game of three postseason series in one October. Foulke, third baseman Bill Mueller, catcher Jason Varitek and rightfielder Trot Nixon—the club's longest-tenured player, known for his pine-tar-encrusted batting helmet—provided gritty ballast.

The love came in e-mails that brought word from soldiers in Iraq with Red Sox patches on their uniforms or Red Sox camouflage hats, the symbols of a nation within a nation. The cannon cockers of the 3rd Battalion 11th Marine Regiment built a mini Fenway Park at Camp Ramadi. Soldiers awoke at 3 a.m. to watch the Sox on a conference-room TV at Camp Liberty in Baghdad, the games ending just in time for the troops to fall in and receive their daily battle briefing.

A woman wrote of visiting an ancient temple in Tokyo and finding this message inscribed on a prayer block: MAY THE RED SOX PLAY ALWAYS AT FENWAY PARK, AND MAY THEY WIN THE WORLD SERIES IN MY LIFETIME.

Besides the e-mails there were boxes upon boxes of letters, photographs, postcards, school projects and drawings that continue to cover what little floor space is left in the Red Sox' offices. Mostly the missives convey profound gratitude.

"Thank you," wrote Maryam Farzeneh, a Boston University graduate student from Iran, "for being another reason for me and my boyfriend to connect and love each other. He is a Red Sox fan and moved to Ohio two years ago. There were countless nights that I kept the phone next to the radio so that we could listen to the game together."

Maryam had never seen a baseball game before 1998. She knew how obsessed people back home were about soccer teams. "Although I should admit," she wrote, "that is nothing like the relationship between the Red Sox and the fans in New England."

Dear Red Sox:
Your first round of drinks is free.
                    —THE LOOSE MOOSE SALOON, GRAY, MAINE

NIGHTFALL, AND the little girl lies on her back in the rear seat of a sedan as it chugs homeward to Hartford. She watches the stars twinkle in between the wooden telephone poles that rhythmically interrupt her view of the summer sky. And there is the familiar company of a gravelly voice on the car radio providing play-by-play of Red Sox baseball. The great Ted Williams, her mother's favorite, is batting.

Roberta Rogers closes her eyes, and she is that little girl again, and the world is just as perfect and as full of wonder and possibilities as it was on those warm summer nights growing up in postwar New England.

"I laugh when I think about it," she says. "There is nothing wrong with the memory. Nothing."

Once every summer her parents took her and her brother, Nathaniel, to Boston to stay at the Kenmore Hotel and watch the Red Sox at Fenway. Nathaniel liked to operate the safety gates of the hotel elevator, often letting on and off the visiting ballplayers who stayed at the Kenmore.

"Look," Kathryn Stoddard, their mother, said quietly one day as a well-dressed gentleman stepped off the lift. "That's Joe DiMaggio."

Kathryn, of course, so despised the Yankees that she never called them just the *Yankees*. They were always the *Damnyankees*, as if it were one word.

"We didn't have much money," Roberta says. "We didn't take vacations, didn't go to the beach. That was it. We went to the Kenmore, and we watched the Red Sox at Fenway. I still have the images . . . the crowds, the stadium, the sounds, the feel of the cement under my feet, passing hot dogs down the row, the big green wall, the Citgo sign—it was green back then—coming into view as we drove into Boston, telling us we were almost there. . . . "

Roberta now lives in New Market, Va., her mother nearby in a retirement facility. Kathryn is 95 years old and still takes the measure of people by their rooting interest in baseball.

"Acceptable if they root for the Sox, suspect if they don't, and if a Damnyankee fan, hardly worth mentioning," Roberta says.

On Oct. 27, two outs in the bottom of the ninth, Boston winning 3–0, Roberta paced in her living room, her eyes turned away from the TV.

"Oh, Bill," she said to her husband, "they can still be the Red Sox! They can still lose this game!"

It was not without good reason that her mother had called them the *Red Flops* all these years.

"And then I heard the roar," Roberta says.

This time they really did it. They really won. She called her children and called "everybody I could think of." It was too late to ring Kathryn, she figured. Kathryn's eyesight and hearing are failing, and she was surely sleeping at such a late hour.

So Roberta went to see Kathryn first thing the next morning.

"Mom, guess what? I've got the best news!" Roberta said. "They won! The Red Sox won!"

Kathryn's face lit up with a big smile, and she lifted both fists in triumph. And then the mother and daughter laughed and laughed. Just like little girls.

Dear Red Sox:
I really want to surprise my whole school and the principal.
—MAINE HIGH SCHOOL STUDENT, ASKING THAT THE ENTIRE TEAM VISIT HIS SCHOOL

"IS THAT what I think it is?"

The conductor on the 11:15 a.m. Acela out of Boston to New York, Larry Solomon, had recognized Charles Steinberg and noted the size of the case he was carrying.

"Yes," the Red Sox VP replied. "Would you like to see it?"

Steinberg opened the case and revealed the gleaming gold Commissioner's Trophy, the Red Sox' world championship trophy. Solomon, who had survived leukemia and rooting for the Sox, fought back tears.

The Red Sox are taking the trophy on tour to their fans. On this day it was off to New York City and a convocation of the Benevolent Loyal Order of the Honorable Ancient Redsox Diehard Sufferers, a.k.a. the BLOHARDS.

"I've only cried twice in my life," Richard Welch, 64 and a BLO-HARD, said that night. "Once when the Vietnam War ended. And two weeks ago when the Red Sox won the World Series."

Everywhere the trophy goes someone weeps at the sight of it. Everyone wants to touch it, like Thomas probing the wounds of the risen Jesus. Touching is encouraged.

"Their emotional buckets have filled all these years," Steinberg says, "and the trophy overflows them. It's an intense, cathartic experience."

Why? Why should the bond between a people and their baseball team be so intense? Fenway Park is a part of it, offering a physical continuum to the bond, not only because Papi can stand in the same batter's box as Teddy Ballgame, but also because a son might sit in the same wooden-slat seat as his father.

"We do have our tragic history," says the poet Donald Hall, a Vermonter who lives in the house where his great-grandfather once lived.

The Sox specialized not, like the Chicago Cubs, in woebegone, hopeless baseball, but in an agonizing, painful kind. Indeed, hope was at the very breakable heart of their cruelty. From the 1967 Impossible Dream team until last season, the Red Sox had fielded 31 winning teams in 37 years, nine of which reached the postseason. They were good enough to make it hurt.

"It's probably the desperately cruel winters we endure in New England," Mike Barnicle offers as an explanation. "When the Red Sox reappear, that's the season when the sun is back and warmth returns, and we associate them with that.

"Also, a lot has to do with how the area is more stable in terms of demographics than most places. People don't move from New England. They stay here. And others come to college here and get infected with Red Sox fever. They get it at the age of 18 and carry it with them when they go out into the world."

If you are born north of Hartford, there is no other big league baseball team for which to root, just as it has been since the Braves left Boston for Milwaukee in 1953. It is a birthright to which you quickly learn the oral history. The Babe, Denny Galehouse, Johnny Pesky, Bucky Dent, Bill Buckner and Aaron Boone are beads on a string, an antirosary committed to memory by every son and daughter of the Nation.

"I've known nothing different in my life," says David Nathan, 34, who, like his brother Marc, 37, learned at the hand of his father, Leslie, 68, who learned at the hand of his father, Morris, 96. "It's so hard to put into words. I was 16 in 1986 sitting in the living room when the ball went through Buckner's legs. We all had champagne ready, and you just sit back and watch it in disbelief.

"I was at Game 7 last year and brought my wife. I said, 'You need to experience it.' The Sox were up 5–2, and my wife said to me, 'They've got this in the bag.' I said, 'No, they don't. I'm telling you, they don't until the last out.'

"I used to look at my dad and not understand why he cried when they lost or cried when they won. Now I understand."

At 11:40 on the night of Oct. 27, David Nathan held a bottle of champagne in one hand and a telephone in the other, his father on the other end of the line. David screamed so loud that he woke up his four-year-old son, Jack, the fourth generation Nathan who, along with Marc's four-year-old daughter, Jessica, will know a whole new world of Sox fandom. The string of beads is broken.

David's wife recorded the moment with a video camera. Two weeks later David would sit and write it all down in a long e-mail, expressing his thanks to Red Sox owner John Henry.

"As my father said to me the next day," David wrote, "he felt like a burden was finally lifted off of his shoulders after all of these years."

He read the e-mail to his father over the telephone. It ended, "Thanks again and long live Red Sox Nation." David could hear his father sobbing on the other end.

"It's nice to know after all these years," Leslie said, "something of mine has rubbed off on you."

Dear Red Sox:

I obviously didn't know what I was talking about.

—FAN APOLOGIZING FOR HIS MANY PREVIOUS E-MAILS,
ESPECIALLY THE ONE AFTER GAME 3 OF THE ALCS, IN
WHICH HE VERY COLORFULLY EXPRESSED HIS DISGUST FOR
THE TEAM AND THE PEOPLE RUNNING IT

IT WAS one minute after midnight on Oct. 20, and Jared Dolphin, 30, had just assumed his guard post on the overnight shift at the Corrigan-Radgowski correctional facility in Montville, Conn., a Level IV security prison, one level below the maximum. The inmate in the cell nearest him was 10 years into a 180-year sentence for killing his girl-friend's entire family, including the dog.

Some of the inmates wore makeshift Red Sox "caps"—a commis-sary bandanna or handkerchief festooned with a hand-drawn iconic "B." Technically they were considered contraband, but the rules were bent when it came to rooting for the Red Sox in October. A few in-mates watched ALCS Game 7 on 12-inch portable televisions they had purchased in the prison for $200. Most leaned their faces against the little window of their cell door to catch the game on the cell block television. Others saw only the reflection of the TV on the window of another cell door.

A Sox fan himself, Dolphin watched as Alan Embree retired the Yankees' Ruben Sierra on a ground ball to end the greatest comeback in sports history. Dolphin started to cry.

"Suddenly the block erupted," Dolphin wrote in an e-mail. "I bristled immediately and instinctively my hand reached for my flashlight. It was pandemonium—whistling, shouting, pounding on sinks, doors, bunks, anything cons could find. This was against every housing rule in the book, so I jumped up, ready to lay down the law.

"But as I stood there looking around the block I felt something else. I felt hope. Here I was, less than 10 feet away from guys that will never see the outside of prison ever again. The guy in the cell to my immediate left had 180 years. He wasn't going anywhere anytime soon. But as I watched him scream, holler and pound on the door I realized he and I had something in common. That night hope beamed into his life as well. As Red Sox fans we had watched the impossible happen, and if that dream could come true why couldn't others.

"Instead of marching around the block trying to restore order I put my flashlight down and clapped. My applause joined the ruckus they were making and for five minutes it didn't stop. I applauded until my hands hurt. I was applauding the possibilities for the future."

Dear Red Sox:
Any player who speaks Latin.
—REQUEST FOR A RED SOX PLAYER TO VISIT THE LATIN
CLASS AT A MIDDLE SCHOOL IN NEWTON, MASS.

ON THE day after Christmas 2003, Gregory Miller, 38, of Foxboro, Mass., an enthusiastic sports fan, especially when it came to the Sox, dropped dead of an aneurysm. He left behind a wife, Sharon, six-year-old twin boys and an 18-month-old daughter. Sharon fell into unspeakable sadness and loneliness.

And then came October and the Red Sox.

Sharon, not much more than a casual fan before then, grew enthralled with the team's playoff run. She called her mother, Carolyn Bailey, in Walpole, as many as 15 times during the course of a game to complain, exult, worry, commiserate and celebrate. She even made jokes.

"My eyes need toothpicks to stay open," Sharon would say during the run of late games. "More Visine. I need more Visine."

Carolyn laughed, and her heart leaped to see her daughter joyful again. She had not seen or heard her like this since Gregory died.

"It was the first time she started to smile and laugh again," Carolyn says. "The Red Sox gave her something to look forward to every day. They became like part of the family."

The day after the Red Sox won the World Series, Carolyn wrote a letter to the team. In it she said of her daughter, "The Red Sox became her medicine on the road back from this tragedy. On behalf of my entire family—thank you from the bottom of our hearts."

Leah Storey of Tilton, N.H., composed her own letter of thanks to the Red Sox. Her father had died exactly one year before the Red Sox won the World Series. Then her 26-year-old brother, Ethan, died of an accidental drug overdose only hours after enthusiastically watching the Red Sox win ALCS Game 5. When the Red Sox won the World Series, Ethan's friends and family rushed outside the Storey house, yelled for joy, popped open a bottle of Dom Perignon and gazed up in wonder at a lunar eclipse, and beyond.

"To us, with the memory of Ethan's happy night fresh in our minds, those games took on new meaning," Leah wrote of Boston's run to the championship. "Almost as if they were being played in his honor. Thank you for not letting him down. I can't express enough the comfort we derived from watching you play night after night. It didn't erase the pain, but it helped."

Dear Red Sox:
I would even volunteer my time to clean up, do the dishes, whatever.
—FAN ASKING THAT THE SOX HOST AN EVENT WHERE
PLAYERS GREET FANS 80 AND OLDER

ON OCT. 25 the Sox were two victories away from winning the World Series when doctors sent George Sumner home to his Waltham house to die. There was nothing more they could do for him. At home, though, George's stomach began to fill with fluid, and he was rushed back to the hospital. The doctors did what they could. They said he was in such bad shape that they were uncertain if he could survive the ride back home.

Suddenly, his eyes still closed, George pointed to a corner of the room, as if someone was there, and said, "Nope, not yet."

And then George went back home to Waltham. Leah knew that every day and every game were precious. She prayed hard for a sweep.

On the morning of Game 4, which stood to be the highlight of Jaime Andrews's life as a "pathetic," obsessed Red Sox fan, his wife, Alice, went into labor. Here it was: the conflict Jaime had feared all summer. At 2:30 p.m. he took her into South Shore Hospital, where they were greeted by nurses wearing Red Sox jerseys over their scrubs.

At 8:25 p.m., Alice was in the delivery room. There was a TV in the room. The game in St. Louis was about to begin.

"Turn on the game."

It was Alice who wanted the TV on. Damon, the leadoff hitter, stepped into the batter's box.

"Johnny Damon!" Alice exclaimed. "He'll hit a home run."

And Damon, his long brown locks flowing out the back of his batting helmet, did just that.

The Red Sox led, 3–0, in the bottom of the fifth inning when the Cardinals put a runner on third base with one out. Jaime could not stand the anxiety. His head hurt. He was having difficulty breathing. He broke out in hives. It was too much to take. He asked Alice to turn off the television. Alice insisted they watch until the end of the inning. They saw Lowe pitch out of the jam. Jaime nervously clicked off the TV.

At home in Waltham, George Sumner slipped in and out of sleep. His eyes were alert when the game was on, but when an inning ended he would say in a whisper, which was all he could muster, "Wake me up when the game comes back on." Each time no one could be certain if he would open his eyes again.

The Red Sox held their 3–0 lead, and the TV remained off in the delivery room of South Shore Hospital. At 11:27 p.m. Alice gave birth to a beautiful boy. Jaime noticed that the baby had unusually long hair down the back of his neck. The nurses cleaned and measured the boy. Jaime was still nervous.

"Can I check the TV for the final score?" he asked Alice.

"Sure," she said.

It was 11:40 p.m. The Red Sox were jumping upon one another in the middle of the diamond. They were world champions.

George Sumner had waited a lifetime to see this—79 years, to be exact, the last three while fighting cancer. He drew upon whatever strength was left in his body and in the loudest whisper that was possible he said, "Yippee!"

And then he closed his eyes and went to sleep.

"It was probably the last real conscious moment he ever had," Leah says.

George opened his eyes one last time the next day. When he did he saw that he was surrounded by his extended family. He said, "Hi," and went back to sleep for the final time.

George Sumner, avid Red Sox fan, passed away at 2:30 a.m. on Oct. 29. He was laid to rest with full military honors on Nov. 2.

On the day that George Sumner died, Alice and Jaime Andrews took home a healthy baby boy. They named him Damon.

Dear Red Sox:

Thank you, 2004 World Series Champs, Boston Red Sox. It was worth the wait.

—CLOSING LINES OF THE OBITUARY FOR CYNTHIA MARIE RILEY-RUBINO IN A HAMDEN, CONN., NEWSPAPER, SENT TO THE TEAM BY ANOTHER FAN

BALLPLAYERS ARE not social scientists or cultural historians. Quite to the contrary, they create an insular fortress in which all considerations beyond the game itself are feared to carry the poison of what are known generically as "distractions."

The Red Sox are not from Boston; they come from all corners of the U.S. and Latin America, and flew to their real homes immediately after a huge, cathartic parade on Oct. 30, during which normal life in New England was basically TiVoed for three hours. ("Three and a half million people there *and* a 33 rating on TV!" marveled Steinberg.)

There is an awful imbalance to our relationship with athletes, as if we are looking through a one-way mirror. We know them, love them, dress like them and somehow believe our actions, however trivial, alter the outcome of theirs, all while they know only that we are there but cannot really see us.

Howard Frank Mosher of Vermont was in northern Maine in the summer of '03 for a book-signing, during which he discussed his upcoming novel, *Waiting for Teddy Williams*, a fanciful tale in which the Red Sox (can you imagine?) win the Series; he heard a small group of people singing in the back of the bookstore. It sounded like, *Johnny Angel, how I love him. . . .*

As Mosher drew closer he realized they were singing, *Johnny Damon, how I love him. . . .* What was going on? he wondered.

"We're performing an incantation," one of the men said. "Damon has been in a slump. We think it's working. He was 4 for 5 last night."

Crazy. How could Damon know this? How could any Boston player know that the Reverend William Bourke, an avid Sox fan who died in his native Rhode Island before Game 2 of the World Series, was buried the day after Boston won it all, with a commemorative Sox baseball and that morning's paper tucked into his casket?

How could Pedro Martinez know that on the morning of World Series Game 2, Dianne Connolly, her three-year-old son, Patrick, and the rest of the congregation of St. Francis of Assisi parish in Litchfield, N.H., heard the choir sing a prayer for the Red Sox after the recessional? "Our Father, who art in Fenway," the singers began. They continued, "Give us this day our perfect Pedro; and forgive those, like Bill Buckner; and lead us not into depression. . . . "

How could Curt Schilling know that Laura Deforge, 84, of Winooski, Vt., who watched every Red Sox game on TV—many of them *twice*—turned the ALCS around when she found a lucky, 30-year-old Red Sox hat in her closet after Game 3? Laura wore it everywhere for the next 11 days, including to bingo. (And she's still wearing it.)

"I've only been here a year," Schilling says, "and it's humbling to be a part of the relationship between Red Sox Nation and this team.

I can't understand it all. I can't. All I can do is thank God that He blessed me with the skills that can have an impact on people's lives in some positive way."

The lives of these players are forever changed as professionals. Backup catcher Doug Mirabelli, for instance, will be a celebrity 30 years from now if he shows up anywhere from Woonsocket to Winooski. The '04 Red Sox have a sheen that never will fade or be surpassed.

The real resonance to this championship, however, is that it changed so many of the people on the other side of the one-way glass, poets and convicts, fathers and sons, mothers and daughters, the dying and the newborn.

The dawn that broke over New England on Oct. 28, the first in the life of little Damon Andrews, was unlike any other seen in three generations. Here began the birth of a new Red Sox Nation, sons no longer bearing the scars and dread of their fathers and grandfathers. It felt as clean and fresh as New Year's Day.

Damon's first dawn also was the last in the fully lived life of George Sumner.

"I walked into work that day," Leah Sumner says, "and I had tears in my eyes. People were saying, 'Did he see it? Did he see it? Please tell me your dad saw it.' You don't understand how much comfort it gave my brothers and sisters. It would have been that much sadder if he didn't get to see it.

"It was like a blessing. One lady told me he lived and died by the hand of God. I'm not religious, but he was blessed. If he was sitting here, he would agree there was something stronger there.

"It was the best year, and it was the worst year. It was an unbelievable year. I will tell my children and make sure they tell their children."

The story they will tell is not just the story of George Sumner. It is not just the story of the 2004 Boston Red Sox. It is the story of the bond between a nation of fans and its beloved team.

"It's not even relief," Leah says. "No, it's like we were a part of it. It's not like they did it for themselves or for money or for fame, but like they did it for us.

"It's bigger than money. It's bigger than fame. It's who we are. It's like I tell people. There are three things you must know about me. I love my family. I love blues music. And I love baseball."

Postscript: I had written a great deal about the Red Sox that October, so when the editors picked them as the Sportsmen of the Year and assigned the story to me, I wondered what could I possibly say about this team that would be fresh. I decided that what really made this championship special was its profound meaning to generations of fans, and was convinced that they could tell this extraordinary tale much better than the players. I'll never forget their voices. While I listened to some of these people tell me their stories, I found myself taking notes through my tears.

I Was a
Toronto Blue Jay

In his five days as a major leaguer, the author saw the splendors of baseball—
and its hard reality—from the best perspective: inside the game

STANDING IN LEFTFIELD DURING A MAJOR LEAGUE GAME—
I am *playing* leftfield—heightens my very sense of being.
There is a vibrancy to the colors and sensations around
me that, even as I stand there, I am cataloging in my most
secure vault of memory. I can feel the tips of my metal spikes knifing
between blades of grass and into the soft, moist earth. I feel the fit and
drape of my uniform, a *major league* uniform, my amazing technicolor
dreamcoat. Gray pants, belted tightly, black-mesh jersey with TORONTO
in metallic silver above the stylized Blue Jays logo on the left breast and
a shimmering silver number 2 on my back. Never can I remember the sky
bluer, the grass greener, the sun brighter.

It is not an out-of-body experience but rather its opposite: a satura-
tion of sensations. With a change in perspective, the familiar becomes in-
tensely intimate, like actually standing on the blue carpet of the Oval
Office or feeling the floorboards of the Carnegie Hall stage beneath your
feet or leaving footprints upon the Sea of Tranquility.

It is also a little like transporting dynamite on your person. A feeling of power, yes, but with a constant undercurrent of danger, especially knowing that Blue Jays first baseman Eric Hinske, who keeps fouling off pitches like a finicky shopper picking through unripe fruit, could at any moment send a curving line drive screaming my way or, worse, loft a fiendish high fly into that bright, cloudless sky and cruel cross-field wind, leaving me to look as if I were chasing a dollar bill dropped from a helicopter.

This is where the long march of a baseball season begins. A team will play upward of 200 games before the curtain falls on the World Series. This is the first for Toronto, an intrasquad game. About 2,000 fans—nearly all of whom, to my dismay as I try to track pitches from leftfield, are wearing gleaming white shirts—ring the backstop of Field 2 at the Bobby Mattick Training Center in Dunedin, Fla., drawn, after a winter of scraping snow shovels against the driveway, by those two lovely words: GAME TODAY.

I am a sportswriter, and sportswriters belong on the other side of the fence with the other unchosen. So why in the name of Kafka is a sportswriter playing leftfield for the Blue Jays? Maybe Kafka, not always the surrealist, can explain. On Oct. 18, 1921, three years before he died at age 40, Kafka cracked open his diary and wrote this entry: "Life's splendor forever lies in wait about each one of us in all its fullness, but veiled from view, deep down, invisible, far off. . . . If you summon it by the right word, by its right name, it will come."

I have come to Dunedin to summon it. Beginning with the team's first full-squad workout on Feb. 25, I have spent five days as a full-fledged player, in spirit and in uniform—attending every private meeting, running every sprint, participating in every live batting-practice session, sharing every clubhouse joke. "The full metal jacket," as manager John Gibbons promised me.

My most modest goals were to make it through five days with my bats and my hamstrings intact. My greater goals were to learn about the game up close, in the first person rather than in the third, about how spring training begins to lay the mortar for the sacred brotherhood of teammates—and about myself.

Five days a Jay, standing there with the vastness of leftfield my responsibility, my head is crammed with newfound knowledge. I've heard the ferocious hum of a 95-mph fastball, taken more than 100 swings a day, been hit by a pitch and heard grown men admonished for not washing their hands after using the bathroom.

Now it is about to end. I will get one at bat in this intrasquad game. One chance at splendor.

Day 1: Beware of Fecal Matter

"RED SOX, Yankees . . . Red Sox, Yankees . . . I don't care about the Red Sox and Yankees," general manager J.P. Ricciardi says. "We have to take care of ourselves. This is the most important year in the four years I've been here. This is your chance, from right now, to decide what kind of team you want to be." ∫

Ricciardi is addressing his troops in a classroom that is down a hallway from the main clubhouse. Like schoolkids the players fill the desks located in the back of the room but leave most of the ones up front unoccupied. This is what is known as the annual orientation meeting, ostensibly to introduce the training, coaching and support staff—and this year one embedded reporter—but also for the manager and general manager to set the tone for the season.

The Blue Jays are a blank slate. After a surprise third-place finish with 86 wins in 2003, Toronto sank to the basement in the American League East last year, losing 94 games. The Jays are Liechtenstein in a division with Cold War superpowers New York and Boston. Toronto's best player, first baseman Carlos Delgado, signed with Florida as a free agent. In front of Ricciardi and Gibbons sit only four players who have made an All-Star team, and only one who has hit 30 home runs, centerfielder Vernon Wells. As if to acknowledge his increased importance to the club, Wells is the one player who dares to sit front and center, where he's casually munching an apple.

"I like this team," Gibbons tells his players. "I like our starting pitching. We have good arms in the bullpen. Our defense is excellent. And we have a lot of very good hitters. What we need to concentrate on is being an aggressive team, being a very good situational hitting team and cutting down on strikeouts. Some people will say this team will not hit a lot of home runs. You never know how that will play out. But we're going to be aggressive on the bases."

Trainer George Poulis also addresses the team. He mentions that he noticed "a couple of guys the other day use the toilet, get up and leave without washing their hands. Now you go to the fruit bowl, you touch some grapes, not taking all of them, and the next guy comes in, takes that grape you touched and puts it in his mouth. And what's on that grape? Fecal matter. That's how you spread virus and bacteria."

There is nervous schoolboy laughter in the room.

"V-Dub," catcher Gregg Zaun calls to Wells, "I think someone touched that apple."

When the meeting ends, the infielders and pitchers leave for Field 2 to work on bunt defense. I join the outfielders in the four covered batting cages for soft toss, a hitting drill in which a coach tosses base-balls to the hitter from behind a protective screen about 20 feet from home plate.

I work with Mike Barnett, 46, who has the rare distinction of being a big league hitting coach without ever having played a day of professional baseball. Barnett's career as a catcher ended in 1978 when he blew out his shoulder at Ohio University. So one day soon after, just to stay in baseball, he walked into the offices of the Pirates' Triple A team in Columbus, Ohio, his hometown, and asked for a job as a bullpen catcher. He got it. He worked his way through various college and minor league coaching stops until the Blue Jays hired him to be their hitting coach in 2002. "I know every day how fortunate I am to be doing what I'm doing," he says.

The art of hitting is the ability to cast aside the preponderance of failure endemic to the task. Only hitters and weather forecasters can be wrong so often and still keep their jobs. To that end a hitting coach is really a confidence coach. He must be vigilantly optimistic. But even in this fraternity of positive thinkers, Barnett stands out. The joke among the front office staff is that Barnett is so sunny that any day they expect him to say, "You know, I think Verducci has a chance to help us . . . . "

Barnett is not, however, a miracle worker. I am 44 years old. Excluding handfuls of pickup games involving other sportswriters, I have not faced live pitching in more than 23 years, since a career at Penn State spent almost entirely as an outfielder on the practice squad. I have not hit with a wooden bat since I was 10, and that one was held together with nails and electrical tape. Not wanting to pretend to be something I wasn't, I didn't visit a batting cage or even swing a bat to prepare for this adventure.

Barnett makes some quick changes that click immediately: He lowers my hands, changes my swing path to a more downward angle and shows me how to shift my weight through the swing for a more balanced follow-through. I fall in love with the solid feel and thwack of hard maple upon a new baseball. Equipment manager Jeff Ross has issued me two bats, one maple and one traditional ash. The maple is noticeably harder.

"A lot of guys who use maple won't use it early in spring training," outfielder Reed Johnson tells me. "It doesn't break as easily, and early on you tend to get jammed more. Guys would rather just break their bat and not feel the pain."

Here it is, first day of camp, and we're supposed to hit live pitching next. That's hard enough after five months off, never mind 23 years.

"Ten, 15 years ago, we'd hit off coaches or machines for five to seven days first," says Merv Rettenmund, the organization's roving minor league hitting instructor. "But it's not the same as live pitching. So you might as well just dive in and get started."

Rain, heaven-sent, forces a change in plans. Pitchers will throw in the indoor cages, where the light is too dim to allow hitters to do anything but stand in at the plate and track the ball.

I step in against righthander Roy Halladay, the 2003 Cy Young Award winner, who is 6' 6", 225 pounds and looks capable of throwing a pitch through the cinder block wall behind the cage. I immediately realize the utter inadequacy of television to capture the power of a major league pitch. Halladay's fastball is angry, announcing its indignation with an audible hum that grows frighteningly loud as it approaches. His slider is even more evil because it presents itself in the clothing of a fastball but then, like a ball rolling down the street and falling into an open manhole, drops out of sight, down and away. His curveball bends more than an election-year politician.

I am so impressed with his stuff—it is *February*—that I will ask him later how close he is to season-ready velocity. Halladay, 27, tells me he's "just about there right now," having thrown off a mound six times before camp opened. Everyone, it seems, hits the ground running these days.

Miguel Batista, 34, follows Halladay on the mound. I am in a group with fellow outfielders Wells, Johnson and Frank Catalanotto, but no one moves to step in. Batista is still waiting when Wells motions to me and says, "Go ahead." I jump in, to the accompaniment of snickers.

It will not be until the next day that Wells tells me Batista hit three players in the head in spring training last year. So I am the royal taster. The three outfielders want me in there to gauge Batista's control. He has about eight varieties of pitches, and all of them move like a rabbit flushed out of a bush. He throws me one pitch that I swear breaks two ways—first left, then right—like a double-breaker putt in golf, only at about 90 mph.

I mention this to the catcher, Ken Huckaby, who laughs and says, "He's filthy. I faced him three times in spring training last year. Struck me out three times on a total of nine pitches."

I don't know how anyone hits Batista, and his teammates' apprehension indicates how uncomfortable he makes hitters. But Batista was 10–13 with a pedestrian 4.80 ERA last year. His gift for making a baseball dance is also his curse. He tends to get careless with his vast repertoire, such as starting weak hitters with errant sliders instead of pumping in a first-strike fastball.

Batista throws me one pitch on which, halfway to the plate, I can see a dot surrounded by spinning seams. Slider! I have cracked its code by reading the telltale dot. Then I realize something: The ball was already halfway to the plate by the time I decoded it, probably too late to do anything with it. Just by tracking pitches from Halladay, Batista,

Scott Schoeneweis and Dave Bush, I have come to understand that there is a race between the ball and my mind, and the ball is winning. By the time I process speed, spin, location and probable path and decide whether to swing or not, it is too late. The ball is past me.

Later we face pitches thrown by coaches from about 50 feet away, or what is called dead-arm BP. The cages become a shooting gallery. As heavy rain pounds the metal roof, all four cages crackle with one solid *thwack* after another. It is so loud that you have to raise your voice to be heard. Coaches take cover behind a protective screen after each pitch as balls whiz past them like shots at a firing range, packing the same deadly force.

During the rainstorm a group of infielders and outfielders huddles in a small dugout nearby while third base coach Brian Butterfield, with a preacher's passion, delivers a sermon on baserunning.

"Make your own legacy," he tells us. "We will always slide into second base. Always. Don't even make that early peel-off an option with two outs. And you know that saying, Don't make the first or third out at third base? Be aware of it, but don't be a prisoner of it. If you get thrown out, that's O.K. Now if it happens again and again, then maybe we have to talk about pulling in the reins. But we're going to be one of the best two-base teams in baseball. Make it a priority."

WHEN BUTTERFIELD is finished, it is still raining too hard to go back to the clubhouse or the batting cages. So, like a bunch of Little Leaguers waiting for the rain to stop, we pass the time telling jokes and needling one another. Second baseman Orlando Hudson, who lovingly refers to 5' 8" infielder Frank Menechino as "Mini-Me," is the team's champion trash talker. Hudson, with Wells and Catalanotto, is considering which players should be allowed to locker near them in the preferred corner of the clubhouse in Toronto. This is serious stuff. The layout of the locker room is like a Monopoly board; some neighborhoods have more intrinsic value than others. Whoever joins those three will gain status, moving in among the tribal leaders.

Johnson, 28, with two years of big league service, wants in on the prime property. He is told he must submit a written application explaining why he is worthy and including a proposed name for the neighborhood. "You want in the hood," Hudson says, "you've got to come up with a name."

Then a single, tremendous crack of thunder fills the air. It sends all of us running through the rain like little boys to the safety of indoors.

In that little treehouselike meeting in the rain, and in the clubhouse over the days to come, I gain a better understanding of the power of camaraderie in baseball. As in the Army, you are thrown together with people of various backgrounds. You might not even like some of them if you met under different circumstances, but wearing the same uniform, sharing the same locker room and shower room and nakedness and fruit bowl, spending so much time together in a confined space—the long, narrow Mattick clubhouse makes me think of a submarine—bonds you to them almost against your will. There is a strange sanctity about a place where guys can pass wind freely without apology.

I am reminded of this unwritten code when I ask lefthander Ted Lilly, who lockers next to me, about Jose Canseco and his steroid tell-all book, *Juiced.* Lilly, who played with Canseco on the 2000 Yankees, has the soft, expressive eyes of a giraffe and such a perpetually concerned look upon his face that pitcher Justin Miller calls him "Eeyore." But Lilly's mien becomes even more somber when I mention Canseco.

"I don't understand it," he says. "You become so close with people as teammates. You share things with them all the time, and then one person violates that trust for what, money? I don't understand how you can do that to teammates, to friends."

Lilly uses the words as synonyms. In the way of the clubhouse, to become a teammate is to become a friend. "I don't doubt that some things he said in general may have some truth," Lilly says. "I know I've been tempted [to use steroids]. You think, What can I do to get to that level? But I have always been very concerned about the health impact."

"I'm sure you've seen guys make money off it," I tell him.

"And there are guys who lost money," he says, "because their bodies broke down. And who knows what problems they still face."

Day 2: Of *Maxim* and Meat Loaf

NOW I FEEL like a big leaguer. I have discovered the miracle of freshly laundered clothes waiting for me in my locker. One day you take off the sweaty stuff and chuck it into a large bin, and the next morning it's all there hanging neatly. My spikes are out-of-the-box spotless. For this I can thank clubhouse manager Kevin Malloy and his crew.

Batista's locker is the talk of the clubhouse. Nothing is on hangers. Everything is folded crisply into neat piles. Finally, Batista walks in and explains: "That's so I'm ready when I'm traded. I've got everything packed up. I just throw it into a bag, and I'm gone. Because you never know when it's going to happen to you in this game."

Everybody laughs, knowing, of course, that he speaks the truth.

At 8 a.m. we are back in the classroom—Wells, with a fresh apple, in the same seat—this time for the annual umpires' presentation, delivered by umpire supervisor Rich Garcia. Garcia notes that the average time of game increased by one minute last year, to 2:51, and players need to be aware of pace-of-game guidelines. He also says more strikes on the upper and lower edges of the strike zone will be called this year—too many were called balls last year, according to the laser-guided QuesTec umpire information system.

Johnson asks Garcia if it is true that QuesTec allows a two-inch buffer zone on each side of the plate when grading umpires. Garcia acknowledges that it's true, and adds that if you include the three-inch width of the baseball, the 17-inch plate actually becomes a 27-inch plate to QuesTec.

There are grumbles in the back of the room.

"Schilling gets more."

"Pedro gets more."

Garcia moves on to beanballs. The quick warnings issued by umpires are designed to cut down on brawls. "And they have," he says. "We had only three last year. Myth: Once a warning is issued, my guy can't pitch inside. Fact: 75 percent of hit batters following a warning did not result in an ejection. So it's working."

"I thoroughly disagree!"

It is Batista, raising a loud objection.

"Last year I was given a warning for throwing a changeup in the dirt," he says angrily. "A *changeup*!"

Garcia admits umpires can make mistakes but reiterates that brawls are terrible for the game's image and the umpires will act aggressively to prevent them.

Today, under a clear sky, the time has come for live batting practice. Wells, Johnson, Catalanotto and I will hit against Francisco Rosario, a 24-year-old righthander whose 94-mph fastball and sharp slider have him on the cusp of making the club.

The outfielders swing rarely and only sometimes make solid contact.

Now it is my turn. I decide to look at the first pitch, a fastball. It seems to hurry at the end, like a car shifting into a higher gear.

O.K., I'm ready. Rosario shows me the palm of his glove, indicating that a changeup is coming. I get a good look at it. It is knee high. As I swing, it disappears, swallowed up by one of those manholes, right under my bat.

The next pitch is a slider off the plate. I let it go. Rosario throws another slider, this time getting more plate than he prefers. I swing and experience that unmistakable feeling of solid contact on my hands, like a hammer delivering the final, perfect blow to a nail. There is no resistance. What looks to the rest of the world like a routine fly ball to rightfield is pure bliss to me.

Jesse Carlson, a nonroster lefthander with a slingshot delivery, is next to pitch.

"V-Dub, should I hit off this guy?" asks Catalanotto, a lefthanded batter.

Just then Carlson throws his first warmup pitch, a searing fastball in the vicinity of where a lefthanded hitter's head would be.

"Forget it," Catalanotto says. "Tom, get in there."

I swing at three of Carlson's pitches and make contact each time, fouling a fastball into the batting cage, hitting another fastball with some authority off the protective screen in front of Carlson and bouncing a curveball in the hole between third base and shortstop. And my bat still is in one piece.

My scariest moment actually occurs when hitting against Double A coach John Valentin. Players don't wear batting helmets for dead-arm BP because the coaches simply groove pitches over the plate. But Valentin lets go of one that is headed straight for my head. It's the last place I'm expecting it, so I freeze for a moment, then finally duck and cover. The ball whacks off the back of my left shoulder. Valentin later apologizes profusely.

"Don't worry," I tell him. "Better you hit me than Halladay or Batista."

Butterfield gives us another baserunning clinic, in which he slips in a mention of an "orange gopher." We all exchange glances, perplexed.

"What's an orange gopher?" Menechino asks.

"'Bout 15 cents a slice," Butterfield replies in his best deadpan.

After practice most everyone hits the weight room for conditioning and strength training. Zaun is twisting his hands in a bucket of uncooked rice to make them stronger without the stress of weights. I am running on a treadmill. The smell of meat loaf is wafting into the room from the players' lounge down the hall, part of the daily breakfast and lunch service that is known simply and affectionately around baseball as the Spread.

"I'm not even sure if it's real ground beef," a player behind me says.

"I like it," replies another. "If it's free, it's me."

I take inventory of the room. There is golf on TV, men reading *Maxim* while riding exercise bikes, Skid Row blasting out of a killer sound system and the aroma of free meat loaf calling the hungry to their caloric satisfaction. The testosterone factor is off the charts.

Day 3: Help from a Higher Power

THE NOTE in a corner of the clubhouse whiteboard reads: CHAPEL. 8:05. I am one of six players to attend, all of us in uniform. The service is led by Gabe Gross, a strapping, fuzzy-cheeked 25-year-old outfielder with a swing as pretty as Easter morning. He is, as if straight out of Central Casting, the Southern ideal of the born *ath-a-lete*, the can't-miss kid who can play every sport, praise God and date the captain of the cheerleading squad with perfect equanimity. The son of an NFL player, Gross played football, basketball and baseball in high school and football and baseball at Auburn. He started six games as a freshman quarterback at Auburn in 1998 after being recruited by Terry Bowden.

"My dad told me, 'Son, once you play quarterback for Auburn, your life is forever changed,' " Gross says. "He was right. To this day, no matter what I do in baseball, people in Auburn know me as the guy who played quarterback at Auburn. And always will."

After Tommy Tuberville replaced Bowden, Gross dropped to third on the depth chart in his sophomore season. Two games after losing his starting job and with fall baseball practice about to begin, he quit the football team. Twenty-one months later the Blue Jays selected him in the first round of the 2001 draft. He made his big league debut last year and is likely to begin this year getting more seasoning in Triple A, though he has the tools to be a star any day now.

Gross reads a few passages from his Bible and relates them to himself and baseball. "I know sometimes I worry so much about baseball, worry about going 4 for 4 that night," he says. "And I know if I put my trust in God, that's really what matters most. And those are the times when I seem to play better too."

The service ends with the players offering special intentions for prayer. Most of them involve immediate family members, left behind but never far from their thoughts in this relentless, isolated pursuit called baseball.

Rain pounds Dunedin again. We repeat our Day 1 schedule: soft toss, tracking pitches from the pitchers, dead-arm BP. I'm amazed at the consistent dead-solid contact that players make in BP. Everyone looks like a star, including 24-year-old Alex Rios, a 6' 5" outfielder and 1999 first-round pick who mysteriously hit only one home run in 426 at bats last year for the Jays. He added 15 pounds over the winter, though, and the ball is jumping off his bat.

"He's going to have a big year," Rettenmund says of a guy who is so quiet that I don't think I hear him say more than two words in five days.

I ask Rettenmund to tell me the difference between a decent hitter and a great one.

"Effort," he says. "The great ones do it easily. There's less movement, better balance. Look at Vernon."

Wells appears to swing casually, but the ball rockets off his bat. He is a fully formed version of Gross: the son of a football player (CFL), he played multiple sports in high school (baseball and football) and was drafted in the first round (1997). He has decided this year, in keeping with Toronto's newfound aggressive approach to baserunning, that he will be a 30-30 player, though his career high in steals is nine. He says it the way you would tick off items on a shopping list. Consider it done.

"Vernon's amazing," Catalanotto says. "Twenty minutes before a game, you start feeling a little nervousness, the butterflies. It's normal. But Vernon will be there not even in his spikes yet, just kicking back. It's like he's going to play a game in the backyard. He makes it look so easy."

I, on the other hand, am one of those hitters whose effort is too visible. I am working at hitting the ball because I lack that sweet, professional flow that actually takes thousands upon thousands of swings to groove. I stick around for extra hitting against a modern pitching machine that delivers the ball out of a video screen so that it appears to be thrown by a two-dimensional life-sized pitcher.

When I am done I tell the machine's operator, "I saw this machine in Winter Haven two years ago."

"Oh, you used to be with the Indians?" he asks.

"Uh, no. SPORTS ILLUSTRATED."

Day 4: O-Dog, Cat and V-Dub, Plus Two

THE COUNCIL of elders convenes. Wells, Hudson and Catalanotto huddle in front of their lockers to review three applications for preferential locker location. They will pick two from among shortstop Russ Adams, infielder John McDonald and Johnson.

"The Pound?" Hudson says acidly of Adams's answer to the name-the-neighborhood portion of the application. "That's not very original."

"He's just trying to suck up to you," Catalanotto says to Hudson, who is known as O-Dog.

"Bad for you," Hudson replies to the player called Cat. "A cat in a pound is a bad idea."

Nicknames are the pledge pins of the baseball fraternity. Earn one and you know you're in. In addition to O-Dog, Cat and V-Dub, Johnson is Reeder, Halladay is Doc, Hinske is Ske or Hendu, Zaun is Zaunie, journeyman catcher Greg Myers is Crash, Rios is Lexi and so on. Smooth-pated third baseman Corey Koskie, signed as a free agent, has not officially been dubbed, though Malloy delivered his spring training allowance in an envelope marked COMMANDANT KLINK KOSKIE.

Players with nicknames are rarely called by their given name. Indeed, when a bat company representative calls Zaun "Gregg" while taking his order, Catalanotto interjects, "*Gregg*? How weird does that sound? I didn't know who he was talking about."

Menechino points to me and tells the rep, "Make sure you get his order."

The bat rep is speechless, trying to figure out who this player is.

"Here's what I need," I tell him. "Ticonderoga. Number 2s."

Wells, Hudson and Catalanotto will later confer briefly with Halladay, also one of the elders, on the clubhouse matter. But I am learning why pitchers cannot fully be team leaders. Pitchers do their own thing. They locker separately, train separately, stretch separately. Pitchers and position players are zebras and wildebeests grazing the same range. They have little in common, but nature has assigned them to the same habitat.

Just before stretching begins on Field 2, Gibbons calls out, "I need everybody here for a minute. These guys have something to say."

The team gathers around Hudson, Wells and Catalanotto. Halladay, the zebra, stands off to the side.

Hudson says, "I'd like to announce that we have a name for our corner of the clubhouse: Oreo Row at Web Gem Way. And we've chosen two people to join us. V-Dub?"

"Our first winner is . . . " Wells says, pausing for dramatic effect. "Reed Johnson." There is applause. "Cat?"

"And the other spot goes to . . . " Catalanotto says, "Johnny Mac. Sorry, Russ."

Adams stalks off indignantly, feigned or not.

"You lost points," Hudson shouts, "because you had spelling mistakes and wrote on a raggedy ol' piece of paper."

Who knew neatness counts in the big leagues? Left unmentioned is the power of tenure. Adams may be Ricciardi's first No. 1 pick and Hudson's double play partner, but he has only 31 days of service time.

More live BP, and Rosario and his 94-mph heater again. I get two swings, both on fastballs. I foul one off into the top of the cage. The other I hit hard toward where a second baseman would normally play.

"Hit and run, that's a base hit," Barnett says. Mr. Sunshine. I love the guy.

My throwing arm feels good, and I can run with everyone just fine. But fatigue in my left shoulder and right quadriceps from four long days of hitting has undermined whatever mechanics I have. I am, however, still far short of the threshold I established to require even stepping into Poulis's training room: displaced fractures or profuse bleeding.

Day 5: One Shot to Summon the Splendor

LAST DAY. Game day. Hitters pack the batting cages every morning as early as two hours before practice officially begins. But today, as I arrive for soft-toss at 8 a.m. before the 9:30 workout, there are no lines for the first time.

"Fifth day," Barnett explains. "Happens every year. Fatigue begins to set in, and guys know when to back off."

Barnett and Rettenmund have improved my swing. I'm exerting less effort but getting better results. Barnett notes that with my downward path and high finish, I've even begun to impart some backspin to the ball, which generates carry.

"Your swing is good," Rettenmund says. "Your timing is terrible."

He's no Mr. Sunshine. By timing, Rettenmund means the synchronicity of body parts, especially the two-part harmony that must exist between the lower body and the hands. "If you have to think about what your hands are doing," Rettenmund says, "it's too late. The ball is past you."

The team is divided evenly for the six-inning intrasquad game. Coach

Ernie Whitt tells me I will be replacing Catalanotto in leftfield after three innings. Gibbons, perhaps extending the aggressive theme of camp a mite too far, tells me, "If you get on, go ahead and take a bag."

The dugout and field are largely quiet. There are one-on-one conversations in the dugout after some at bats, in which every pitch gets a full-blown autopsy. But chatter of the Little League variety is essentially nonexistent, except for one master practitioner: Hudson, whose lips cease flapping only when he sleeps, or so rumor has it. Hudson is to chatter what the machine gun is to ammunition. Even in the middle of a play, when Menechino stabs a hot bouncer at third base and prepares to throw to first, Hudson yells, "Attawaytogo, Mini-Me!"

Our side, the home team, is winning 2–0 when I replace Catalanotto in leftfield in the fourth. Hinske, the finicky hitter, does launch a fly ball in my direction, but it lands far foul. No other projectiles come anywhere near me for my three innings.

McDonald begins our turn at bat in the fifth with a triple, which thrills me because I am next. The infielders play in, which means they can cover less ground against me.

As I step in to hit, a fan behind the backstop says to no one in particular, "Who's this guy? I don't have a number 2 on my roster."

"He's a new guy," says Ricciardi, who is seated with Gibbons behind the backstop. "We just signed him."

The pitcher is Chad Gaudin, 21, a freckle-faced, 165-pound righthander from Louisiana who somehow conceals a 94-mph fastball and hellacious slider beneath his Huck Finn looks. Gaudin (pronounced GO-dan) reached the big leagues with Tampa Bay in 2003 just two years removed from high school. He threw a perfect game in the minors that year and set an organizational record with a 1.81 ERA. After Gaudin finished with a 4.85 ERA out of the Devil Rays' bullpen last year, Ricciardi traded Kevin Cash, a 27-year-old catcher, to add Gaudin's live arm to his bullpen. Cash left behind some of his bats. The black maple one that I have in my hands, still intact after numerous turns in the cage, is one of them.

What I don't know is that among AL pitchers who faced at least 200 batters last year, only 12 hit batters more frequently than Gaudin (correction: pronounced go-DOWN). It may be a fool's naiveté, but I don't even think about the possibility of getting hit.

During one of our tracking sessions in the cage, I had asked Johnson if he ever dwelled on the possibility of getting struck by a pitch. He told me, "There is no fear factor as a hitter. You're so locked in on hitting that you don't allow that thought. You wouldn't be here if you did. When I'm going good is when I usually get hit. It means I'm staying in there longer."

I step into the batter's box, placing my right foot in the hole McDonald scraped inside the back chalk line. I am aware of nothing but Gaudin—not the crowd, not the infield in and, Lord knows, not the blue sky.

This moment is the essence of the game, its molecular core. It is why we love baseball as we love a family member, while the other sports have to manage with our lust, infatuation or uncommitted affection. Either I will win or Gaudin will win, and even the most rudimentary fan will immediately know it. No one will have to wait for the game films. And no teammate can help me.

A baseball game will stage about 80 of these batter versus pitcher matchups, all of which appeal to our American sense of democracy—we must *take turns* at bat—and our thirst for conflict and for quick and clear resolution, the backbone of prime-time television, our real national pastime, as well. Eighty miniversions of *CSI*.

Since sportswriters fall significantly below utility infielders and pitchers in the food chain of big league hitters, I assume Gaudin will attack me with a first-pitch fastball. I have committed to swing at the first pitch since I woke up and ate a bowl of instant oatmeal from the Spread. Gaudin swings his arm down, back, up and through in that familiar, graceful but orthopedically damning circle of a big league pitcher.

Here it comes. It is a fastball and it is a strike. I have prepared for everything about this pitch except one thing: its speed. The baseball jumps on me so incredibly quickly that I am transfixed. The ball has not just outraced my mind, it has fried its circuitry. Synapse shutdown. I cannot swing.

"*Huuuuh!*" bellows the umpire.

I am in a hole, 0 and 1. Worse, I have a slightly gnawing feeling in my stomach that I will never again see a pitch that good.

Now I *must* swing. Here it comes again. Fastball. Inner half. I swing. Just as I do, the ball is gone. Manhole. It drops so unkindly beneath the path of my bat that I can almost hear it laugh.

I am in hitter's jail, 0 and 2, and Gaudin is not bound by the Geneva Convention. He can do whatever he wants with me—spin one, waste one, shave my whiskers. This much I know: If it is within the 34698 ZIP code, I am swinging. You do not leave eagle putts short, you do not miss the birth of your children, and you do not go down looking in your only major league at bat.

Here it comes again. Fastball. Up. Farther in. I swing.

Contact!

Wait. What? My bat. Weightless. Gone.

I look in my hands. Only about eight inches of maple remain. The other 26 inches are gone to I-don't-know-where. Sawed in half. The palm of my right hand is vibrating like a tuning fork and will for the next 30 minutes.

The baseball? I look up. There it is. A pop-up toward first base. I run. I see Hinske, 235 pounds of Wisconsin beef, in the base line tracking it. Panic is a rapid transit system to the brain, and I have time to imagine a collision, the pain and the ignominy of a sports-writer blowing out the knee of the starting first baseman. But Hinske catches it uneventfully. I am out. Though the bat died in vain, there is a measure of victory to be extracted from merely making contact.

Huckaby, hitting next, strikes out, but Shea Hillenbrand picks up both of us with a single to drive in McDonald. We win 3–0.

In the locker room I run into Gaudin, towel around his waist, head-ed for the shower.

"You know what?" he says. "I didn't even know it was you up there until after the at bat. I was just so locked in on trying to get an out with the man on third. I threw that two-seamer down [on the sec-ond pitch] and figured I'd come back up for a different look. Change your eye level. Then after the out, I looked over and thought, Man, that was Verducci. You did real good."

I head to the weight room, where Butterfield finds me.

"Skip wants to see you in his office," he says.

"Now?"

"Right now."

I walk into Gibbons's office. Ricciardi and his assistant, Tim Mc-Cleary, flank Gibbons's desk.

"Close the door," Gibbons says. "Have a seat.

"This is one part of the job that's never easy. You gave a great ef-fort out there. We appreciate it, but . . . it's a good thing you have an-other job. We've got your unconditional release papers right there. Sign both copies."

That's it. It is officially over. I walk back to my locker, toss my copy of the release onto the top shelf and plop down on my chair. And suddenly I see, tucked behind the miraculously laundered and hung undergarments, my maple bat in its two-piece eternal repose. And I have to smile. For it is then that I know for certain that I have summoned the game's splendor in all its fullness.

Postscript: The most reader feedback I ever received was for the Red Sox Sportsmen of the Year story—until this one. I think it resonated not just with fans who were devoted to one team, but with anyone who ever dreamed of wearing a big league uniform or wondered what it was like to face a 95 mph fastball, which pretty much covers the general population of baseball fans.

I had wanted to write about baseball this way—up close—for years, inspired by curiosity, a brilliant 1973 essay by poet (and cameo Pittsburgh Pirate) Donald Hall and a longstanding love for playing the game. I chose the Blue Jays because I wanted a low-profile team on which my presence would not become a media event. I could not have picked a better ballclub. The Jays made this story possible by granting me full access and treating me as one of their own.

An unexpected bonus—which I didn't learn about until the day the issue printed—was becoming the first SI writer to appear on the magazine's cover. Cover or no cover, the experience was more than I ever could have hoped for. It made me think of a 19th-century saying, often associated with the Gold Rush: "I have seen the elephant," which was a way of saying you had been somewhere most others had not, and had probably endured significant tribulations along the way. I came away from the experience with a distinct feeling that I was a little wiser than I'd been, certainly more privileged.